Welcome to **SOCIAL THEORY**

Sara Miller McCune founded SAGE Publishing in 1965 to support the dissemination of usable knowledge and educate a global community. SAGE publishes more than 1000 journals and over 000 new books each year, spanning a wide range of subject areas. Our growing selection of library products includes archives, data, case studies and video. SAGE remains majority owned by our founder and after her lifetime will become owned by a charitable trust that secures the company's continued independence.

Los Angeles | London | New Delhi | Singapore | Washington DC | Melbourne

Welcome to SOCIAL THEORY

Tom Brock

SAGE

Los Angeles | London | New Delhi
Singapore | Washington DC | Melbourne

$SAGE

Los Angeles | London | New Delhi
Singapore | Washington DC | Melbourne

SAGE Publications Ltd
1 Oliver's Yard
55 City Road
London EC1Y 1SP

SAGE Publications Inc.
2455 Teller Road
Thousand Oaks, California 91320

SAGE Publications India Pvt Ltd
Unit No. 323–333, Third Floor, F-Block
International Trade Tower, Nehru Place
New Delhi 110 019

SAGE Publications Asia-Pacific Pte Ltd
3 Church Street
#10-04 Samsung Hub
Singapore 049483

Editor: Natalie Aguilera
Assistant editor: Rhoda Ola-Said
Production editor: Martin Fox
Copyeditor: Richard Leigh
Proofreader: Thea Watson
Indexer: Silvia Benvenuto
Artist: Joshua Harrison
Marketing manager: Ruslana Khatagova
Cover design: Francis Kenney
Typeset by: C&M Digitals (P) Ltd, Chennai, India

Library of Congress Control Number: 2022944850

British Library Cataloguing in Publication data

A catalogue record for this book is available from the
British Library

ISBN 978-1-5297-3262-7
ISBN 978-1-5297-3261-0 (pbk)

For Mom and Dad

CONTENTS

LIST OF CASE STUDIES

ONLINE RESOURCES

Welcome to Social Theory! is supported by online resources for lecturers to use with students, which are available to access at: **https://study.sagepub.com/brock1e.**

For lecturers

PowerPoint decks featuring figures from the book, which can be downloaded and customised for use in your own presentations.

ABOUT THE AUTHOR

Dr. Tom Brock is a Senior Lecturer in Sociology at Manchester Metropolitan University where he teaches social theory and the philosophy of social sciences to undergraduate and postgraduate students. Tom's research interests include social theory, games and digital consumption. He has published widely on these topics in journals including *The Sociological Review, Journal for the Theory of Social Behaviour, Information, Communication and Society, Games and Culture*, and the *Journal of Critical Realism*. Tom is the Book Reviews Editor of the *Journal of Consumer Culture*.

1

Introduction

Chapter Objectives

This chapter will:

- Introduce the classic and contemporary social theories that this book covers.
- Offer ways of thinking about social theory and identify how social theories connect to a broader landscape.
- Examine key themes across different social theories, including structure and agency, social ontology and epistemology, and modernity.

Keywords

Social theory, knowledge, structure and agency, social ontology, social epistemology, modernity, realism, idealism, scepticism, the Enlightenment, secularism

Welcome!

Welcome to my book! Welcome to social theory! I am very excited to be sharing this book with you because my reason for writing it is deeply personal – I want to try to make the core theoretical arguments behind a range of ideas as accessible as possible without compromising their complexity or historical context. This is no easy task, but I have set about it nevertheless because I am deeply passionate about social theory and I genuinely find it inspiring and many of its ideas insightful. I believe social theory makes social and cultural research meaningful and relevant. It is what helps social and cultural researchers turn their descriptions of the world into perspectives that can challenge taken-for-granted assumptions and expose new ways of understanding and living in society. We exist in a world with all sorts of structural constraints and **power** relations, as well as interactions between humans and non-humans, individuals, networks, and global authorities. These processes actively shape the way we behave daily, often without us realising or being able to comprehend fully. Social theory helps students pierce the surface of everyday reality to begin to analyse, explain and understand it. It also helps students grasp life's social complexity in a way that gives them the confidence to develop their own ideas and progress them into original research projects.

I have also written this book because I am very familiar with the struggles of trying to understand social theory. Many existing textbooks introduce the problems of teaching social theory by noting that students experience anxiety or boredom at the prospect of learning about its ideas. These textbooks suggest that these ideas either do not make sense or are so abstracted away from real life that social theory becomes irrelevant to the reader. There is some truth to this. When I first began studying social theory at university, I found the experience profoundly isolating. There were just *so many words*, many of which I could not pronounce, let alone understand. I do not mind confessing that I felt embarrassed on more than one occasion when asked if I knew the meaning of the phrase **social ontology** and if I could use it in a sentence. As a working-class student from Birmingham, it was difficult for me to grasp the ideas behind these words as they became a barrier to my understanding and development – I certainly didn't feel confident saying them in my Brummie accent! This experience is not far removed from what Diane Reay talks about in Chapter 7 when discussing the 'cultural habitus' of the classroom; there are taken-for-granted inequalities embedded within social theory that shape *who* can engage with it and why. Of course, these inequalities relate not only to class but also to race and gender, which is a core theme of social theory explored in Chapter 8.

My experiences with social theory are inseparable from the approach I have taken in the design and writing of this textbook. First, the book uses lots of images. These images offer students analogies and metaphors to help understand the core message that grounds a particular concept or idea. One of the first things that I explain to my students is that behind every theorist and every concept there is a philosophical assumption about how the world 'works'. If they can grasp this assumption, then the verbose (!) or wordy language is less of a barrier to understanding its insight. Consider, for example, the following passage from Karl Marx (1844; emphasis in original):

> First, the fact that labor is *external* to the worker, i.e., it does not belong to his intrinsic nature; that in his work, therefore, he does not affirm himself but denies himself, does not feel content but unhappy, does not develop freely his physical and mental energy but mortifies his body and ruins his mind.

Though Marx is a poetic writer, it can be difficult to establish from the original texts what the take-away message is and how one develops this in practice. As I explain in Chapter 2, one of the core ideas behind Marx's critique of capitalism and modern working conditions is his view of human nature, which stipulates that people, above all else, are labourers. This assumption is core to Marx's view of what is wrong with the modern world. It sets forth many of his concepts, such as alienation, exploitation and **ideology**, which have become foundational to social and cultural research. Many of the images within this book illustrate these concepts in a way that invites students to reflect on these take-away messages as well as their ongoing relevance today.

Second, the book uses lots of contemporary examples. These are to support students in developing their critical thinking skills. It is important to note that, mainly when writing essays, it is one thing to understand a concept by describing it, and it is quite another to apply a concept to a case study or example. When students apply concepts to examples, they evidence their analytical and critical evaluation skills. Consider, for example, the case study in Chapter 6 on 'metric power', which discusses research that applies Michel Foucault's understanding of surveillance and disciplinary control to a range of examples, from Apple Watch, Facebook and Google Scholar. This example and others aim to encourage a way of approaching social theory as a 'tool' (see Craib, 1997), mainly to interrogate society to reveal its structural constraints, power relations and interactional processes. Indeed, the examples in this book aim to offer students the means to develop a critical eye on society, one that pierces the surface of everyday life to analyse and explain its underlying processes (or even question this very assumption, which theorists do in Chapters 6 and 10!).

Third, the book also points the reader to 'focus on facts'. This feature is not because I want students to memorise some particular ideas. On the contrary, social theory is about gathering and generating new insights into life about things previously taken for granted. Yet, there are many times when it is helpful to highlight the interconnectedness of theories and ideas across chapters or themes. For example, in Chapter 3, I discuss why it is essential to reflect on the relationship between the ideas of Friedrich Nietzsche and Sigmund Freud, and in Chapter 6, I talk about the influence of these ideas on poststructuralists like Jacques Derrida.

'Focus on facts' is also a way to single out essential concepts and ideas that do not always fit into the narrative or history (or histories) of particular theorists but are nevertheless crucial for the generation of ideas. For example, in Chapter 10, I highlight the significance of Gilles Deleuze and Félix Guattari's concept of **affect** in influencing the 'affective turn' in the social sciences and the critical writings of feminist scholars such as Sara Ahmed and Rosi Braidotti. The point is that these facts serve as a frame of reference, guide critical issues and act as a medium to support students in making non-obvious connections.

What these design features all have in common is my intention to help students understand the arguments behind core theories and concepts in social and cultural research. I want this book to support the reader to see the 'wood-for-trees' – the landscape of social theory and how particular ideas connect, even if they might be by different theorists, separated by history or focus on diverse areas of society. To this end, I want to stress that students can develop confidence in social theory once they connect with its basic arguments.

Focus on Facts

Some of the primary arguments that this book covers are listed below:

- Capitalism is a political and economic system in which workers are vulnerable to exploitation through management and business practices that pursue profit and growth over appropriate workers' rights and protections (*Karl Marx*).
- Giant corporations use mass media and advertising to exercise a monopoly over culture and secure a dominant economic and cultural position over the masses (*Theodor Adorno and Max Horkheimer*).
- The ruling classes secure ideological control and social domination over the working classes by shaping social and cultural attitudes – 'cultural hegemony' (*Antonio Gramsci*).
- There is no objective meaning to life; we are all individually responsible for our actions, who we are, and the world we live in (*Friedrich Nietzsche*).
- Humans have an unconscious mind in which sexual and aggressive instincts are in continual conflict for control against social norms and other psychological defences (*Sigmund Freud*).
- The modern world is like an 'iron cage': a system of rational and secular forces creating disciplined yet disenchanted workers (*Max Weber*).
- The moral constitution of the modern world is shifting towards individualism and egoism (*Émile Durkheim*).
- The human mind structures the world around us, not objective or material conditions (*Immanuel Kant*).
- Consciousness is intentional; when we think, we direct our thoughts towards particular objects and things (*Edmund Husserl*).
- The practical task of living our lives structures our experiences of the world and how we relate to other people (*Alfred Schütz*).

- Social inquiry is not about explaining society through facts but interpreting people's methods for accomplishing everyday activities (*Harold Garfinkel*).
- When we perceive objects, we do not merely represent them but project our tastes, intentions and values onto them, shaping our experience (*Maurice Merleau-Ponty*).
- Language is an essential feature of human interaction because it provides the shared system of symbols and signs needed for interpersonal communication (*George Herbert Mead*).
- Other people interpret our social behaviour, and we reflect on these interpretations to shape a vision of ourselves (*Erving Goffman*).
- The structure of language shapes meaning (*Ferdinand de Saussure*).
- Language obscures or hides ruling-class ideologies (*Roland Barthes*).
- We can deconstruct texts to reveal that language has multiple meanings and interpretations (*Jacques Derrida*).
- There is no such thing as 'truth', but claims to 'know' the truth often reveal acts of power (*Michel Foucault*).
- Social structures condition human behaviour by generating practices that reflect the opportunities and constraints of particular social positions (*Pierre Bourdieu*).
- Social structures do not determine social behaviour; agents act to reproduce or change them through their everyday practices (*Anthony Giddens*).
- Social structures and human agents are distinct entities with their own properties and powers that social research should not conflate (*Margaret Archer*).
- Men create values and practices that subordinate women by restricting their activities and experiences (*Simone de Beauvoir*).
- Sex and gender are not things that people 'have' but things people perform (*Judith Butler*).
- Feminism largely ignores women's differences by presenting feminist issues from a white, middle-class, heterosexual perspective (*bell hooks*).
- The law does not recognise or understand that Black women's lived experiences reflect racial and gender-based issues (*Kimberlé Crenshaw*).
- Histories of colonialism reveal various racial prejudices that link closely to capitalist exploitation (*Franz Fanon*).
- European culture uses preconceptions of the East to reinforce itself as a site of power (*Edward Said*).
- There are many deep-seated anxieties within colonial power (*Homi Bhabha*).
- Histories of colonialism often marginalise the experiences of the most disenfranchised, particularly women (*Gayatri Spivak*).
- Agency extends beyond humans to non-humans and inanimate objects (*Bruno Latour*).
- The point of social theory is not to classify and categorise the features of the world but explain how the world changes over time (*Gilles Deleuze*).
- We must focus on the intrinsic value of animals and the natural environment when thinking about the future of Earth (*Rosi Braidotti*).

Of course, any attempt to write a textbook about social theory will produce an incomplete list of ideas and perspectives. What I try to do in this book is strike a careful balance between making the 'canon' of social theory accessible while paying attention to debates concerning its lack of diversity and inclusivity. As Alatas and Sinha's (2017) book *Sociological Theory Beyond the Canon* makes clear, there is a need to critique the **Eurocentrism** that dominates the historical development of social theory. I agree, and this book draws attention to these concerns, particularly in Chapter 9, which deals with the need to 'decolonise sociology' through the works of Ali Meghji and Gurminder Bhambra. It also draws attention to the need to push beyond the traditional boundaries of the 'canon' and engage more substantially with new materialist and posthumanist scholarship. As Chapter 10 discusses, some of the most problematic aspects of social thought are rooted in a mixture of European colonialism and **anthropocentrism**, raising critical questions about the future of social theory and the dangers of theorising about humans (or what constitutes the 'human') as above and beyond non-humans, such as animals and the natural environment. From this perspective, I hope the book not only brings students into conversation with recent debates in social and cultural theory (rather than solely revisiting the 'classics') but does so in a way that helps them to identify the historical connections between these ideas. In my view, this is an integral part of 'thinking about theory'.

Thinking About Theory

One of the first things I explain to my students is that social theory, at its most fundamental, involves 'thinking' about the social world. When we theorise about society, we often try to explain how a social event occurs or why a specific person or group behaves in a particular or patternable way (though some theorists challenge this assumption about theory and research; see Chapters 6 and 10). As Ian Craib (1992) argues, social theory is less a matter of just learning what theorists have said and more about learning to think theoretically; learning what we can from ideas to use them to explain and understand some kind of experience or general processes within the world. In other words, social theory helps us to reach explanations, but to do this we must 'think' about the world critically – we must perform some kind of mental abstraction as we 'step away' from the observable events in the world and 'theorise' about what might be causing them to happen or what their potential effects might be.

One of the most challenging things about social theory is that this process of thinking can, at first, seem entirely unfamiliar. We might consider it akin to being transported to an unknown world with a new and mysterious language. This can feel like quite an isolating experience, but, in truth, many of the problems that social theorists deal with are ones we face in our everyday lives. As Steven Miles (2001, p. 6) writes, everything we do involves some measure of theory: we might theorise about why our sports teams never appear to succeed, despite substantial financial investment. We might theorise about the cost of living and whether our student loans are sufficient to survive. We might also theorise how best to achieve a first-class degree or graduate employment. The critical point is that we are very used to 'thinking' through everyday problems and social theory is no different: it provides a way to understand what is happening around us.

One way I invite my students to start thinking about theory is to ask them to reflect on the possible conditions for why a given phenomenon occurs and what some plausible answers might be. Consider, for example, the theorising involved in making a medical diagnosis or coming to a verdict in a court case. In medicine, a doctor is given a set of observable symptoms and must think through what disease or illness best explains them. Likewise, when a jury listens to evidence in a criminal case, they must think through all of the evidence and consider whether the defence or prosecution has provided the best explanation. In each case, what is taking place is a process of exploring observable events and considering the (many) possible explanatory conditions.

Social theory is similar: it proposes ways of making sense of society through reasoned consideration of why things happen. Yet, as Craib (1992, pp. 5–6) notes, it is also different. Social theory provides us with the principles, frameworks and concepts to start reasoning through the world more systematically and logically. These principles will shape and guide the kinds of conditions that we think explain social phenomena. For example, as Chapter 8 discusses, there are many different types of feminist theory, each focusing on different aspects of social inequality and injustice – from legal and economic to psychological and cultural conditions. Each theory guides how we think about feminist issues differently, which is also why it is essential to get the broadest possible exposure to theoretical ideas before making up our minds about what the social world is like and why!

Theory also shapes our arguments, such as when writing an essay or research paper. As Tom Chatfield (2017) notes, an argument is simply an attempt to persuade someone of the truth through the reasoning of ideas. Theory helps us make persuasive arguments as we integrate certain principles or concepts into our thinking and use them to reason through particular examples. This is why I recommend to students that they reflect on how theorists construct convincing arguments through the reasoning of their ideas. Think about the ways in which theorists 'set up' their assumptions about the world and then try to find ways to support these assumptions through empirical research. There is something very persuasive about arguments which clearly introduce their 'truths', that is, what they are saying about society, before reasoning through the different concepts and examples that support this particular vision.

Roots and Branches

Another way I encourage my students to think about theory is by using the metaphor of a 'tree' with various roots and branches. As Peter Kivisto (2020) argues, we can conceive of social theory as emerging through two stages. The former comprises the 'roots' – a period roughly between the mid-nineteenth and twentieth centuries in which sociology emerges as a distinctive discipline by distinguishing itself from philosophy and the life sciences. Kivisto (2020, p. xxiv) writes:

During this time, the first explicit advocates of this new field of inquiry appeared
on the scene and created what might seem as the infrastructure needed to sustain it,
particularly the carving out of a legitimate place in the university system, with all
that implies. This time frame represents sociology's classical period. The individuals
associated with this era were responsible, even when they were not trying to do so, for
giving sociology its initial identity.

In this book, I identify these individuals as Karl Marx, Émile Durkheim and Max Weber. They,
alongside crucial thinkers such as Auguste Comte, Immanuel Kant, Georg Hegel, Friedrich
Nietzsche and Sigmund Freud, constitute the central figures of an early history of social theorising. Again, this list is not exhaustive and, where possible, I have tried to identify alternative
histories and perspectives (see, for example, the discussion of Harriet Martineau in Chapter 4
or W.E.B. Du Bois in Chapter 9), but it does capture the broad consensus that these thinkers are
at the 'roots' of social theory. This book examines these individuals precisely because they get
us thinking in 'intellectually productive ways' (Kivisto, 2020, p. xxvi) and provide the foundations for contemporary social thought.

For example, Marx's concern with capitalism and ideology has become productive grounds
for thinking critically about a range of contemporary issues, from mass media, consumerism
and digital labour (see Chapter 2) to questions concerning the nature of structure and agency
(see Chapters 6 and 7) and feminist and postcolonial politics (see Chapters 8 and 9). Durkheim's
work also remains a fruitful way of discussing **social epistemology** and what constitutes
social scientific research and knowledge, particularly in dialogue with interpretivist and phenomenological perspectives (see Chapters 3, 4 and 5). Durkheim's ideas influence cultural sociology, shaping how we understand social participation in rituals and collective events, such
as sports and games (see Chapter 4). The ideas of Nietzsche, Freud and Weber also continue to
be foundational. They each offer critical insight into the nature of power and social control,
foreshadowing the emergence of various postmodern, feminist and new materialist perspectives
(see Chapters 6, 8 and 10).

Kivisto characterises the latter stage of social theory from the mid-twentieth century to the
present day as the 'branches' of a tree. Kivisto (2020, p. xxix) writes that 'many inside and
outside the world of social theory would describe the situation as a cacophony of competing
approaches'. Indeed, today, few attempt to unify social theory around a single theoretical school
or model. Instead, multiple perspectives guide social and cultural research, some of which have
very different beginnings and trajectories. One way to discuss these differences is to consider
three 'branches' of social thought: 'consensus', 'conflict' and 'action' theories.

Consensus perspectives focus on the role of human socialisation and learned behaviour in
explaining the order and predictability of societies. They have their roots in the philosophy
of writers like Aristotle, Thomas Aquinas and John Locke, who conceive of society in terms of
people's consensual nature and the possibility of living in complete and free agreement with
one another. This perspective is exceptionally influential on early functionalist thinkers,

like Durkheim and Talcott Parsons (see Chapter 4), who argue that societies socialise people into agreement and consensus through structural norms, roles and responsibilities (see Bernard, 1983).

Conflict perspectives are different. They describe societies in terms of the conflict they generate, whether as a result of either socioeconomic and cultural inequalities or because conflict is an inevitable part of human life. In the former case, it is philosophers like Plato, Jean-Jacques Rousseau and Marx who suggest that if we eliminate the (social, economic and cultural) sources of conflict in society then freedom for agreement and consensus may be possible (Bernard, 1983). On the other hand, writers like Niccolò Machiavelli, Nietzsche and Freud suggest that true consensus is never possible because societies always need to exert control over overt expressions of conflict. This assumption leads conflict theorists to focus on power rather than consensus and how social and cultural ideas act as an instrument of force and social control (see Chapters 3, 6, 8 and 9).

Action perspectives are different again. They move away from structural explanations of society to focus on the *interpretations* of individual actors and how these interpretations shape or construct orderly behaviour in society. Action perspectives suggest that the most crucial influence on an individual's behaviour is the behaviour of other individuals, rather than structures such as the unequal distribution of socioeconomic resources or social and cultural norms. Indeed, action perspectives attend to the beliefs and values of actors to understand why, for example, a person might choose to act in one particular way over another. Action perspectives have their origins in the ideas of Weber (see Chapter 3) but also in Edmund Husserl's phenomenology and the philosophy of George Herbert Mead (see Chapter 5). Where Weber constructs a typology to help classify the different ways people interpret the world, Husserl considers the nature of experience, and Mead considers the methods people use for interpersonal communication. These perspectives contrast with consensus and conflict views because they question the assumption that 'real' structures determine the actions of agents. Instead, action perspectives suggest that social reality is a construct that is dependent on the ongoing interpretations and activities of individuals. This view is a frequent theme within social theory (see below).

Outside of consensus, conflict and action perspectives, there are other 'branches' within social theory worth highlighting. One is the 'linguistic turn' within social theory, which refers to perspectives that focus on the role of language in shaping communication and meaning (see Chapter 6). The linguistic turn generates a series of essential questions about how we gain access to the world through language and whether meaning is fixed or conditional on the structures of particular texts and words. The linguistic turn is exceptionally influential on poststructuralist and postmodern theorising, which challenges fundamental assumptions within the social sciences, such as whether it is possible to identify certain 'truths' about social life in a 'neutral' or 'objective' manner. The linguistic turn is also an example of where ideas within the arts and humanities (mainly through literary studies) begin to shape social and cultural research. Another recent development in social theory is the 'materialist' and 'affective' turns. These 'branches' refer to developments in new materialism: a set of perspectives that share an interest in discussing the properties and agency of material things while raising important questions about how humans relate to non-humans, such as animals, technology and the natural environment of planet Earth (see Chapter 10). New materialism also challenges fundamental assumptions within the social sciences, particularly the idea that the human should be the central feature of our theories and practices.

I think the metaphor of a tree, then, is a helpful way to begin visualising the landscape of social theory: behind each theorist and perspective is a set of assumptions that give way to ideas, concepts and frameworks that other thinkers borrow, take up or criticise. No social theory is fully self-enclosed, yet it is crucial to recognise that some contrasting assumptions about the world lead to different trajectories. This book, then, is divided into chapters that deal with these different paradigms, starting with the 'roots' and moving through to the 'branches'.

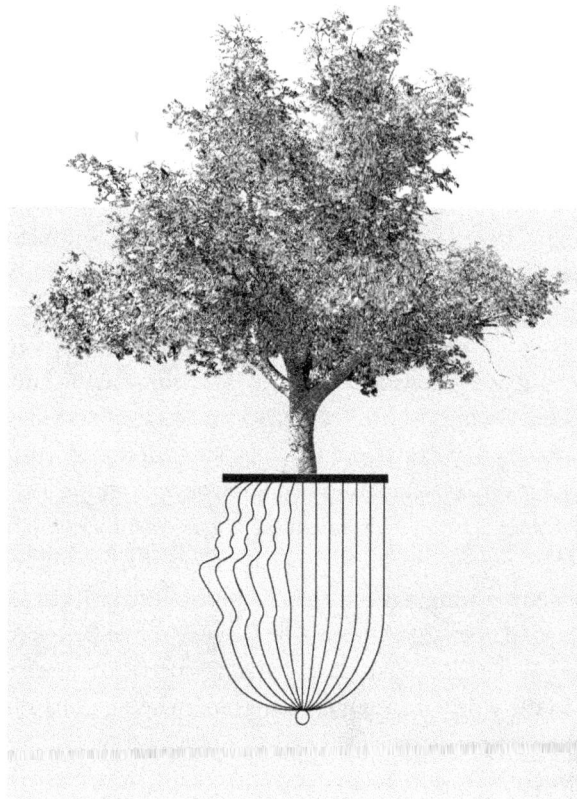

Figure 1.1   Roots and branches

Think about social theory as a 'tree' with various roots and branches. The 'roots' cage in certain assumptions about the world but also give way, allowing new perspectives to grow and flourish in the form of various 'branches' of contemporary theory.

Frequent Themes

The final point of this chapter is to suggest that some frequent themes run across social theory. They are structure and agency, knowledge and modernity.

Structure and Agency

In one way or another, most social theories deal with the question of structure and agency, which concerns the relative importance of 'social structure' or 'agency' (or individual actions) in an analysis of how society works. This theme begins in the writings of Marx and Durkheim, who suggest that social structures determine aspects of society, whether through exploitative wage-labour relations or the social roles and rules that generate consensus within society (see Chapters 2 and 4). Weber's methodological writings introduce an alternative perspective: that it is the actions of agents, particularly their beliefs and values, which shape social behaviour (see Chapter 3). Freud and Nietzsche's perspectives are a little more complex. Freud suggests that normative social structures penetrate the mind to constrain an individual's instincts and sexual desires, leading to repression. Nietzsche outwardly rejects the idea of an objective society, suggesting that individuals are responsible for their actions and the world in which we live (see Chapter 3).

The interest in structure and agency continues with phenomenology and symbolic interactionism (see Chapter 5). Phenomenologists like Husserl do not entertain the idea that individuals are passive agents of social structures. Instead, phenomenologists consider how individuals experience the world to become subjectively engaged social actors who actively order and make sense of their daily realities. This is a theme that is also central to the phenomenological sociology of Alfred Schütz and the ethnomethodology of Harold Garfinkel. Symbolic interactionism is also interested in agents, focusing mainly on the role of the **self** and how individuals develop their identities through interpersonal communication and language. Notably, a sense of structure re-emerges within symbolic interactionism, particularly through the works of Erving Goffman, who points to how social institutions exercise control over individuals through the use of signs, symbols and labels. Indeed, it is through Goffman's work that we get a sense of how the micro-dimensions of face-to-face interactions might 'carry' structural rules and obligations – something that Anthony Giddens develops explicitly in 'structuration theory' (see Chapter 7).

Structuralists, poststructuralists and postmodernists interrogate the potential for language, especially within written texts, to impose meaning on the world (see Chapter 6). They view written texts and, later, discourse as a means to confer power over individuals and encourage researchers to deconstruct these texts to reveal their inconsistencies and paradoxes. This approach becomes the basis for a sceptical view about objective 'truth' claims, including the possibility of generating knowledge about external social structures and their impact on agents. Indeed, the idea of power becomes more diffuse or 'fluid' in the context of these writers. For Foucault, power is not simply a 'top-down' exercise, such as through the use of force. Instead, it is more sutble and complex, working through techniques of surveillance and self-governance to shape people's **subjectivity** in complex ways. For Lyotard, social life is far too ambiguous and contradictory to attempt to use social structures to explain the 'truth' of society. Indeed, Lyotard is critical of the politics that often hides behind (social) scientific explanations – an idea also developed within actor-network theory and new materialist approaches (see Chapter 10).

This question of structure and agency is dealt with acutely by theorists like Anthony Giddens, Pierre Bourdieu and Margaret Archer (see Chapter 7). These theorists engage with earlier accounts of social structure and agency to 'reconcile' their differences and offer an account of how social structures produce societal change (or maintain the status quo). Their respective arguments focus on either 'merging' structure and agency together or keeping them analytically separate. In the first instance, structure and agency come together in people's practices and interpersonal communication, meaning that people 'carry' structural rules and resources in their actions. This 'carrying' takes the form of either their embodied practices (Bourdieu) or the language that people use (Giddens). In the second instance, researchers must keep structure and agency analytically separate (Archer). Archer's point is an ontological one (see social ontology): that social structures have properties and powers that are fundamentally different from agents or people. We must understand what these different powers and properties are before proceeding to explain how they interact. Archer's work, in particular, pays attention to the importance of human **reflexivity** and how it enables people to mediate their structural circumstances.

Finally, the question of structure and agency also appears in debates concerning feminism (see Chapter 8) and new materialism and **posthumanism** (see Chapter 10). Regarding feminism, there are different theoretical perspectives, which map to different understandings of the importance of structure and agency in determining aspects of inequality and **patriarchy** within society. For example, where Marxist feminists argue that socioeconomic structures are responsible for gender inequality, postmodern feminists suggest we must deconstruct social scientific understandings of sex and gender to reveal their power relations (see **dualism**). Through the work of Donna Haraway (see Chapter 8) and others, postmodern feminism is also influential on new materialist and posthuman social theory. Again, these theorists question the assumption that social structures govern social action at 'depth', preferring to argue that **assemblages** of human and non-human 'agents' make things happen. As with postmodernism, there is a sense here of the fluidity of social life and the possibility that things are constantly changing over time. There is no interest among theorists like Gilles Deleuze and Félix Guattari (see Chapter 10) in revealing the 'truth' of society by describing the characteristics of particular social structures. Instead, the focus is on the nature of change itself and the affect(s) this has.

Knowledge

The second frequent theme in social theory is knowledge. Every type of social theory makes claims about the world, but some theories have very different understandings about what is 'real' or not (Inglis with Thorpe, 2019, p. 4). As highlighted above, some theories suggest that society has 'real' social structures that determine people's behaviours. Other theories suggest it is people's experiences that are 'real' and which drive social behaviour. Others reject the idea of the 'real' entirely, suggesting that it is impossible and politically problematic to try to define and explain the social world scientifically. These theories each express a different assumption or social ontology about the world and the nature of its existence.

I teach my students to consider the fundamental differences between three ontological positions: **realism**, **idealism** and **scepticism**. Realism asserts that scientific theories can provide descriptions and explanations about the world that are approximately true. This position implies not only some kind of 'depth' to reality but also that it is possible to generate knowledge about its underlying mechanisms or causal laws. Realism is the basis for many social theories, including Marxism, functionalism and **critical realism**. Idealism, alternatively, assumes that our thoughts and ideas shape reality. It rejects the assumption that reality can exist independently of what is happening in our minds and suggests that human experience is vital in understanding what it is to exist in the world. Idealism is the basis for social theories, including phenomenology and **ethnomethodology**. Scepticism is altogether different again. It challenges the idea that we should be making these assumptions about the world. Sceptics recognise that there is politics and power involved in the creation of knowledge and 'truth' claims. As such, they question the foundations on which these claims are often made, thereby exposing any shortcomings in trying to define, explain (or control) what society is like. Scepticism forms the basis of the works of Nietzsche, Foucault and a range of postmodern, posthuman and new materialist thinkers.

There is also another dimension to knowledge within social theory: social epistemology. Social epistemology refers to how social theories intend to study what they think of as 'real' or not in the world. Crucially, social epistemology maps closely to social ontology as different theories match their assumptions about the world to the kinds of knowledge that they think essential to identify. For example, Chapter 4 discusses the 'positivism' of theorists like Comte and Durkheim. Positivism is an epistemology that suggests that the social sciences should generate knowledge about facts and causal laws similar to the natural sciences, often by collecting and analysing statistics. This perspective contrasts with the interpretive tradition (see Chapters 3 and 5), including the methodological works of Weber but also phenomenologists and phenomenological sociologists (see Chapter 5). These epistemological positions suggest that social research should look for knowledge that helps us understand people's beliefs and values by interpreting either what is happening in their heads or the methods by which they organise their daily lives.

Social ontology and epistemology are frequent themes throughout social theory because they shape the methods researchers adopt as they undertake their studies. It is important to recognise that our assumptions about the world shape the knowledge that we think is appropriate and relevant, informing the approaches we take to collecting and analysing data. As such, when reading social theory, always keep in mind the following questions:

- What is this theory saying about the nature of society?
- What is this theory saying about the kinds of knowledge appropriate for the study of society?
- What are the types of method that might be relevant for use with this theory?

Modernity

The third and final theme is modernity. Generally speaking, the 'roots' of social theory typically concern what society is like, how it operates and the direction in which it is going. Early social theorists such as Marx, Durkheim and Weber all agree that there are some core socioeconomic and cultural features of this modern landscape and that these raise particular threats or problems for social consensus. These features include the shift from feudal to capitalist-based societies (see **feudalism** and **capitalism**) due to **industrialisation,** in which new types of working and living arrangements dramatically alter the fabric of social life. As Chapter 2 details, capitalism brings with it a shift from agricultural labour (farming) to factory-based wage relations focused on mass production. It also brings a new type of consumer and an urbanised populace: shopping and living within sprawling cities, rather than farming food or crafting their own clothes. Marx, Durkheim and Weber each find a way to contend with these features of modern societies. For example, Marx argues that modern societies organise work (or wage labour) in contradictory and exploitative ways. Durkheim argues that modern societies are responsible for an emerging **individualism** that is changing social and moral bonds (see Chapter 4). Weber argues that modernity brings **disenchantment** through new forms of social and economic organisation (see Chapter 3).

Alongside these central features are the **Enlightenment** and **secularism**: two broad movements in social thinking that contextualise early theorists' interest in modern societies. The Enlightenment refers to an intellectual and cultural movement from the eighteenth century onwards that emphasises science, reason and logic over and against non-rational beliefs and forms of social organisation such as religion or monarchy. The Enlightenment became integral to the self-understanding of modernity in Europe because it suggested that, for the first time in history, people could produce knowledge for social progress. Indeed, it is often associated with initiating key events, such as the French Revolution in 1789 (which eventually led to the collapse of the French monarchy), and the development of French sociology through writers like Alexis de Tocqueville, Claude Henri Saint-Simon, Comte and, later, Durkheim (see Ritzer, 2008, pp. 9–18). Indeed, many of the values of the Enlightenment, such as reason-based change, scientific innovation and social advancement, became a core part of Durkheim's vision for sociology as a science of society.

Linked closely to the Enlightenment is secularism: a movement that refers to the general decline in the significance of religious thinking and practices (in some countries) while also leading to the separation of religious affairs from the running of state institutions. Before

Figure 1.2 The Enlightenment

Some refer to the Enlightenment as a 'light bulb' moment in human history because of its role in generating new ideas informed by scientific research.

the Enlightenment, experts would produce knowledge about the world by translating and interpreting religious texts to explain what God and other deities had in mind for them. The Enlightenment brings a radical change of direction here: it brings the power of reason and rationality to these interpretations and, in many instances, reveals religion as a human creation full of contradictions and power relations. This is certainly the perspective of writers such as Nietzsche and Freud, who, as a result of science, question the value of religious belief and knowledge in the modern world (see Chapter 3). Secularism also shapes Weber's view of modernity, albeit from a different perspective. Weber describes the process of **rationalisation** through which logic and reason come to strip people and European societies of their religious values and beliefs, leading to an overarching absence of meaning and conviction.

Since the 1960s, particularly with the emergence of poststructuralism (see Chapter 6), social theorists have increasingly tended to reflect on and challenge this idea of modernity and its central features. Indeed, the idea of 'postmodernity' speaks to moving beyond the assumption that societies have these overarching features (sometimes referred to as 'metanarratives'). A significant part of social theory has become about questioning the ontological and episte-mological assumptions on which the idea of modernity rests and how theorists of modernity reinforce particular social and cultural biases. This is particularly apparent in feminism, where debates take place over the conceptualisation of inequality and patriarchy and how it rein-forces binary categories of sex and gender (see Chapter 8). It is also apparent in postcolonial theory, which explicitly challenges the idea of the Enlightenment and its role in establishing European power through colonial and imperial conquest of other nations (see also Bhambra, 2007; Connell, 2007).

With these themes in mind, I now encourage you to explore the prominent thinkers, issues and debates in classical and contemporary social theory. I really hope that they inspire you to think, research and act about the world in new ways.

Summary

- This book offers many images, contemporary examples and other facts to support the reader in understanding the core message behind particular theoretical perspectives and ideas.
- There are many productive ways to 'think about theory' that make it easier to grasp. The first is to recognise that social theory is less a matter of just learning what theorists say and more about thinking about what we can learn from these ideas to use them to explain and understand the world. The second is to recognise that there are many plausible explanations for social phenomena or events, which is why it is vital to have a broad grasp of different theoretical perspectives. The third is to reflect on how theorists construct their own arguments in reasoned ways, starting with their assumptions about how the world works and then moving to prove those assumptions through research and evidence.
- We can also 'think about theory' in terms of the relationship between its different 'roots' and 'branches' and how different perspectives emerge around different ontological and epistemological assumptions
- Some frequent themes run throughout social theory, including structure and agency, knowledge and modernity. Each one speaks to many of the similarities and differences between theoretical perspectives.

Review Questions

- What are the main differences between conflict, consensus and action perspectives across social theories?
- What makes the following ontological perspectives different: realism, idealism and scepticism?
- What is the role of modernity in the development of social theory?

Annotated Reading

For a historical sketch of early social theory, notably the works of Marx, Durkheim and Weber, try George Ritzer's (2008) *Classical Sociological Theory* (New York: McGraw-Hill), now in its fifth edition.

In the third edition of their book *Introducing Social Theory* (Cambridge: Polity Press), Pip Jones and Liz Bradbury (2018) provide a more detailed introduction to the relationship between consensus, conflict and action perspectives.

Those interested in better understanding the role of social ontology and social epistemology in the research process will benefit from reading Michael Crotty's (1998) *The Foundations of Social Research: Meaning and Perspective in the Research Process* (London: Sage).

2

Marx and Marxism

Chapter Objectives

This chapter will:

- Introduce Karl Marx, particularly his concern with capitalism and the contradictions it raises for work and wage labour.
- Familiarise critical concepts, including alienation, exploitation, class conflict, ideology, and commodity fetishism.
- Consider the continuing relevance of Marx's arguments through contemporary examples of modern factory settings and the 'gig economy'.

Keywords

Capitalism, wage labour, alienation, exploitation, class, ideology, commodities, production, consumption

Introduction

This chapter shows that Karl Marx was a critical thinker whose concern with **capitalism** led him to expose the organisation of work (or wage labour) as contradictory. In particular, Marx reveals that, by exchanging labour for a wage, workers are vulnerable to exploitative management and business practices. Marx encourages social and political resistance, and we can see examples of that resistance today in the movements that challenge wealth inequalities and call for better working conditions. Marx also alerts us to the power of **ideology** in obscuring the problems of capitalism by moving critical attention away from workers' experiences. Marxists develop this idea by revealing that the problems of capitalism are not bound to the economy but penetrate social and cultural activities. Mass media, consumerism and digital labour remain essential areas for thinking critically about capitalism's hold over everyday life and what alternative possibilities exist. This ongoing commitment to questioning the organisation of work and the economy is Marx's legacy.

What Is Capitalism?

Before we can understand Marx's ideas, we must first explore what capitalism is. Since the earliest of times, human societies have crafted and traded goods for consumption and means of subsistence through various forms of labour. In pre-capitalist European societies, many people met their needs by farming the land or producing goods through trade skills, such as woodworking or weaving. Capitalism changes this arrangement by turning people into wage labourers (see **wage labour**). Rather than living and working on the land of another (i.e., a king or nobleman), exchanging their labour for the resources and tools needed to feed, dress and entertain themselves, capitalists employ workers to produce goods in return for a wage. A wage (or salary) is the price paid by the employer in exchange for their labour time. In early capitalist European societies, workers produced goods for capitalists to sell within a marketplace. These goods were sold at a price higher than the cost of paying these workers' wages, thereby generating profits for the capitalist. As such, capitalism is about pursuing profit through efficient production and reinvestment practices. Capitalists make money by keeping the costs of production low and reinvesting their profits back into their businesses. As such, economic growth involves managing the labour force, sometimes through cutting wages or increasing productivity.

Basing production on wage labour creates division and conflict under capitalism between the owners of capital, who own what Marx calls the 'means of production', and those who sell their labour in exchange for wages. In pre-capitalist societies, members of the ruling classes, such as feudal lords, owned the land, machinery, materials and workplaces needed to make goods. These lords would exploit peasants or 'serfs' by forcing them to produce essential goods. The aim of this production was consumption. Serfs would cultivate the land to meet the needs of the feudal lord. This system changes under capitalism as wealthy people take ownership over these means to employ workers to make these goods. A characteristic feature of this system is that production is for accumulation, not just consumption. Wealthy people accumulate capital (often in the form of money) by generating profit through this wage-labour relation. Capitalists are free to invest this money in any activity that will bring about future profit and business growth, and workers are 'free' to find any employment that pays them a wage.

What is unique about capitalism is that wage labour is free and unfree. Wage labourers are relatively free to decide whom they work for and where. They can move around geographically to find suitable work and transfer within occupations to secure better pay conditions. This method of organising labour is preferable to feudal serfdom (see **feudalism**), where owners force their workers to labour and physically bind them to their land. Nevertheless, it is difficult to survive under capitalism without paid work, and many people have little choice in what jobs are available. Many wage labourers are also subjects of tight employer control through disciplinary techniques, such as performance reviews, operating as a check on employee productivity. The threat of unemployment may also bind wage labourers into accepting these controls, for the alternative is to struggle without money. People are 'slaves' to a wage, as Marx (1844) puts it.

As Fulcher (2015, pp. 15–16) suggests, capitalism is also about a change in consumption: wage labourers can neither access the raw materials nor create what they need to survive. What results is a demand for a range of new capitalist businesses that supply subsistence: the food, clothing, shelter and other basic amenities, including leisure and entertainment, needed to sustain life. Fulcher argues that this creates a 'double role' for the wage labourer – they are both a producer and a consumer – which explains why capitalism continues today. Workers reproduce their wage-labour relations by participating in consumer culture, that is, by shopping. That people will work overtime or borrow money to consume is evidence of the contradiction that living in a capitalist society presents.

Capitalism as a Contradiction

Now that we have a basic idea of what capitalism is, we can consider the ideas of Marx in more detail. Marx was a philosopher, economist and political activist born in Germany. The legacy of his ideas is in the way Marx questions the organisation of work within capitalist economies. Marx saw a contradiction at the heart of capitalism, between wage labour and capital accumulation, and argued that it was responsible for a great deal of human suffering and social inequality. In his book *Das Kapital*, published in 1867, Marx addresses what he thinks the causes of this contradiction are and why. We, wage labourers, must change how capitalist economies organise work. That a new system could come to supplant capitalism is the focus of his book *The Communist Manifesto*, co-authored with Friedrich Engels and published in 1848.

Georg Hegel

To understand what Marx saw as a contradiction within capitalism, we need to engage with the ideas of Georg Hegel. Hegel was a German philosopher who was very influential on Marx during his early years of study. Hegel asks a simple question, 'what is human history?' or, in other words, 'how might we characterise human progress?' Hegel's response is to suggest that what defines human history is our capacity to reason. Humans progress through history by reasoning their way through challenges, confrontations and conflicts. Hegel's response sounds abstract, but it is essential to remember that he is writing during the **Enlightenment** period, when intellectuals saw scientific knowledge as a means of advancing values, such as liberty, tolerance, **secularism**, and human progress. Hegel agrees, suggesting that human reason drives history forward.

A key concept of Hegel is the dialectical method (see **dialectics**), which, dating back to Ancient Greece, refers to the way that reasoned debate takes place. Two intellectuals would debate a subject. The first would present an argument or 'thesis', such as 'The colour of the ocean is blue'. The second would present a counter-argument or 'antithesis', such as 'The colour of the ocean is green'. A great debate would ensue between the two intellectuals, each providing evidence to support their argument while appraising their opponents' position. Finally, they reach a resolution or 'synthesis' – 'the answer is in how the water reflects the light!' Hegel proposes that this dialogue, reasoning through the collision of opposing ideas, leads to a heightened sense of human freedom. Hegel sees the dialectical method as securing human progress because it generates new insight into the human condition and its consciousness of the world. As history progresses, humans have become more self-conscious and, therefore, more rational and freer.

Hegel's philosophy might sound far-fetched, but consider how we 'level up' through everyday life. Each day, whether through education, work or training, we gain experience that grants us access to more skills and knowledge about the world around us. The more skills we have access to, the more choices we have when solving problems. Hegel's point is that, as time passes, humans are levelling up, breaking past systems of rulership by creating societies based on rationality. Freedom is the endpoint of human history, suggests Hegel, where the dialectical method serves to unify humanity by resolving all contradictions and thereby harmonising human culture through reason.

Hegel's philosophy is very theoretical, but its impact on a young, radical Marx should not be understated. Marx also sees human history as marked by struggle, conflict and confrontation but takes Hegel's understanding of the dialectical process in a decidedly different direction.

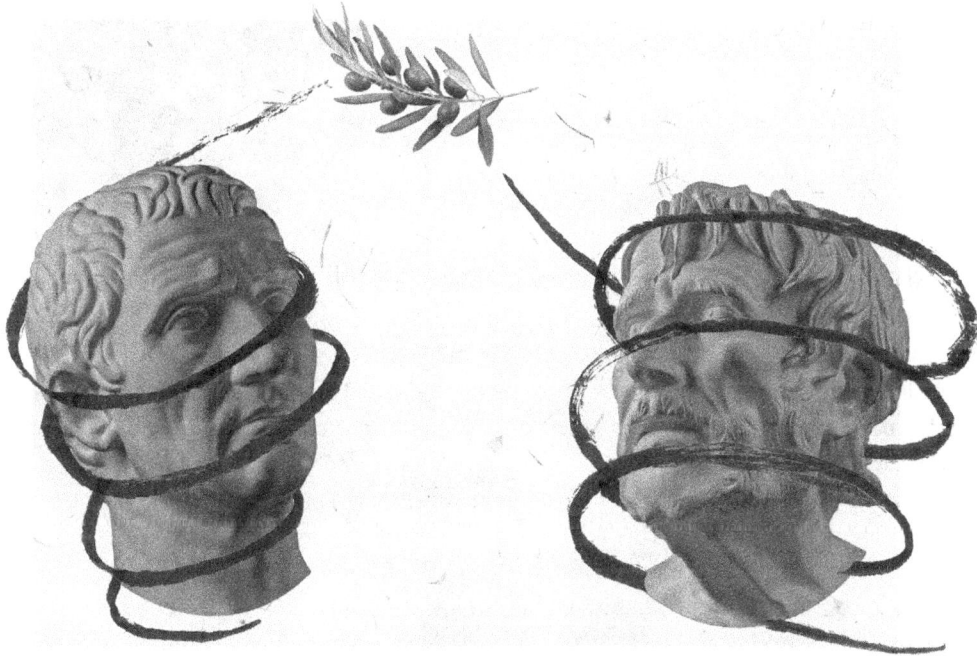

Figure 2.1 Dialectics

Think about how two speakers with opposing views try to find common ground through the ability to reason and debate. In Ancient Greece, the more we can reason and debate, the closer we are to freedom, progress and peace. The olive branch is a symbol of such resolution and reconciliation.

Young Karl Marx

As a young man beginning his doctoral studies in Berlin, Marx was a member of a student group known as the 'Young Hegelians', a group of radical thinkers who met to criticise the state, religion, politics and culture from a leftist perspective. Hegel's philosophy captivated these young academics, but many regarded it as abstract and incomplete. One criticism, in particular, was with Hegel's view of human history as the pursuit of freedom as it unfolds through the dialectical process. The importance that Hegel afforded thought over action concerned Marx and others within this student group. The dialectical process suggests we must unify through careful deliberation and debate to resolve the world's problems. Marx did not support this view. He was critical of Hegel's **idealism**: the idea that our consciousness comes before our material existence. Marx (1845) rejected the view that we can simply reason or think our way through social ills, saying, 'Philosophers have hitherto only interpreted the world in various ways; the point is to change it'.

Marx's point is that the dialectical process does not account for people's material circumstances. Hegel's view of history obscures the real relationship humans have with the material world – how it structures our basic needs, such as food, clothing, shelter and entertainment. Marx brings Hegel down to earth. He embraces the idea that we need to understand how humans experience the material world by examining the economic conditions of their labour. The dialectical method remains essential here, but its focus shifts. Freedom is no longer about resolving the opposition between ideas but identifying the contradictions within people's working lives.

Marx had a personal reason to question Hegel's lofty account of freedom: he had observed the social misery that an economic crisis brings. Marx's family owned a vineyard in Trier, part of the Mosel wine region of southwestern Germany. During the 1830s and 1840s, these vineyards were in crisis due to economic policies implemented by the Prussian government. Many winemakers found themselves in a state of uncertain desperation as the government's policies opened up the region to market competition, leading to falling prices and debt. Marx (1843) published articles angrily criticising the government's policies, critical of how the Prussian government positioned the vine growers' distress as the result of producing inferior products. The truth, as Marx saw it, was that the vine grower's unfortunate circumstances were the result of the government's social, political and economic decisions.

There was nothing 'natural' about the increasing economic competition between winemakers. It was the result of a political economic structure that created winners and losers. This encounter with the winemakers is what, in part, drives Marx's critique of Hegel. Marx writes that Hegel's understanding of the dialectic must be 'inverted' to reveal the truth about modern societies: that the structuring of work is the basis of a real, material contradiction. People need to recognise that the political economic structures of capitalism are at odds with our human nature.

Human Nature

> Labour is, in the first place, a process in which both man and Nature participate, and in which man of his own accord starts, regulates, and controls the material reactions between himself and Nature. ... By thus acting on the external world and changing it, he at the same time changes his own nature. (Marx, 1867)

Marx argues that our ability to labour is what makes us human. What defines us as a species (as separate from other animals) is our capacity to produce our food, clothing, shelter and other means of subsistence. Marx argues that humankind has the physical and mental prowess required to be free to produce whatever goods are needed to survive. Humans are a species-being, Marx suggests, by which he means that it is of our nature to be practically and theoretically engaged in the production of our physical environments. What makes us human is that we plan ways to transform the world's materials to meet our needs. We develop recipes, craft tools, and build structures of the imagination, capable of feeding, clothing, housing and transporting many millions of people.

What is crucial about modern societies – and capitalism – is that this particular moment or 'historical epoch' has twisted human nature. The essence of our labour is no longer in keeping with our species-being as capitalism changes how humans relate to the production of their physical environments. More specifically, under capitalism, humans no longer produce what they need or use but, rather, labour for wages.

For example, consider the changing role of a baker in society. Baking bread was once at the heart of everyday life, with its practical and theoretical skillset affording valuable opportunities for rewarding work and social experience. Bakers knew the ingredients, recipes and techniques needed to turn raw materials into valuable goods, crucial for nutrition. The craft of baking was a way of expressing human creativity while also fulfilling key physical, social and familial needs. Baking and eating bread connected families and local communities together.

However, under capitalism, the role of the baker changes. Following **industrialisation**, and the automation of baking by factory machines, the baker no longer produces bread for immediate use or subsistence needs. Instead, the baker exchanges their labour for a wage to purchase the commodities they need to survive. Marx argues that capitalism fundamentally changes labour: it shifts value away from what humans produce for use to the exchange of labour for wages. As a factory worker, the baker sells their time to another to earn a wage. Marx sees this shift as people losing their freedom to produce for themselves in rewarding ways, which is at odds with their human nature.

In distinction to Hegel, then, Marx believed that transforming our needs through labour was the engine of human history – not merely dialectical reasoning. The social, political and economic relations that allow people to labour creatively and collectively drive the shift from pre-modern to capitalist societies. True human potential resides in how people work together to conquer their material needs. The problem, as Marx sees it, is that people are no longer labouring for themselves in capitalist societies. Workers labour for others and, with it, are chained to wages. People become 'slaves' to wage labour to survive (Marx, 1844). So Marx (1852) famously remarks:

> Men make their own history, but they do not make it as they please; they do not make it under self-selected circumstances, but under circumstances existing already, given and transmitted from the past.

What this means is that individuals cannot escape their human nature. They cannot escape the labour that historically places them under conditions that are not of their choosing. Under capitalism, exchanging labour for wages is one such condition. People can make history by working together to transform labour in ways that better reflect humanity – meeting our needs through creatively free production. Of course, that idea – of collective labour making for a better world – only emerges because Marx conceives of **alienation**.

Alienation

Marx's theory of alienation brings together the different strands of thought previously covered. Marx uses the term to capture what he feels is wrong with modern society's structure of labour relations. Marx expresses these concerns most clearly in *The Paris Manuscripts*, an initial analysis of the conditions of modern industrial societies and how they result in the estrangement of wage labourers from their work. Marx argues that industrialisation perverts the inherent relationship between labour and human nature by hiring employees to work for paid wages. Marx (1844; emphasis in original) writes:

> First, the fact that labor is *external* to the worker, i.e. it does not belong to his intrinsic nature; that in his work, therefore, he does not affirm himself but denies himself, does not feel content but unhappy, does not develop freely his physical and mental energy but mortifies his body and ruins his mind.

Labour is not our own under this new arrangement as modern industrial relations alienate us from it. Labour is no longer an end in itself, an expression of human capability and creativity, but a means to an end: a way of earning money. Marx argues that this process has four essential components:

1   Modern industrial societies alienate workers from their 'productive activity'. Workers no longer produce objects to their ideas nor immediately satisfy their needs through the objects they create. Instead, they work for others – capitalists – who sell the products that workers create in exchange for a wage. For Marx, under this arrangement, the worker becomes as much a commodity as the thing that they produce. Wage-labour relations remove the worker from their work. Workers do not see themselves within their labour.
2   Industrial working conditions of modern societies alienate workers from the object of their labour activities – the product itself. Workers do not own the products their labour creates, nor can they afford to buy such products through their wages.
3   Marx argues that people need and want to work cooperatively to appropriate from nature what they require to survive. Industrial working conditions disrupt this cooperation by forcing strangers to work together, side by side, isolating them into cubicles, or by telling them that they are in constant competition for jobs or promotions. These conditions alienate workers from their fellow workers. Modern industrial relations turn fellow workers into adversaries rather than allies.
4   Finally, capitalism alienates workers from their very nature, that is, from their human potential. Labour is no longer a source of satisfaction or personal investment. Instead, work is where people feel the least human. Workplaces script and programme employee activity to ensure efficiency and productivity. Indeed, there is little room for creativity or autonomy on the assembly line. For Marx, controlling labour in this way dulls human consciousness and, ultimately, people's capacity to be freely creative.

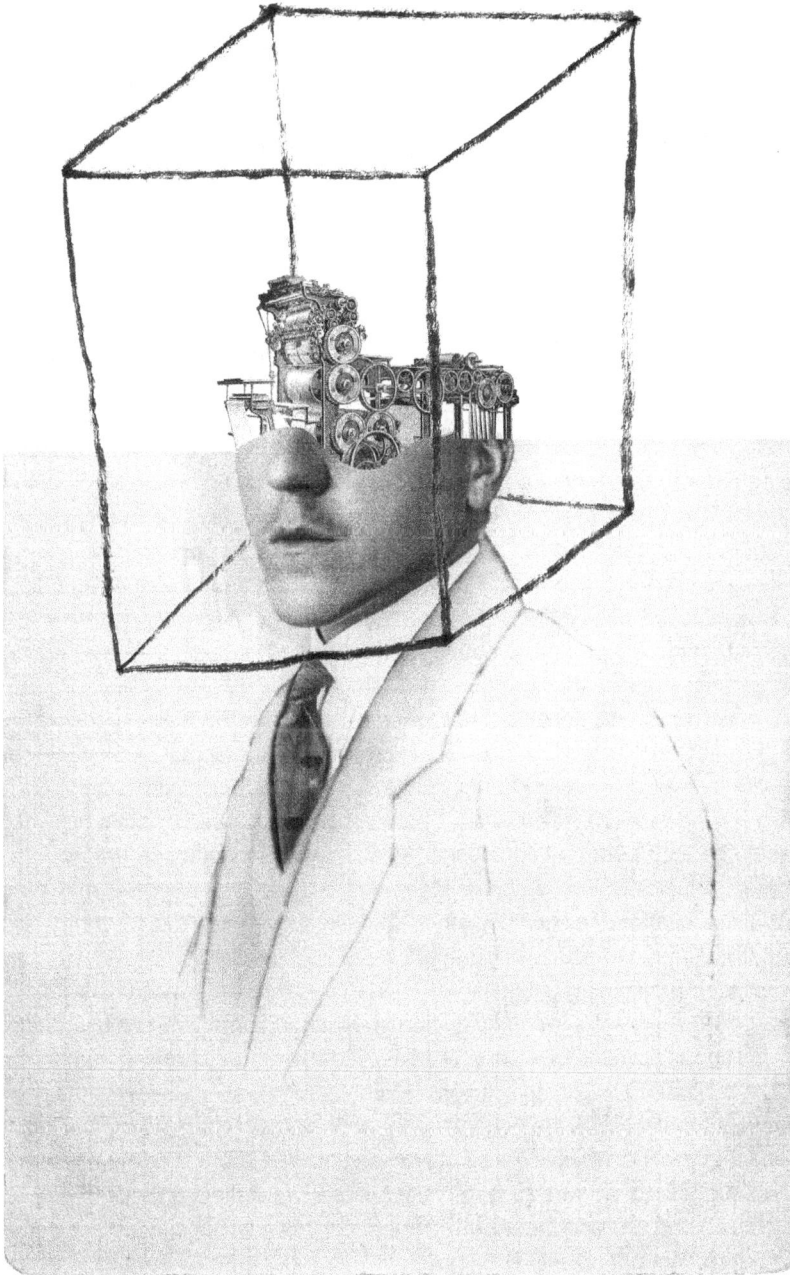

Figure 2.2 Alienation

Reflect on how workers might lose aspects of their autonomy and identity to become part of a mechanised social class. They are 'boxed off' or disconnected from the product of their labour and confined to and defined by industrial production processes.

Marx and Apple Inc.

Brian Merchant's (2017) account of the working conditions in the Foxconn factory in Shenzhen, China, connects closely to Marx's four types of alienation. Merchant argues that the factory, which produces Apple products, is illustrative of the 'brutality' of assembly-line work, revealing the immense stress, long workdays and harsh management practices that come with manufacturing Apple (and other technology) products.

First, consider how the assembly line operates at Foxconn to alienate workers from their 'productive activity'. Since Apple products, like the iPhone, are compact, complex machines, their assembly requires sprawling lines of hundreds of people to build, inspect, test and package each device. Up to 450,000 workers perform these tasks in 141 steps over 24 hours. Merchant (2017, p. 329) estimates that workers spend 1,152,000,000 hours screwing, gluing, soldering and snapping iPhones together in a single three-month period. Following Marx, this exhaustive labour operation confers no creativity on the part of the workforce. The workers have no direct impact on the broader design of the product nor complete control over its delivery. Designers at Apple's headquarters in Silicon Valley do the creative work and strategic planning. Merchant (2017, p. 314) paints a bleak picture of the assembly line at Foxconn, suggesting that managers humiliate workers who fail to meet productivity quotas, speak to one another during working hours, or leave their work stations without permission.

Second, consider the relationship these workers have with the Apple products they create. In part, Apple's financial success hinges on exploiting cheap labour to produce its products efficiently and effectively. Merchant (2017, pp. 319, 333–335) argues that Foxconn assembly-line workers earn around $20 a day. Their wages barely meet basic needs, and many work overtime to compensate for their poor pay conditions. As such, very few of these workers can afford to own the Apple products they manufacture. Merchant (2017, p. 335) suggests that many workers 'laugh off' the idea of affording such a luxury item. Instead, workers must 'scrimp' and 'save' to purchase unofficial Apple products through the local black market.

Third, consider the working relationships inside Foxconn, which Merchant (2017, pp. 312, 316, 318, 322, 339) suggests are particularly cruel. Managers regularly scold workers for being too slow or making mistakes by insulting or punishing them in front of one another to make an 'example'. These rituals of public humiliation, Merchant suggests, create a culture of high-stress work, anxiety and control. Workers become managers as they 'adapt' to the use of shame and embarrassment as tools to discipline their coworkers. Indeed, there is an expectation, Merchant (2017, p. 316) suggests, that workers who make a 'costly' mistake prepare a formal apology – a letter, read publically, promising that they will not make this mistake again.

Why would workers put up with such practices? Merchant (2017, pp. 312, 315) argues that the work culture within Foxconn (and China, more broadly) makes quitting difficult. There is an expectation that workers must organise their lives around work and the factory's timetable. Workers eat, sleep and live within the factory's compound. As Merchant (2017, pp. 330–331) recollects, if Apple's manufacturing schedule changes, Foxconn can summon thousands of workers and hundreds of engineers to begin production or make last-minute product changes.

This organisation of wage labour speaks to Marx's fourth point: that alienation comes from the way that workplaces, to ensure productivity, demand control over workers' lives. Merchant (2017, p. 308) accounts for the immense stress, depression and desperation that these conditions create, including, sadly, examples of employee suicide.

These four understandings of alienation play an essential role in how Marx conceives of not only capitalism but also **exploitation**.

Capitalism as Exploitation

The previous section raises four essential points about Marx's work:

1   Marx identifies a problem with capitalism in how it organises labour relations.
2   He calls this problem a 'dialectical contradiction', following the work of Georg Hegel.
3   This contradiction concerns how capitalists accumulate value through wage labour.
4   Marx sees a shift in society from people labouring for themselves to labouring-for-capitalists. This process perverts people's natural relationship to labour, making them feel alienated.

This section develops these points by considering the arguments from Marx's later works, such as *Capital*. These works are more 'structural' in perspective, focusing on the way that the economy in modern societies shape labour relations. Here critical concepts such as commodities, exploitation, **class** and ideology emerge. This section will consider these concepts and how they inform Marx's critique of capitalism as a site for exploitation.

Commodity Fetishism

Marx reveals the true nature of capitalism through his examination of commodity fetishism, which refers to his analysis of commodities in society. Commodities are goods (e.g., food or clothing) or services (e.g., haircuts or mail delivery), the qualities of which satisfy human needs. Marx uses the term 'fetishism' to capture how social and material relations (or society) imbue these goods with fantastical powers that go beyond their natural properties. Marx argues that commodities exist in a contradictory dual state that obscures the origins of labour to create a society of relations between things, not people. Indeed, for Marx, what characterises capitalism is that commodities, not people, organise social and material relations.

For example, consider a loaf of bread sitting on a supermarket shelf. When we look at this commodity, we can describe it in different ways. First, we can describe it physically in terms of its natural properties or essential ingredients, such as flour and water. Second, we know its intended use or purpose: to provide nutrition through eating. What we do not know, however, is who makes the loaf or where or how. This production process is an essential part of the commodity too. The loaf requires the employment of all sorts of workers, including people who source the raw materials and operate the machinery, to mix, bake and package the goods. For Marx, as these workers bring the loaf into existence, it creates or renews social and material relations, such as between the factory owner and the worker or the owner of the distribution company and the lorry driver. The production process also includes social relations between consumers and the names and identities of the workers that they do not and cannot know. Commodity fetishism, then, refers to how commodities, like the loaf of bread, possess the magical ability to create or renew all kinds of social relations while also being something as simple as a mixture of flour and water.

Marx suggests that consumers cannot see or know who produces commodities because labour in the capitalist system happens privately, whether on farms or in factories. This privatisation of labour changes how people value the production process at the point at which labour becomes social. In pre-capitalist societies, labour was about producing goods to meet our immediate needs, such as sourcing and producing loaves of bread for ourselves. Marx calls this 'use-value', which captures the idea that the object of labour was once primarily based on needs. These goods are not commodities, for we recognise, socially, the skill, creativity and labour that goes into producing them. Marx argues that private labour, under capitalism, is different. Private labour is given value when commodities enter a marketplace for exchange. Marx calls this 'exchange-value', which captures the idea that labour is only worth what the market values. Indeed, he suggests that all commodities float free of their physical properties, taking on a life of their own. Under this system, there are no interactions between individuals per se, just interactions between commodities. People sell their labour by exchanging it for wages to buy commodities that, in both cases, the market determines the value of. For Marx, the complexity of this process is what characterises commodity fetishism: that the exchanges happening in the system take place between things, not people, thereby obscuring the origins of labour and the forces that influence working conditions. Marx's concern is that this structuring of social life, through commodities, gives way to exploitation and social control.

Exploitation

A simple definition of exploitation is the act of maltreating someone by benefiting from their work. Marx argues that capitalism is an exploitative economic system because capitalists benefit from the work of others. Remember, capitalism is a system based on commodity production in the service of capital accumulation. A principle of this system is reinvestment: capitalists take a percentage of the sale of the products that labourers create and reinvest it back into the business for expansion and growth. Reinvestment might sound like good economics, but for Marx, such a system hides relations of **power** and social control. Indeed, Marx challenges the idea that capitalism is a neutral force, arguing that it is an inherently political system because of the way that it benefits privileged social groups through the organisation and exploitation of working people.

Marx argues that wage labour is a social, political and economic relationship that divides labour into two main groups or classes in society – the workers and the capitalists. Workers are wage labourers who produce commodities. They do not own the resources or tools by which to meet their needs. The workers are also consumers: they can only buy what they need by exchanging their labour for wages. Capitalists, on the other hand, own the means of production and are the ones who pay the wages through the capital – in the form of money – that labourers generate through production. It is by this generation of capital through wage-labour relations that Marx captures the division between classes.

Marx argues that capital exists within a circuit that achieves growth by exploiting wage labourers. Capitalists are business owners who, in the search to generate profit and maximise growth, must drive down the costs of commodity production. Marx argues that wage labourers will suffer within this circuit, as sacrifices to the cost of labour and the conditions of work will generate the profit needed to fund growth. Indeed, Marx suggests that the constant tendency of capital is to force the cost of labour back towards zero. His overwhelming concern was that capitalists were making labour so cheap that workers could not purchase the precious commodities they needed to survive. This contradiction between wage labour and capital is what Marx terms exploitation: that, through the exchange of labour time for wages, capitalists gain a disproportionate amount of wealth. Exploitation describes how capitalists maltreat workers, often by twisting work conditions, to accumulate capital.

Remember that, for Marx, it was once only workers who could produce objects of (use) value. Under capitalism, business owners find a way to generate (exchange) value from workers' labour. Poor pay, stress, sickness, dangerous conditions, unemployment and poverty are all examples of the exploitation that follows this shift in the organisation of the economy and work. Marx rails against any suggestion that these social conditions are in some way 'natural' or 'neutral'. The economy is not neutral. Marx sees it as a form of social domination, where decisions about worker lay-offs, student loans, interest rate rises, bank bail-outs and tax loopholes are political decisions that benefit one group of people over another.

Why is the concept of exploitation important? Workers might appear to be 'free' under capitalism, but they are not, as modern labour relations coerce workers into accepting poor pay and working conditions. The clearest example of this coercion is through what Marx (and Engels) term the 'reserve army of labour': the relative surplus population awaiting employment. Marx suggests that, under capitalism, part of the working population becomes excess to requirements as the workforce grows and machines replace the need for labour. This surplus availability influences the pay rate of wages and working conditions because a large workforce of unemployed people will force wages down while potentially intensifying the exploitation that workers experience (i.e., bosses might coerce workers to work longer hours and for less because of the availability of replacement labour). This circuit where exploitation thrives is what Marx argues will cause class conflict.

Class Conflict

The term 'class' typically refers to a grouping of objects or people. Marx defines the term differently, describing class in terms of its potential for social conflict. Marx argues that people form a class in so far as they are in common conflict over their exploitation. There are two main classes in capitalist society for Marx: the workers (or the proletariat) and the capitalists (or bourgeoisie). As highlighted above, capitalists own the means of production – the resources, tools and knowledge – needed to produce goods. The workers are dependent on the wages that capitalists provide to live. This arrangement affords capitalists the social and economic power to exploit labourers. Marx argues that the continuing exploitation of the workers will generate conflict between classes as capitalists force the cost of labour towards zero. This contradiction in the organisation of the economy and work cannot continue without conflict. Marx (1867) writes:

> We have seen how this absolute contradiction between the technical necessities of modern industry, and the social character inherent in its capitalist form, dispels all fixity and security in the situation of the labourer; how it constantly threatens, by taking away the instruments of labour, to snatch from his hands his means of subsistence.

Marx argues that it is a self-defeating act on behalf of capitalists to exploit labourers whose productive activity is indispensable to the economy. By mistreating workers, Marx sees capitalists as creating the material conditions for social revolution. Change is possible because of the extent of exploitation, which evidences the need to oppose the structures organising modern labour production. Marx argues that workers' revolts are powerful because they resist the processes that organise the productive activity. For example, by withdrawing their labour through strikes, workers remove the power of employment structures to generate economic value. Marx argues that a social revolution that targets these 'forces of production' can cause the supporting institutions to change. Culture, law and social policy are the functions of 'relations of production' that tend to prevent changes to the organisation of the economy and work. For example, some laws prevent workers from striking under certain circumstances or penalise those who withdraw their labour without proper notice. Marx argues that laws and cultural ideas, such as the suggestion that striking workers are 'lazy', which prevent social change, perform the function of ideology. In essence, they hide the contradictions in the exploitative organisation of work in modern societies.

Ideology

Marx uses the word 'ideology' in two senses. First, ideology refers to those ideas that emerge from living in a capitalist society but reflect the reality of capitalism in an inverted manner. Marx uses the metaphor of a 'camera obscura' to describe this: a device that employs an optical quirk to show an image reflected upside down. The fetishism of commodities characterises this type of ideology or upside-down image. We know that money is nothing but a piece of paper and that its value is a social construct, and yet we treat money as though it has tremendous value, using it to determine how people eat, sleep and live.

Marx argues that this ideology is vulnerable to social, political and economic disruption by examining its underlying material contradictions. In one sense, this is what Marxism is about: raising awareness that human value is not dependent on money and that people may form caring relationships or perform social actions without need of financial reward. By raising people's awareness of this, Marx suggests that the contradictions that drive capitalism will come into view, righting our inverted view of money and showing people that the economy is a political entity. As such, Marxism is about supporting workers to become aware of their structural exploitation by revealing how governments, businesses and other elites use legal and economic tools for social and political control.

However, consciousness-raising might not be enough. Marx is aware of a second, more deceptive, form of ideology that attempts to obscure these efforts. Marx argues that within religion, philosophy, literature and law there are ideas that attempt to make any contradictions in wage-labour relations appear coherent – such as that (economic) competition, domination and control are part of human nature. These ideas typically explain away workers' experiences of labour conditions as personal problems or individual idiosyncrasies. For example, conservative or right-wing political commentators might suggest that exploitation is natural: that economies of production will always lead to an unequal distribution of wealth. Marx's point is that such ideas are purposively abstract to draw attention away from workers' experiences to justify the status quo. Ideology here renders social change implausible by presenting any problems with labour relations as examples of contradictions in human nature, not capitalism.

Importantly, this second type of ideology shapes our very understanding of freedom. Marx (1973/1939, p. 652) argues that capitalist practices invert our view of freedom:

> This kind of individual freedom is therefore at the same time the most complete suspension of all individual freedom, and the most complete subjugation of individuality under social conditions which assume the form of objective powers....

The act of exchanging labour for wages, or wages for commodities, presupposes that we are all free. Indeed, one might suggest that no one forces a consumer to buy the latest Apple iPhone nor the Foxconn factory worker to labour in excessively challenging conditions. However, Marx argues that people are not free. Freedom means the ability to have control over our productive activity. In this sense, the worker is neither free nor equal to the capitalist. Marx goes on to suggest, more philosophically, that *it is capital that is free:* free for exchange as people accept it freely without prejudice. Money does as it wishes in so far as no one questions its validity in structuring our daily lives.

Our inverted view of freedom is such that governments can introduce policies and measures that portray inequalities as equality. For example, consider the idea of 'regressive taxation': governments uniformly apply a tax to all situations, such that it affects people with low income more severely than people with a high income. Value-added tax (VAT) or sales tax is an example of regressive taxation. In the UK, all consumers, regardless of their income, pay 20% VAT on a wide range of goods and services. Imagine two consumers, each purchasing a £180 rail ticket, of which VAT totals £30. The first consumer earns £1000 per week, making the VAT cost 3% of their income. The second consumer earns £200 per week, making the VAT cost 15% of their income. In this case, though the tax rate is the same, the person with the lower income pays a higher percentage, making the tax 'regressive'.

All this means is that, for Marx, ideology is not just a by-product of social relations but a material force capable of gripping the masses in practical concerns and activities. This material form makes ideology challenging but provides the impetus for Marxists to examine the qualitative ways that exchange relations impact workers' lives.

After Karl Marx

Since Marx died in 1883, there have been many attempts to interpret his ideas and define what Marxism 'is'. Many different groups claim to be Marxists and continue to identify the relevance of his work by drawing parallels between his thinking and contemporary society. The most notable are those formulated by left-wing thinkers in western Europe following the end of the First World War. Here, two of the most recognised versions of Marxism are the 'critical theory' associated with the Frankfurt School and Antonio Gramsci's theory of **hegemony**.

Frankfurt School

The Frankfurt School was a group of academics at the University of Frankfurt in the 1920s. In its earliest days, the Frankfurt School set out to produce a critical theory of capitalist societies by identifying mechanisms of ideological repression and social control. Members of the school include Theodor Adorno, Max Horkheimer, Herbert Marcuse, Eric Fromm and, later, Jürgen Habermas. The Frankfurt theorists were living in a politically turbulent time involving Adolf Hitler's rise to power and the Nazi Party in Germany. **Fascism** was a central theme in their work, and the theorists were critical of National Socialism in Germany and Soviet Communism. Moving to the USA to escape Nazi rule, these theorists reflected on how mass media (radio, television, cinema, newspapers) in these 'democratic' countries were also powerful agents of social control and ideological repression. Their analysis of mass media was the first social theoretical analysis of media forms and their apparent effects on audiences.

Adorno and Horkheimer (1997/1944) draw on Marx's ideas and on writings from Sigmund Freud and Max Weber (see Chapter 3) to analyse how mass media became a central pillar of ruling-class ideology and social control. Where Marx saw contradictions in capital accumulation

as generating chronic instability through competing classes, Adorno and Horkheimer were sceptical that such competition was a prelude to a socialist economy. Instead, Adorno and Horkheimer
argue that capitalism has entered a monopoly phase, where large businesses (e.g., Coca-Cola, Ford
Motors and, later, Starbucks) replace competition with social controls through mass media
and advertising.

In this situation, cultural activities become crucial to the ongoing functioning of capitalism as giant corporations use mass media to exercise a monopoly over cultural life. For
example, consider the use of advertising. For Adorno and Horkheimer (1997/1944), advertising is an ideological media: it is a way of securing social and economic power through
cultural domination. Many of us can recall the world's biggest companies only by identifying
their logo or brand (there is even a board game based around this premise!). For Adorno and
Horkheimer (1997/1944), the power of advertising is that it not only keeps us consuming the
products and services of these companies but also works to block out from people's minds
anything that does not bear a company's particular brand or logo. Thus, it may be difficult
for us to think of using any other computer operating software than Microsoft Windows, or
search engine other than Google, or taxi company other than Uber. Advertising is ideological, then, in so far as it obscures how these companies secure a dominant economic and
cultural position within everyday life.

Adorno and Horkheimer use the term 'culture industry' to capture this process and examine how companies commodify culture. In particular, they suggest that companies produce
cultural goods to be sold and mindlessly consumed by audiences en masse. Rarely do consumers thoughtfully engage with radio shows, films, and magazines. On the contrary, these
commodities serve the status quo by reproducing the ideology of mass media. For example, Adorno and Horkheimer were very critical of how the culture industry ransacks art,
poetry and philosophy to create products for monopoly capitalism. Their work also draws on
the psychology of Freud (see Chapter 3) to argue that constant exposure to these products
(through advertisements) keeps capitalism working by reducing the audience's capacity for
critical thinking and fixing consumerism into the unconscious. For example, watching television, with its simplistic content and patternable structure, promotes a lack of thought on
behalf of its audience, whereas looking at a piece of art with its deep symbolism promotes a
much more thoughtful response. Adorno and Horkheimer make a sharp distinction between
'art' and 'mass culture' for this reason, suggesting that mass-produced consumer goods are
not genuine expressions of individual freedom but the products of false needs unconsciously
implanted by the culture industry.

Adorno and Horkheimer's view of culture has come under severe attack, most notably
from other critical thinkers who question their pessimism and suggest that the potential for social change requires a recasting of the way popular culture and agency operate
(Arvidsson, 2006; Hall, 2001/1973). Nevertheless, Adorno and Horkheimer's ideas remain
essential in helping us to understand how culture becomes ever more tightly integrated
with economic control.

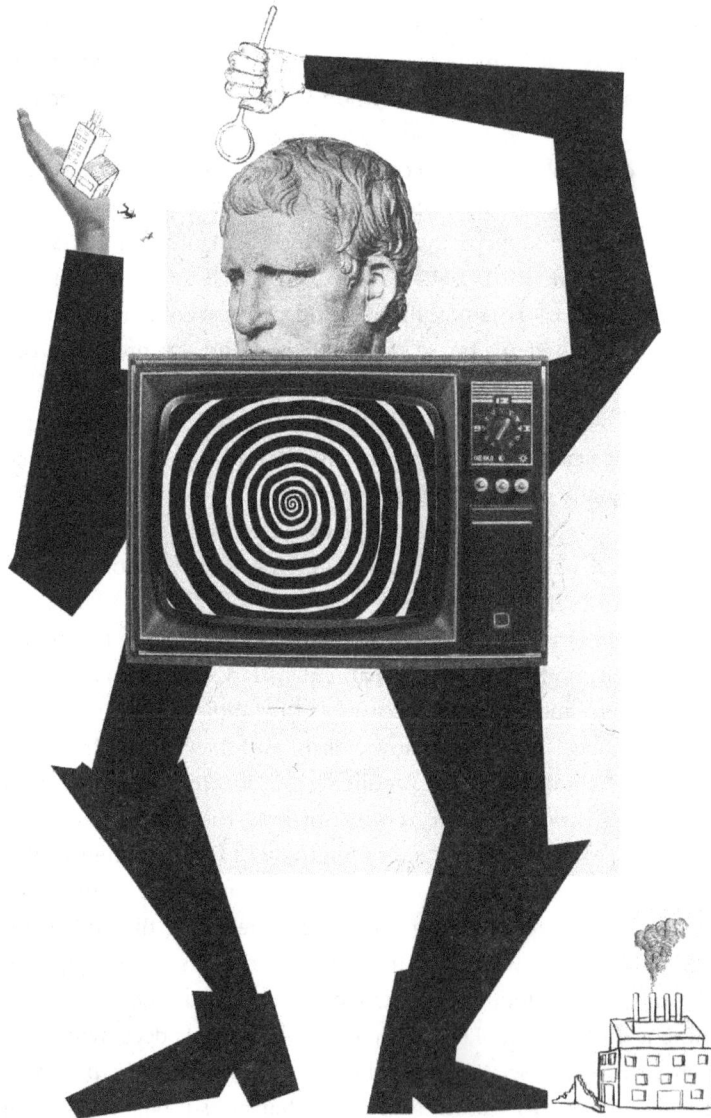

Figure 2.3 Frankfurt School

How does mass media, like television, operate as a method of social control, limiting our critical thinking and keeping us from resisting the status quo? The Frankfurt School argues that mass media works like a 'Big Brother' in society: first, it takes on a colossal form, shaping the relations between work, labour and culture; second, it sits at the heart of the modern subject, shaping how individuals see themselves and others.

- Jürgen Habermas, also a member of the Frankfurt School, was critical of Adorno and Horkheimer's disdain for modern culture and political scepticism. Habermas's (1984/1981) theory of 'communicative action' is more optimistic, suggesting that culture allows for conversational freedoms and reasoned debate. Culture is full of 'ideal speech situations' where people communicate rationally, free from coercion or power, thereby creating spaces for social consensus.

Antonio Gramsci

A leading member of the Italian Communist Party, Antonio Gramsci develops another influential form of Marxism during his imprisonment by Italian fascists (see fascism) between 1929 and 1937. In his *Prison Notebooks*, Gramsci develops Marx's notion of ideology through the concept of hegemony. Hegemony refers to a relationship in which one person or group consents to the leadership of another because it is advantageous. Gramsci uses this idea to examine how ruling classes secure social domination by shaping social and cultural attitudes. In particular, Gramsci argues that physical repression by the ruling classes, whether through violence or economic coercion, is never enough to secure a stable social order. Instead, ruling elites, such as the government, must develop and maintain a set of beliefs and norms that present their interests as common-sense values of benefit for all. Gramsci suggests that the values of working people will align with the values of ruling elites in these circumstances and uses the term 'cultural hegemony' to describe this process.

Artz and Murphy (2000) give examples of 'cultural hegemony' in the context of the United States, arguing that a range of social practices, relationships and structures ensure that people consent to and participate in capitalism. In particular, they argue that the capitalist class maintains cultural hegemony by convincing working-class people that this political economic system will (always) provide for their material well-being. Thus, by providing social security, unemployment compensation, federal jobs programmes and agricultural subsidies, the US government continues to find ways of renewing popular consent to capitalism and its class relations (Artz and Murphy, 2000, p. 25). Indeed, the notion of the 'American Dream' achieves something similar: it is the belief that anyone, regardless of background, can attain success through the hard work and sacrifice that social mobility affords. This idea ensures mass consent in capitalism by making individuals responsible for their economic circumstances and prospects.

Of course, as the gap between rich and poor widens, the future of this cultural hegemony is under threat. Gramsci insists that ruling-class hegemony is a fragile social phenomenon, particularly as it faces regular opposition from below, or what he calls 'counter-hegemonic forces'. A counter-hegemonic force is a social movement or political grouping that appears to try and change the existing social fabric. For example, consider the practices of the Occupy Wall Street movement in 2011. As Green (2015) argues, this movement emerges rather spontaneously to oppose economic inequality through existing social and political relationships. The movement was dynamic, using social demonstration and spectacle across multiple sites to draw the public's attention to financial greed and political corruption. Green (2015, p. 171) argues that the movement's goal was to destroy capitalism by proposing alternative possibilities and developing a new agenda and vision within the context of the political movement. This politics 'prefigures' any notion of the existing (capitalist) system, thereby challenging its cultural hegemony.

Gramsci's account of hegemony captures a sense of the complexity of social struggle as various and contesting worldviews. Ruling classes must work to manage this situation by introducing new social practices or policies and often in response to counter-hegemonic struggles. In his theory, there is no such thing as a ruling class in the singular. Instead, in modern societies, ruling groups, such as government officials, business leaders, religious leaders, and medical and justice professionals, make up different 'blocs', each with their specific interests and viewpoints. These 'blocs' may work together on a particular issue to retain cultural hegemony. For example, various 'blocs' might come together to justify austerity measures in times of economic crisis. Gramsci insists that there is no guarantee that these 'blocs' will reach an agreement or secure mass consent. This need for compromise means that counter-hegemonic struggles are always possible.

Focus on Facts

- Stuart Hall (1987) captures this sense of ideological and counter-ideological struggle in his paper 'Gramsci and Us'. Hall uses Gramsci to examine the emergence of **neoliberalism** within Britain in the 1980s and the failure of the political left to counter Margaret Thatcher's 'authoritarian populism'.
- Ernesto Laclau and Chantal Mouffe (1985) develop a postmodern reflection on Gramsci's concept of hegemony, suggesting that the dominance of social attitudes can change swiftly, leading to rapid changes in leadership and new political agendas.

Case Study 2.2

The Gig Economy

From Uber to Deliveroo and Amazon, we are all aware of the digital platforms driving changes in how we work, travel, eat and live. Marx's ideas continue to be relevant for examining what life is like in this 'gig economy', especially for those workers whose livelihoods are contingent upon temporary or zero-hour contracts. As Woodcock and Graham (2020, pp. 11–19) argue, Marx's ideas provide critical insight into how digital platforms continue to disadvantage wage labourers through the reorganisation of work. In particular, they suggest that these platforms dismantle the employment relationship by, first, casualising vast numbers of staff onto independent contracts (or forms of 'self-employment') and, second, by atomising the worker into an individual unit, which prevents the formation of sustained or successful worker resistance. Together, these platforms fail to provide appropriate rights and protections for workers, including workplace training, statutory sick pay, predictable working conditions and measures to prevent abusive practices.

As with Marx, Woodcock and Graham (2020) argue that a critique of these platforms must come through the perspectives of gig workers. After all, they are the wage labourers that make sense of the relationship between work and capital. Woodcock and Graham (2020) show that the gig economy connects to longer histories of worker exploitation by examining this relationship, including the ways that the 'casualisation of contracts' operates to cut labour costs. Woodcock and Graham (2020) argue that the contractual trick of self-employment allows platforms to access labour at short notice, in abundant supply and with limited commitment. These agile environments allow digital platform companies to respond quickly to demand without paying various overhead expenses.

Cant (2020, pp. 43–51) provides another critical example of the 'gig economy' by considering how Deliveroo uses algorithms to save the company money. He argues that Deliveroo has a system of 'algorithmic management' that uses complex calculations to manage worker labour at a lower cost. Algorithms significantly reduce the time (and therefore the cost) it takes to order, make, dispatch and deliver food. These algorithms directly impact the gig worker, intensifying the work process by keeping it under constant surveillance and leveraging competition (between workers) to increase productivity. For example, Cant (2020, pp. 52–53) recalls how the app induces workers to compete for wages based on the number of deliveries made. Workers would distance themselves from one another, sitting close to shops or restaurants, hoping that the app would hire them first for jobs.

It is essential to recognise that resistance and political action also characterise gig work. Both Woodcock and Graham (2020) and Cant (2020) stress that workers are finding ways to draw attention to the inequalities in the gig economy. Indeed, a series of strikes and public demonstrations from 2018 onwards raises questions about platform work and its relationship to class composition. What are the possibilities for change as workers of global platforms connect to global struggles for working rights and protections? As of 2020, policy-makers in the European Union are also moving to boost workers' rights by passing legislation that affords minimum protections to gig workers.

Figure 2.4 Gig work

Today's employment can be as flexible and accessible as couriering food for companies like Deliveroo. However, many workers find themselves trapped within this digital gig economy as unstable pay, limited progression and ambiguous workers' rights restrict and exploit their labour.

Summary

- Karl Marx was a critical thinker whose concern with capitalism led him to expose the organisation of work (or wage labour) as contradictory. In particular, Marx shows that, by exchanging labour for a wage, workers are vulnerable to exploitative management and business practices.
- Marx encourages social and political resistance, which we can see today in protests and social movements that challenge wealth inequalities and call for better working conditions.
- Marx also alerts us to the power of ideology in obscuring the problems of capitalism by moving our critical attention away from workers' experiences. Marxists develop this idea by revealing that the problems of capitalism are not bound to the economy but penetrate social and cultural activities.

- Mass media, consumerism and digital labour remain essential areas for thinking critically about capitalism's hold over everyday life and what alternative possibilities exist. This ongoing commitment to questioning the organisation of work and the economy is Marx's legacy.

Review Questions

- What do you think of Marx's theory of alienation? Why might it still be relevant today?
- To what extent would you agree with the claim that the modern world is created unequal and contradictory?
- What examples of 'class struggle' can you think of?

Annotated Reading

Ernest Mandel's introduction to Marx's (1990) first volume of *Capital* (London: Penguin) provides an accessible overview of the context and scope of the work.

For a more detailed account of Marx's ideas and influence, try Gregory Claeys (2018) *Marx and Marxism* (London: Penguin).

Terry Eagleton's (2011) *Why Marx was Right* (New Haven, CT: Yale University Press) provides a humorous and vigorous defence of Marx's ideas against the usual criticisms.

For those interested in a Marxist analysis of the Internet and digital technologies, read Christian Fuchs's (2010) 'Labour in Informational Capitalism and on the Internet', *Information Society*, 26(3), 179–196.

Karen Gregory and Jathan Sadowski's article 'Biopolitical Platforms: The Perverse Virtues of Digital Labour', *Journal of Cultural Economy*, 14(6), 662–674, interviews Deliveroo workers to examine how the design of the company's app makes their workers more productive but also exhausted and anxious.

3

Nietzsche, Freud and Weber

Chapter Objectives

This chapter will:

- Introduce Friedrich Nietzsche, Sigmund Freud and Max Weber, particularly their critical perspectives on modernity, religion and power.
- Outline critical concepts, including power, repression, the unconscious, disenchantment and legitimacy.
- Show the relevance of these critical thinkers through reference to contemporary arguments and case studies.

Keywords

Power, repression, subjectivity, the unconscious, rationalisation, disenchantment, sublimation, nihilism, *Verstehen*, existentialism

Introduction

Karl Marx is not the only social theorist to raise critical questions about society. Friedrich Nietzsche, Sigmund Freud and Max Weber also offer a critical perspective. Yet, these theorists depart from Marx's focus on the political economy by turning their attention to **power** and its relationship to human consciousness. Put straightforwardly, these three thinkers critique the mind and how modern social living subjugates (see **subjugation**) and controls people's thoughts, feelings and actions. The problem of modernity is not, as Marx argues, about industrial working conditions and exploitative labour relations but, rather, **repression**: that moral values and social norms have the power to dominate people's beliefs and control their practices. Nietzsche, Freud and Weber ask questions about why people obey rules or repress traumas or legitimate authorities. In asking these questions, they recognise that social structures shape modern **subjectivity** through psychological tensions and conflicts. Indeed, all three theorists examine the impact of culture on human consciousness – a topic that foreshadows the emergence of postmodern social theory in the late twentieth century (see Chapter 6).

Each theorist starts from a unique perspective. Friedrich Nietzsche shows us the shortcomings in our consciousness by questioning the very foundations of morality and religious belief. In particular, he exposes the inconsistencies and falsehoods within Christian religious teachings, arguing that they are fabrications created to control human behaviour through notions like 'good' and 'evil'. Sigmund Freud is different. He argues that it is not enough to be critical of consciousness. Instead, he develops a theory and therapy that asks patients to confront the thoughts and feelings that drive (un)happiness and (dis)contentment in society. Freud is the originator of psychoanalysis, a school of psychology that interrogates the **unconscious** to help patients resolve traumatic experiences. Like Nietzsche, Freud thinks that society has the power to control social behaviour, but it is through the repression of (sexual and aggressive) instincts that social norms restrict human consciousness. Max Weber is different again, but carries forward ideas from Nietzsche and Marx to examine the role of religion in creating the ethical foundations for capitalism. Weber examines the beliefs and values of Protestantism, a religious movement whose relationship to God pivots on an ethic of hard work, discipline and frugality. Weber argues that this ethic is part of the ideological framing of capitalism and suggests that it has a particularly dark side through his theory of **rationalisation:** that reason and instrumental calculation replace traditional values as human motivation. As such, Weber clashes with Marx about the problems of modernity, suggesting that acts of power and domination, not the economy, drive human history towards a bleak future. Famously, Weber characterises this future through the term **disenchantment**, which reveals the oppressive nature of modernity.

Friedrich Nietzsche

The son and grandson of a Lutheran pastor, Friedrich Nietzsche spent his early years in and around local church dwellings before studying theology at the University of Bonn in Germany. After a short period, Nietzsche resigned from his religious training and went to study classical philology (the examination of language in oral and written historical sources) at the University of Leipzig. His time in academia was full of personal challenges. Nietzsche suffered from recurring bouts of illness (terrible migraines, violent indigestion) and sustained permanent injuries due to military service. Indeed, pain, suffering and the determination needed to overcome sickness are an essential theme of Nietzsche's **existentialism** – a philosophy that explores the nature of human existence through experience. Nietzsche died in 1900, following several years of mental and physical health issues.

Notwithstanding these challenges, Nietzsche was a prolific writer, publishing many books and essays that provoke the reader into questioning the foundational values and ideas we use to affirm human existence. Of note are the works that Nietzsche wrote towards the end of his life, *Thus Spoke Zarathustra* (2006/1883), *Beyond Good and Evil* (1966/1886), *On the Genealogy of Morals* (1989/1887), and *The Anti-Christ* (2005/1888). Each book questions the nature of religious belief and works to discredit Christianity and other belief systems by subjecting their teachings and practices to critical scrutiny. In doing so, Nietzsche not only rejects religious attitudes (a 'neurosis' as he calls it) but toils with the prospect of what is left when science and culture 'kill' God. Some of Nietzsche's most engaging concepts, like the Übermensch and the 'will to power', emerge from this critical analysis, prompting us to consider the human condition from a radical perspective.

Focus on Facts

Nietzsche's view of life is quite philosophical. He sees it as a battle between two forces: chaos and order. In *The Birth of Tragedy* (1992/1872), Nietzsche suggests that the soundest (or healthiest) option is to find a balance by bringing more art, play and creativity into an otherwise sobering, rational world. Without this balance, Nietzsche suggests that humanity will fall into the meaninglessness of a cold, ordered world. As such, Nietzsche characterises life as the 'will' to live – to find beauty and imagination in the world, despite evidence that pain and cruelty exist. This philosophy of life is why Nietzsche is so hostile to religion – he views it as an escape from these dynamics.

Religious Neurosis

Nietzsche's critique of religion begins from a simple premise. Religion has, for centuries, been the singular governing force over what any given society considers morality to be – what is 'good' and 'evil' in the world. Nietzsche responds by arguing that science and education pose a direct challenge to these traditional belief structures. Reason and rationality are the tools of **secularism**, the rejection of religion and the belief that it should not form part of the state or public education. As Nietzsche sees it, science will dismantle faith by revealing its inadequacies to structure social life. Nietzsche's works, then, contribute to this vision by questioning the effects of religion on human consciousness and the qualities of religious belief.

Though an atheist, Nietzsche's criticisms do not focus on analysing arguments for the existence or proof of God. Instead, Nietzsche concentrates on how belief in God comes about and the role it plays in people's lives. Nietzsche sees Christianity as a 'neurosis' (Southwell, 2009, p. 142) or 'sickly imagination' (Ingraffia, 1995, p. 65): a value system that creates irrational attitudes that run contrary to human instinct and survival. Nietzsche evidences such beliefs by examining Christian teachings, ranging from personal sacrifice and self-denial to expressions of pity, hope and love. What emerges is a series of rebuttals of religious attitudes that reveal irrationalities at the heart of what is moral. For example, consider these essential teachings from the bible (Southwell, 2009, p. 142):

> Blessed are the poor in spirit: for theirs is the kingdom of Heaven.
>
> Blessed are the meek: for they shall inherit the earth...
>
> An eye for an eye, and a tooth for a tooth: But I say unto you, That ye resist not evil: but whosoever shall smite thee on thy right cheek, turn to him the other also...
>
> Love your enemies, bless them that curse you, do good to them that hate you, and pray for them which despitefully use you, and persecute you.

On first reading, such statements appear as messages of selflessness, humility and compassion. Yet, Nietzsche questions this meaning. He argues that such beliefs betray social interests when subject to critical scrutiny (see also **scepticism**). Religion, Nietzsche notes, is nothing but an attempt by the powerless to wrestle authority and control away from dominant social classes. Indeed, he develops the concept of 'slave morality' to suggest that the historical origins of Christianity are but an attempt by the weak to turn powerlessness into a virtue. Nietzsche's argument here is far-reaching (see Southwell, 2009, pp. 142–144), but the crucial point is that he sees Christianity as a subtle means of turning life-affirming values (strength, pride, pleasure) into *sins* while making *virtues* of weakness (pity, hope, love). Consider, for example, Nietzsche's (2005/1888, p. 6) words on pity:

> Christianity is called the religion of *pity*. – Pity is the opposite of the tonic affects that heighten the energy of vital feelings: pity has a depressive effect. You lose strength when you pity. And pity further intensifies and multiplies the loss of strength which in itself brings suffering to life. Pity makes suffering into something infectious...

Nietzsche's point here is that Christian teachings about pity do not alleviate suffering or change the experience that pain inflicts. Instead, empathising has the opposite effect: it saddens, disheartens and discourages action. To show compassion does little, in Nietzsche's view, to mitigate difficult circumstances. This view might sound unusually cold, but Nietzsche's concern is that Christianity is a religion that worships inaction. He sees its teachings as a method of praising ideas that run against the instincts needed to survive life. Indeed, the strength of a person, Nietzsche asserts, relates to how much 'truth' they can tolerate (or how much suffering they can endure) without the need for a religious 'crutch'.

Nietzsche expresses similar concerns about other Christian notions, such as hope and love. In *Thus Spoke Zarathustra*, Nietzsche (2006/1883, p. 6) warns, 'do not believe those who speak to you of extraterrestrial hopes!' Here, he captures an argument familiar throughout his work: that religious people appeal to an otherworldly entity to escape life's problems and difficulties. In God or Jesus Christ, Nietzsche argues, hope is an example of how the faithful deny the responsibility needed to take control and live life. Indeed, he argues that hope never offers a resolution to a problem: it prolongs inaction. This sentiment is also apparent in Nietzsche's (2005/1888, p. 20) critique of love, which he argues is a means of manipulating human emotion:

> Love is the state in which people are most prone to see things the way they are *not*. The force of illusion reaches a high point here, and so do the forces that sweeten and *transfigure*. People in love will tolerate more than they usually do, they will put up with anything. A religion had to be invented where people could love: it gets them through the worst in life – they stop noticing the bad aspects completely.

Nietzsche's point here is that love (in God or Jesus) is an emotion that blinds us from the realities of everyday life. Through love, we endure more pain and suffering than we would otherwise accept. As such, we can devote ourselves, that is, our sense of self and well-being, to meet with all of God's commandments. This dedication is a dangerous illusion for Nietzsche, which misleads and deceives. Indeed, as many broken hearts may attest, devotion deludes us into bearing painful situations because we treat them *as if they did not exist*. Nietzsche's critique of love speaks to this power of religion to take hold of people, such that they experience unnecessary anguish in the name of an imaginary entity.

By exposing these irrationalities, Nietzsche rejects Christianity as a form of extreme self-denial. He argues that its attitudes represent a 'neurosis' that attributes morality to acts of sacrifice and restraint. Nietzsche's concern is that such messages carry an implicit pessimism about human existence and obscure the possibility for progress through acts of self-determination. These irrationalities give Nietzsche grounds to reject God and consider what must follow.

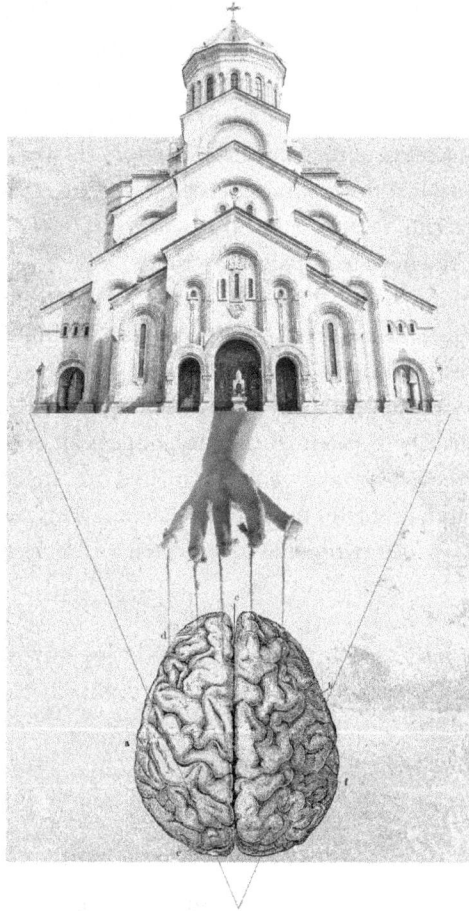

Figure 3.1 Religion and control

What is Nietzsche's view of religious power and social control? Nietzsche suggests that Christianity uses the authority of the Church to manipulate people into action through teachings that deem powerlessness a virtue.

Killing God

Perhaps one of Nietzsche's (1974/1882, p. 181) most famous quotes is when he pronounces the death of God:

> God is dead. God remains dead. And we have killed him. 'How shall we comfort ourselves, the murderers of all murderers? What was holiest and mightiest of all that the world has yet owned has bled to death under our knives: who will wipe

this blood off us? What water is there for us to clean ourselves? What festivals of atonement, what sacred games shall we have to invent? Is not the greatness of this deed too great for us? Must we ourselves not become gods simply to appear worthy of it?...'

Nietzsche is not suggesting here that God is literally 'dead'. Instead, he questions whether education and science challenge religion so much that it no longer offers a viable source of morality. As his arguments suggest, there are inconsistencies and irrationalities within Christian teachings that reveal them as social constructions rather than examples of divine intervention. As such, Nietzsche warns of a coming crisis in morality as God's death inevitably leads to revaluating ethical standards. Moreover, Nietzsche recognises that Christianity provides many people with a basis for objective truth and purpose in the world. Nietzsche's concern is that, without God, society will likely fall into meaninglessness and despair: what he refers to as 'nihilism', or a belief in nothing.

The problem of nihilism is significant for Nietzsche. He sees it as a threat to humanity. Nietzsche believes that, by killing God, humankind, for the first time in history, must self-reflect on what 'humanity' means. Humankind must address itself and ask what morality is without the presence of God or Christian teachings as a guide. Nietzsche (1968/1901, p. 318) says: 'It is a measure of the degree of strength of will to what extent one can do without meaning in things, to what extent one can endure to live in a meaningless world...'. What Nietzsche is saying here is that humankind must find the strength to overcome nihilism. Only by finding a morality that reflects the human condition, rather than the unachievable standards set by Christianity, will society thrive. Where the death of God creates a gap in morality, Nietzsche sees an opportunity for humankind to reveal inner strength and self-determination, or what he terms the 'will to power'.

Nietzsche's response to nihilism comes through two essential concepts. The first is the 'will to power', which refers to how morality resides within human strengths, including people's abilities, ambitions and survival instincts. Nietzsche takes the view that robust, healthy and confident people express their will more readily. This perspective is not to say that Nietzsche advocates the pursuit of power. Instead, he appreciates its redirection through creative and life-affirming pursuits. Nietzsche praises those whose expressions of art, music, and culture harness talent to create beauty. The will to power is about self-mastery and the prospect of finding virtue through wilful and creative endeavours. This perspective is why Nietzsche is so critical of Christianity – he believes it is an escape from human nature's painful but also artistic nature.

Secondly, Nietzsche uses the term 'Übermensch', which roughly translates to the 'Overman', to identify the superior being who will lead humanity out of nihilism. The expression comes from a character that Nietzsche develops in his book *Thus Spoke Zarathustra*. The Übermensch is a man willing to overcome conventional Christian morality by creating a new value system. This system will confront truths about the human condition, such as that life is a constant struggle to balance pain and pleasure. Nietzsche writes of the Übermensch as someone whose inner strength, rather than religious belief, will renew humanity's sense of meaning. This perspective may sound abstract, but Nietzsche seeks a strong leader whose self-mastery and critical thinking will expose shortcomings in human consciousness and social attitudes. Admittedly, this perspective did not work out how Nietzsche intended. His sister, Elisabeth, promoted these ideas to justify Nazi beliefs in a superior Aryan race.

Through provocative ideas and creative writing, Nietzsche scrutinises morality to show us that the beliefs and values that guide human consciousness may disguise irrationalities or betray social interests. This idea – that critical theory questions the value behind values – is an essential part of social thinking and reappears again in contemporary work. Indeed, Nietzsche's scepticism is very influential not only in poststructuralist and postmodernist scholarship (see Chapter 6) but also in aspects of new materialism and posthumanism (see Chapter 10).

Focus on Facts

Nietzsche's arguments about religion anticipate the ideas of Sigmund Freud and psychoanalysis. Freud and Nietzsche share the perspective that religious belief is a projection of individual or societal values, which refers to when a person projects their anxieties onto another. Nietzsche sees slave morality as a projection: judging the behaviour of others to disguise one's weakness. Freud considers religion a coping mechanism that originates in childhood experiences of helplessness.

Sigmund Freud

Sigmund Freud is best known as the founder of psychoanalysis: a school of psychology that develops theories and therapeutic techniques to study the unconscious mind and provide treatments for mental illness. Some of Freud's ideas, particularly concerning sex and the origins of psychological illness, raise crucial questions about the relationship between socialisation and human psychology. In particular, Freud develops a deep insight into the tensions that characterise human development as people establish social contact and build the foundations for social life. As a critical theorist who shares similarities with Nietzsche, Freud reckons with the human condition to reveal that tragedy – or, at the very least, unhappiness – is at the heart of civilisation. Indeed, his significant concepts within psychoanalysis, such as **repression** and sublimation, speak to this theme: that progress in life concerns painful self-awareness.

Hysteria

Some of Freud's founding concepts for psychoanalysis, such as the unconscious and repression, connect to his early work of treating female patients suffering from 'hysteria': an out-of-date term to describe a range of psychological disorders that present with physical symptoms, including paralysis, amnesia, convulsions, and hallucinations. As Thurschwell (2000, p. 16) explains, during Freud's time, most medical practitioners saw hysteria as attention-seeking or a physical disease affecting females only. Indeed, there is a long history of connecting notions of female insanity to female sexuality through the concept of hysteria, which comes from the Greek *hysteron* or 'womb' (see Parker et al., 1995, p. 42). Freud was unconvinced by these explanations. In *Studies on Hysteria*, Freud shows that the disorder has psychological origins in traumatic events in a patient's past. Patients attempt to repress early traumatic events and find them awkward or painful to recall. Freud argues that hysteria symptoms emerge as unresolved psychological conflicts, often beginning in childhood (Bocock, 2002, p. 17).

It is important to note that Freud's study of hysteria is also where we see the beginnings of his famous 'talking cure' approach, which he develops through collaborative efforts with his mentor, Josef Breuer. The method starts from a simple premise: that, through talking, the patient confronts the repressive activity of the mind (see Parker et al., 1995, p. 19). Psychoanalysis relies on the idea that the cure for mental illness comes from patients unearthing their unconscious wishes, anxieties and traumas. As such, Freud and Breuer saw talking as a means of 'catharsis': as patients speak, they begin to discharge the energy or emotion that accompanies deep-seated psychological conflicts (see also Corsini and Wedding, 2008, p. 23).

For example, consider the case of Bertha Pappenheim (or Anna O.), a significant patient in Freud and Breuer's study of hysteria. Pappenheim was a 21-year-old woman whom Breuer began treating in 1880, after she had spent a long time caring for her elderly, sick father. Pappenheim approaches Breuer following her father's death, as she was suffering from headaches, disturbed vision, episodes of paralysis, and speech impairment (Launer, 2005, p. 465). Under hypnosis, Breuer encourages Pappenheim to revisit painful memories of her father's care and subsequent passing. He notes that Pappenheim recalls these memories precisely and expresses them with striking emotion (Launer, 2005, p. 465). Indeed, Breuer suggests that Pappenheim's sessions were 'cathartic' as talking through the distress of her father's death brought relief to her symptoms.

The case of Bertha Pappenheim was critical to Freud's thinking about the relationship between repression and trauma. Freud saw Pappenheim as an example of how patients repress the memories of traumatic events alongside the deeply unpleasant emotions that accompany them. This view is still accurate today in cases of 'post-traumatic stress', in which patients experience a traumatic incident (e.g., car crash, childbirth, war) and then develop symptoms including flashbacks, nightmares, anxiety attacks and insomnia. For Freud and Breuer, the 'talking cure' was pivotal in helping patients recover traumatic memories and discharge the emotions accompanying these experiences, such as fear, sadness and anger. Indeed, the link between repression and catharsis becomes the cornerstone of Freud's thinking about hysteria and leads to his interest in sexuality.

Sexual Repression

Freud's study of hysteria leads him to the critical realisation that there is a sexual component to repression. He asserts that, in many cases of hysteria, the trauma that provokes the onset of symptoms may be too trivial to determine the cause of a patient's behaviour. Freud begins examining the wishes, daydreams and infatuations accompanying the desire to consummate sexual activity. Indeed, Freud determines that sexual desire (also known as the libido) is an instinctual part of human life and begins to express interest in his patients' intimate affairs to understand the sexual nature of repression.

For example, in one case study, a young girl came to Freud with an obsessive fear of urinating whenever she was in a public place. Freud traces the obsession back to an episode at a theatre, during which the young woman experiences intense genital sensations and sexual fantasies upon seeing an attractive male acquaintance. This experience leaves her wanting to urinate, forcing her to leave the theatre. The patient recalls her attempts to fend off subsequent episodes by repressing her erotic thoughts, leading to her phobia. Freud effects a cure by helping the patient recover her original memory and presumably recognise and accept her sexuality (see Storr, 2001, p. 22).

Other examples from Freud also suggest a sexual component to repression. For instance, in one case, that of 'Elizabeth von R', Freud suggests that her hysterical symptoms result from an antagonistic sexual drama involving her brother-in-law. Freud explains that Elizabeth's 'secret love affair' with her dead sister's husband creates a psychological conflict between her sexual desires and traditional moral values. Freud writes, 'This girl felt towards her brother-in-law a tenderness whose acceptance into consciousness was resisted by her whole moral being' (Freud, 1895d, cited in Boag, 2012, p. 10). Strange as this may sound, Freud's point is that the origins of hysteria are sexual. He elicits patients' sexual desires, dreams and fantasies to identify the antagonistic thoughts and processes that hide their emotions. As such, Freud is convinced that sexual satisfaction is a primary part of human happiness and argues that a lack of sex life is a chief characteristic of hysterics (Storr, 2001, p. 25). Later, this idea informs his critique of religion and civilisation, suggesting that moral attitudes and social norms repress human instincts.

Focus on Facts

- Freud traces the repressive memories of his patients back to infantile sexual development and the beginnings of human socialisation. He develops the concept of the 'Oedipal complex' to describe how children form emotional attachments and develop personalities. Freud's study of children informs his theory of the mind, most notably, his concept of the 'superego', which describes the internal voice that prohibits children (and adults) from breaking moral boundaries through guilt.

- Freud examines the dreams of his patients to understand the causes of hysteria. In *The Interpretation of Dreams* (1997/1899), Freud suggests that dreams are expressions of wishes and desires that patients repress, some of which come from early childhood. The content of these wishes and desires is unacceptable and potentially disturbing to current social and moral norms. As such, Freud argues that dreams give patients a way to experience them indirectly – dreams are a catharsis between social censorship and the body's need to release impulses and desires.

Religious Discontent

Freud's studies of hysteria inform his critique of religion. He argues that religious belief is akin to hysteria – an illness, the symptoms of which emerge from psychological tensions between human impulses and the contexts of socialisation. Freud's analysis begins by reflecting on the psychology of spiritual needs, which he argues are a form of projection: a psychological defence mechanism in which the human ego denies unconscious impulses by attributing them to others. Put simply, Freud argues that religious belief is a coping mechanism for the anxieties and uncertainties that characterise human life.

Freud arrives at this critique of religion by suggesting that believers seek a version of the 'internalised, punishing father' (Thurschwell, 2000, p. 102). This phrase may appear unusual, but it comes from Freud's theory of the 'superego', which indicates that children develop the ethical component of their personalities by internalising patriarchal power (e.g., a father's ability to punish and protect them; see Thurschwell, 2000, p. 47). Freud argues that Christianity and Judaism attempt the same thing – they are, as he calls them, 'religions of the father' (Thurschwell, 2000, p. 102). This means that Christianity and Judaism have teachings and practices that ask believers to internalise the patriarchal power of God. For example, they mix threats of punishment, through notions like 'sin', 'evil', or 'hell', with promises of protection, through ideas like 'salvation' and 'heaven'. As such, Freud argues that these religions attempt to recreate what parents offer children: a sense of protection by internalising threats of punishment. Freud (1930, cited in Thurschwell, 2000, p. 104) writes:

> The derivation of religious needs from the infant's helplessness and the longing for the father seems to me incontrovertible … I cannot think of any need in childhood as strong as the need for a father's protection.

Freud's point here is that religion presents itself as the father figure to a helpless child. It is a coping mechanism that gives people the illusion of security. Moreover, Freud sees religion as resembling symptoms of psychological illness – a kind of 'psychic infantilism' (Thurschwell, 2000, p. 104) whereby believers use religion to repress the unconscious anxieties and feelings of insecurity that begin in childhood.

From this perspective, Freud, like Nietzsche, questions whether religion provides an appropriate base from which to guide human endeavours. Helplessness, and a desperate need for a father figure, are not the happiest foundations for establishing a conscience or a sense of responsibility towards others. Freud argues that a conscience based on repression is a tool of submission rather than a forward-looking, progressive agency (Thurschwell, 2000, p. 104). In Freud's view, the civilised 'moral' human being is a repressive formation. People are, in reality, driven by a range of human impulses, some of which include intensely sexual and aggressive drives. Freud sees religion as holding civilisation back – its teachings and practices working to repress rather than confront human instinct (Thurschwell, 2000, p. 104).

Freud (2002/1930) broadens this thinking to encompass society more generally in his book *Civilization and Its Discontents*. Here, Freud argues that civilisation emerges from humanity's need to conquer the Earth and to turn its harsh conditions into serving human needs and desires. This process, argues Freud, requires cooperation: an ability to put aside individual interests and work together to maintain an orderly society. Freud recognises that this step is not an easy task for humans, whose aggressive impulses drive conflict and war. As such, Freud concludes that there is a paradox at the heart of civilisation: that it requires repression or, more accurately, sublimation to exist. Sublimation turns instinctual urges and energies into non-instinctual behaviour (Thurschwell, 2000, p. 104). Freud makes the point that humans must sublimate their instinctual behaviour if they are to cooperate and establish relationships of mutual benefit. Sublimation is how humanity comes to conquer the Earth.

Why is this important? Freud suggests that discontent or unhappiness sits at the heart of this paradox. Through the sublimation of instincts (particularly the libido), the individual suffers civilising demands. In other words, individuals must deny themselves, their desires, wishes and impulses to maintain social order. Freud suggests that such a process creates a constant source of dissatisfaction in the human psyche, leading to neuroses on an individual and collective level. For example, as a society, we may bear external restrictions that regulate the morality of sex, legislating on what constitutes a legitimate or illegitimate relationship. For Freud, such governance imposes internal limits on what the human conscience considers acceptable moral behaviour. As such, what religion or civilisation believes to be an 'unnatural' coupling might generate feelings of guilt and unhappiness. Freud's point is that civilisation pivots on such antagonisms between instinctual demands and repressive societal structures (Thurschwell, 2000, p. 106).

Freud offers no solution to the discontentment that these antagonisms create. Instead, he draws his analysis to a conclusion by arguing that the religious have the most to suffer from attempts to repress instinctual gratification. Freud suggests that the individual who tries to live the most moral life is likely to spend their time suffering from an acute sense of guilt. Indeed, Freud infers that a sign of mental illness begins with obsession and neuroses, that is, those who regularly punish themselves or have the most acute sense of civic duty and responsibility. As such, Freud brings a decidedly sociological point to bear on human psychology: that social norms have the capacity to bind people into repressive ties (Thurschwell, 2000, p. 107).

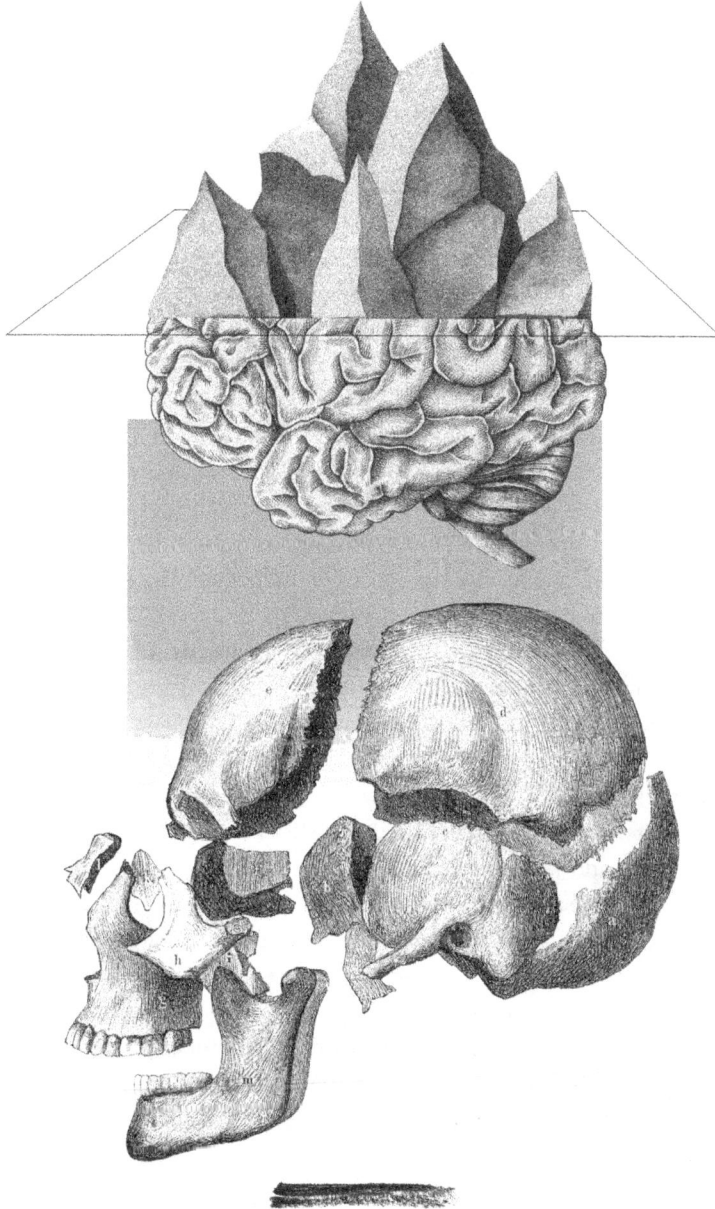

Figure 3.2   Freud and the unconscious mind

Reflect on the idea that the human mind is like an iceberg, with the root causes for human suffering and unhappiness hidden deep underneath the surface. Repression means that the causes of an individual's behaviour are never immediately visible and that catharsis may provide insight into different fragments of human experience.

Freud's Legacy

Where Freud's ideas might appear peculiar to some, his examination of human consciousness informs much of social and cultural theorising. As Outhwaite (2015, pp. 79–86) notes, the twentieth century sees several scholars attempt to bring Freud's ideas forward, often by merging them with Marx. Eric Fromm, Herbert Marcuse and Theodor Adorno were prominent among these, all associated with the Frankfurt School (see Chapter 2). For example, in *The Sane Society* (2001/1955), Eric Fromm draws on Freud and Marx to argue that capitalism has produced 'the manipulated personality': a form of social estrangement that dehumanises people through overconformity to bureaucratic structures. *Contra* Freud, Fromm suggests that personal freedom is still possible but must come through a rejection of capitalist and communist ideologies.

Fromm's perspective differs from that of Herbert Marcuse, who indicates that capitalism restricts human possibilities through scarcity of resources and the social control of people's needs. In *Eros and Civilisation* (1987/1955), Marcuse coins the term 'surplus repression' to capture the notion that capitalists introduce social controls above those indispensable for civilisation. This perspective influenced Theodor Adorno (see Adorno and Horkheimer, 1997/1944), whose critique of the 'culture industry' applies Freud's ideas to show how individuals accommodate capitalism in their lives (see Chapter 2). In particular, Adorno uses Freud to consider how the entertainment industry influences the human psyche to internalise capitalist logic, such as the imperative 'to consume'. Adorno felt that culture (in the form of leisure) was a false projection, an illusory reality that was as mechanical, formulaic and empty as the workplace.

Freud's legacy extends beyond the Frankfurt School to critical theorists such as Frantz Fanon (see Chapter 9) and Jacques Lacan (see Chapter 6). For example, in *Black Skin, White Masks* (2008/1952), Franz Fanon draws on psychoanalysis and Marxism to consider the detrimental effects of colonial domination on racial identity. Fanon argues that colonialism is a configuration of power that denigrates and dispossesses Black people of economic, cultural and sociopolitical possibilities. This process has a profound impact on the psyche of colonised people who, Fanon contends, seek empowerment by identifying with the language, appearance and desires of white colonisers. Fanon's work makes an essential contribution to postcolonial studies. Jacques Lacan, a French psychoanalyst and psychiatrist, takes Freud's work in a very different direction. He develops the concept of the 'mirror phase' to describe the first moments a child recognises themselves within a mirror. Lacan urges that the mirror is a one-dimensional reflection that cannot attest to the many thoughts, feelings and desires that constitute a child's psyche. As such, the mirror reflects an uncomfortable truth to the child: that they will never fully realise their identity. Lacan argues that this realisation creates feelings of loneliness (or a 'lack of being') that become a core part of human subjectivity by motivating people to take control of their external appearances. Lacan's work has been influential in research into language and **discourse** (see Chapter 6).

The diversity of approaches inspired by psychoanalysis speaks to the richness of Freud's work and his influence on critical social theory. This impact is particularly apparent in the ideas of Max Weber, who draws on Freud but also on Nietzsche and Marx to develop his approach to religion, culture and society.

Max Weber

Max Weber was a German sociologist, philosopher and political economist known for his significant influence on social theory and research methods. Three of Weber's ideas stand out as particularly essential. The first is his study of social action, mainly through the concept of **Verstehen**, which anticipates qualitative research into meaning, interpretation and subjectivity. The second is Weber's political sociology, in which he discusses different types of inequality and authority relating to state power and domination. The third is his sociology of religion, in which he considers the role of religious belief in generating capitalism. Through these ideas, Weber raises critical questions about modernity and warns of the dangers of disenchantment.

Weber's Method

Weber's sociology begins from the perspective that science is an attempt to interpret social action to arrive at causal explanations. He argues that general laws, which statistical analyses try to discover, cannot add anything to *why* people act in particular ways. As such, Weber argues that sociology needs a method – *Verstehen* – that examines people's motivations by considering their historical and cultural context. In his own words, *Verstehen* means 'to identify a concrete "motive" or complex of motives "reproducible in inner experience"' (Weber, 1975, cited in Allen, 2004, p. 72). Weber's point here is that people choose to act and that the outcomes of such activities become part of the structures for future social action.

Weber notes that there are two types of *Verstehen*. The first is through direct observation, whereby sociologists grasp people's intentions by noticing facial expressions or outward behaviour. The second type seeks to place social action in a 'sequence of motivation' by considering the contexts of why it is occurring (Allen, 2004, pp. 72–73). In both cases, the idea is that sociologists can put themselves in the place of others, appreciate their structural circumstances, and take account of their motives to interpret social action. Weber sees this as a distinguishing feature of sociology and suggests that this focus on motivations is as 'scientific' as the natural sciences when done rigorously. Indeed, as his account of religion and capitalism shows (see below), people's beliefs play a crucial role in history and social change.

It is important to note that *Verstehen* reveals Weber's view about the causal complexity behind historical configurations, like capitalism. His method acknowledges that small-scale social interactions form part of society's broader cultural and structural landscape. Studying how individuals attach meaning to behaviour and develop value systems is challenging.

Indeed, Weber recognises that the complexity of human interpretation makes it difficult to generalise arguments across societies. Any conceptual framing a person uses, including a sociologist, is contextually dependent. As such, Weber argues that sociologists should adopt a wide range of explanatory devices (called 'ideal types') to help them unearth the significance and meaning behind social actions. Weber classifies these into four types (see Allen, 2004, pp. 77–78):

1 'Instrumental rational action' refers to utility maximisation or rationally calculating the ends and means to effectively achieve a goal.
2 'Value rational action' refers to when people commit to behaviours that reflect a set of concerns of the utmost importance.
3 'Affective action' refers to how emotional feelings, such as love, motivate behaviour.
4 'Traditional action' refers to those practices or habits that develop over time as a result of historical, cultural or social trends.

These classifications reveal the level of **reflexivity** that characterises social action. Indeed, each type speaks to a different way humans meaningfully orient themselves towards the world. As such, Weber's method highlights the complexity of consciousness that accompanies social action.

Inequality and Power

Like Marx, Weber saw relations of inequality as central to modern capitalist economies; however, he rejects the Marxist notion that class inequality is the salient feature. For Weber, **social stratification** results from different types of power and the struggle for economic advantage within 'market situations' (Allen, 2004, p. 3). Weber determines that the possession of productive property does not determine class position. Instead, he argues that other factors, such as prestige and political influence, are significant for affording life chances. Weber recognises that the market has the power to distribute differences between individuals within a society. Weber defines class as an individual's capacity to solicit rewards for selling skills in a marketplace. This perspective rejects Marx's polarisation of classes and the idea of the proletarian revolution (see Chapter 2). Indeed, Weber recognises that propertyless workers do not necessarily occupy the same situation if the market values their skills differently.

Arising from this, Weber also rejects the Marxist notion that class membership determines power. His view is broader than the economic factors that characterise Marx's work. As Weber puts it, power 'is the probability that one actor within a social relationship will be in a position to carry out his will despite resistance, regardless of the basis on which this probability exists' (Weber, 1978, cited in Allen, 2004, p. 99).

Like Nietzsche, Weber sees society as comprised of shifting power struggles as people impose their will on others to survive. Indeed, he is interested in understanding how the powerful come to legitimate their authority, despite others acting in resistance. Weber suggests that power involves different appeals for legitimacy by the powerful and defines domination as the probability that a person will obey a command. Consider, for example, the practice of governments during the coronavirus pandemic. Weber suggests that power works by the government trying to internalise what they want the public to do (e.g., stay at home, self-isolate, wash your hands regularly). He writes: 'Every genuine form of domination implies a minimal form of voluntary compliance, that is, an *interest* (based on ulterior motives or genuine acceptance) in obedience' (Weber, 1978, p. 212).

For Weber, the essence of legitimacy is a minimal form of obedience. People internalise the actions of the powerful based on self-interest. Thus, governments issue social restrictions, such as curfews or lockdowns, on the basis that self-isolation is of benefit to all. From this perspective, legitimacy only works if people have some rational reason to accept authority, thereby submitting to its rule to a greater or lesser extent. As such, Weber identifies different types of domination/authority to consider the grounds for claiming obedience (see Allen, 2004, p. 100):

- 'Traditional authority' is a system or person in which the sanctity of moral traditions legitimates the powerful.
- 'Charismatic authority' is a system or person in which exceptional qualities or unusual circumstances legitimate the powerful.
- 'Legal-rational authority' is a system or person in which belief in the rule of law legitimates the powerful.

This apparatus affords Weber a sophisticated view of human motivation by revealing that power drives social life beyond economic interests. Indeed, one of Weber's primary arguments is that social action is rarely about just economics. Instead, he argues that a range of beliefs, meanings and values shape rational decision-making, of which productive relations are one part. Weber begins to unearth these intricacies in his analysis of capitalism and its relationship to the religious beliefs of Protestants.

Religion and Capitalism

One of Weber's most significant works, *The Protestant Ethic and the Spirit of Capitalism*, was published in 1905. Here, Weber challenges some of the fundamental components of Marxism by considering the causes of capitalism from an alternative perspective. In particular, Weber departs from Marx by suggesting that it is essential to examine the social actions of religious believers (or, in this case, Protestants), for these generate the values and meanings that support money-making practices. Weber's concern is understanding *why* people work hard, save money or invest, even after meeting their basic needs. He is not convinced that Marx has an explanation for this.

Weber's approach is to consider how wealth becomes an ethical imperative. His analysis begins by examining the expansion of Protestant religious denominations and the moral values they preach. Weber suggests that the growth of Protestant belief systems, coupled with an interest in money-making, was necessary to create the conditions of capitalism. For example, he cites the writings of Benjamin Franklin, a Puritan and one of the Founding Fathers of the United States, as an example of this money-making ethic. He writes:

> [Franklin] saw his discovery of the 'usefulness' of virtue as a revelation from God, who wished to direct him toward virtue *by this means* … this 'ethic' is the *making of money* and yet more money, coupled with a strict avoidance of all uninhibited enjoyment. (Weber, 2002/1905, p. 12)

Weber's point here is that Protestantism gives the act of money-making ethical value by connecting it with God. The Protestant faith reinforces the relationship between money and religious belief by asserting that success in economic activities is proof of being 'blessed' by the Almighty. Weber suggests that teachings within Protestantism confer this life lesson, such as Luther's notion of 'calling': a concept that signifies that a saintly life corresponds to performing well in work. From this perspective, Weber argues that Protestants understand the need to pursue or exhibit hard work and discipline if they are to honour God's will.

We still hear these values today in phrases such as 'time is money', 'money begets money' and 'always pay your debts'. These sayings reveal the value that people attribute to rational money-making practices. For example, the phrase 'time is money' clearly implies that efficiency and productivity are essential parts of making money effectively. Similarly, the slogan 'money begets money' captures the importance people attribute to acts of investment, turnover and profit. Such phrases capture what Weber calls the 'spirit of capitalism'. He writes:

> Furthermore, and even more important, a religious value was placed on ceaseless, constant, systematic labor in a secular calling as the very highest ascetic path and at the same time the surest and most visible proof of regeneration and the genuineness of faith. This was inevitably the most powerful lever imaginable with which to bring about the spread of that philosophy of life which we have here termed the 'spirit' of capitalism. (Weber, 2002/1905, p. 116)

Weber's point is that this Protestantism provides a sober, conscientious, and diligent workforce. God justifies hard work by suggesting that it leads to a moral life. This understanding closely connects to the idea of 'predestination' within the Presbyterian church, which indicates that God predetermines salvation (or damnation) at birth. Protestants believe that no amount of religious ritual, sacrifice or celebration can change this fate. Indeed, the Presbyterian church is quintessentially rational. There are no displays of extravagance, such as gold relics, expensive paintings, or grandiose statues. Protestants cannot 'buy' themselves into Heaven. Instead, they must look for signs from God that they are on the right trajectory. Protestantism suggests that disciplined, hard work is such a sign.

The Protestant lifestyle stressed hard work, the accumulation of wealth, its reinvestment, and the creation of profit to assure a connection with God. What Weber establishes, then, is an 'elective affinity' – a harmony – between Protestant religious beliefs and the beginnings of capitalism. Weber is not saying that Protestantism *causes* capitalism. Instead, he suggests that an independent change in theological teachings (from Catholicism to the Protestant Reformation) creates the conditions of possibility for capitalism to emerge. In other words, capitalism requires a suitable ideological framing to be possible, and Weber (2002/1905, p. 19) suggests that this is the religious pursuit of economic gain, 'We shall nevertheless provisionally use the expression "spirit of capitalism" for that attitude which, *in the pursuit of a calling* [*berufsmäßig*], strives systematically for profit for its own sake'.

One of the downsides that Weber notes about the spirit of capitalism is that, over time, instrumental rational action becomes a routine part of everyday life. Indeed, Weber suggests that calculability becomes a primary driver for human motivation, replacing the traditional or emotional motives once core to religious practices. Weber argues that, eventually, capitalism strips the 'magic' from the ethical imperative behind Protestantism, leaving in its place a modern world characterised by the triumph of efficiency. Weber refers to this process as rationalisation: the notion that strategic cost–benefit actions come to define every aspect of social life. Weber sees this process as the central problem for modern civilisation, suggesting that these instrumental pursuits are without magical or spiritual grounds. Indeed, he warns that modern life is in danger of disenchantment, of being ethically anchorless, as people and institutions conduct their activities with one goal in mind – making a profit.

Focus on Facts

In *The Protestant Ethic*, we see some resonance between Weber and Nietzsche's account of nihilism. Weber argues that rationalisation leads to a valueless life, whereby instrumental calculation and cost–benefit analysis supplant art, creativity and spirituality. Famously, Weber suggests that modernity is akin to an 'iron cage': the idea that life pushes people to disciplined, hard work without any of the philosophy or spiritual calling that once drew the Puritans.

Case Study 3.1

Weber Online

Graeme Kirkpatrick (2002) presents a modern take on Weber's ideas in his essay, 'The Hacker Ethic and the Spirit of the Information Age'. Here Kirkpatrick develops an interesting historical analogy between the pioneers of personal computing in the 1970s and the Protestant groups that Weber describes. Kirkpatrick argues that the two groups have psychological, cultural and sociological affinities. Where Weber's Protestants instigate cultural change conducive to capitalist development, Kirkpatrick argues that the worldview of hackers has contributed to ideas – embodied in personal computing – that enable capitalists to exploit information technology.

(Continued)

Kirkpatrick explains that the similarities between the two groups point towards the ironic historical fate of value systems in the construction of capitalism. He notes how both were victims of success; their advocacy of practices tending towards eliminating their spiritual calling. For example, a life of Protestant diligence became valued for its utility rather than virtue. Likewise, Kirkpatrick notes that hackers once advanced the goal of personal computing to ensure autonomy and empowerment through technological mastery. He argues that the design features of contemporary personal computers neutralise these ideas while keeping the ethos of hard work and utility maximisation.

To elaborate, Kirkpatrick suggests that a history of hackers reveals their spiritual motivations alongside broader countercultural trends in the 1960s and 1970s. Hackers were interested in how computers afford possibilities for experimentation, self-expression, and social transformation. Kirkpatrick quotes Steve Wozniak, the creator of the Apple Mac, saying that he came from a 'group of beatniks or hippies' who 'were going to totally change the world' (Kirkpatrick, 2002, p. 173). As such, Kirkpatrick positions hackers as 'priests' who share a religious devotion to the spiritual side of technological mastery. Indeed, he suggests that hackers wanted to know what was happening inside computers to open up new worlds of communication and interaction. The emergence of modern interface design changed this process, argues Kirkpatrick. Users became accustomed to the experience of controlling devices without the knowledge or skill to understand how they work. As such, personal computers became about a user's ability to achieve practical goals that had nothing to do with computing. Indeed, many of the computer devices we use today have simple interfaces that enable us to quickly and efficiently complete tasks, including working, shopping, playing video games, and controlling 'smart' machines. Kirkpatrick argues that these devices no longer require an understanding of how computers work. Instead, their function is goal-oriented: we use them, sometimes instrumentally, to achieve rational goals.

From this perspective, Kirkpatrick argues that contemporary capitalism's demands supplant hacker countercultural aspirations. Friendly interfaces now act as authorities on how to connect to global networks, legitimating software engineers' power and enabling a sober workforce for the information age. From this perspective, Kirkpatrick suggests that the personal computer has become implicated in processes of social rationalisation. These devices are necessary for work but have nothing to do with the principles of the pioneers who developed them. Kirkpatrick concludes that, like the Puritans whose work ceased to be 'virtuous' and became mundane, so is true of the radical spirit behind the hacker ethic.

Bureaucracy and Rationalisation

Weber considers the emergence of bureaucratic systems evidence of social rationalisation and disenchantment. A bureaucracy is a social structure that organises people through a central-ised administrative hierarchy. We see them in businesses, governments and education, where administrators operate to maintain order by controlling rules and resources. Indeed, many modern institutions have a human resources department that acts as a typical bureaucracy. Weber argues that such administrative governance epitomises legal-rational authority and instrumental action, linking bureaucracy to rationalisation. He argues:

Bureaucratic rationalization ... changes the material and social orders, and through them the people, by changing the conditions of adaptation, and perhaps the opportunities for adaptation, through a rational determination of means to ends. (Weber, 1968, cited in Ritzer, 2013, p. 32)

Weber's point here is that modern societies organise human activity into bureaucracies because they constitute the most efficient and rational means to maintain order and maximise efficiency. Bureaucracies will divide complex tasks into components, with each department responsible for a section of the overall project. Employees in each department manage their part of the task separately, according to a set of rules, regulations and predetermined sequences (Ritzer, 2013). A quick, accurate and efficient means of completing tasks appropriately emerges. If this task sounds similar to the factory conditions that Marx critiques (see Chapter 2), then it is because bureaucracies turn the task of social organisation into an assembly-line-like experience.

Weber expands on this position by identifying five elements of bureaucracies that ensure they operate at the height of instrumental rationality (see Ritzer, 2013, pp. 35–47):

- Predictability: bureaucracies operate in a highly predictable manner as employees understand how others will behave and can respond with a high degree of certainty.
- Efficiency: bureaucracies are an efficient way of achieving complex tasks by sorting them into small, separate projects that many people can complete quickly.
- Calculability: bureaucracies quantify as many activities as possible so that employees can perform their duties through a series of specific steps at a calculated speed.
- Control: bureaucracies control people by replacing human judgement with non-human technology, eventually becoming an automatic process.
- The irrationality of rationality: over time, bureaucracies become unpredictable, inefficient and uncontrollable as instrumentalism leads to unnecessary rules and processes, which delay results (i.e., too much 'red tape').

Weber recognises the dual-sided nature of bureaucracies. On the one hand, they have advantages in organising the sizeable institutions that modern capitalist economies demand. Bureaucracies can discover and implement decisions quickly and effectively, often at a low cost. However, Weber also warns of the irrationalities of organising social institutions in this instrumental manner. As bureaucracies grow, they become unpredictable and inefficient as conflicting rules and processes create tension and uncertainty between employees and service users. Equally, quantifying every aspect of work will lead to rushing jobs and poor-quality outcomes. Weber notes that bureaucracies will lose control of their workers if employees begin to recognise that technology is undercutting or sabotaging their role. This highly rational operation can lead to somewhat irrational ends (Ritzer, 2013).

Weber concludes with a rather pessimistic view, suggesting that more and more people will become encased in this bureaucratic life. The 'iron cage' of capitalism, to which he refers, captures the idea that instrumental rationality will structure all future social organisation and interaction. Indeed, Weber argues that the rationalised principles of the bureaucracy will lock people into instrumental forms of work and recreation. From here, we see Weber's notion of disenchantment most clearly as it refers to the dehumanising grind of the bureaucratic machine, alongside an obsession with efficiency and calculability that typifies modern existence. Like Nietzsche, then, Weber considers the problem of modernity as the absence of any fundamental spiritual, emotional or aesthetic considerations in life.

Focus on Facts

The sociologist George Ritzer (2015/1993) develops the concept of **McDonaldisation** to examine the rationalisation of work, production and consumption in late twentieth-century societies. Ritzer applies Weber's model of bureaucracy to contemporary life, arguing that it adopts the characteristics of a fast-food restaurant.

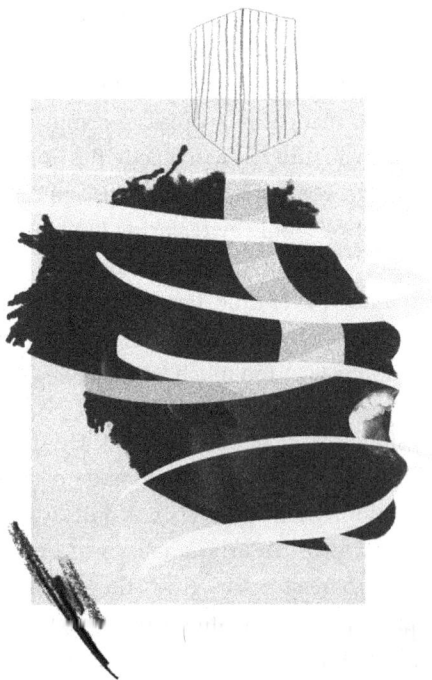

Figure 3.3 Irrationality of rationality

Consider what it is like to live in a world where every aspect of social life must be assigned a value or be cost-effective. Think about how systems of administration or bureaucracy become so restrictive that it feels as if one is confined into a cage. This is what Weber means by the irrationality of rationality.

⌐Case Study 3.2¬

Re-enchanting Social Life

The works of Nietzsche, Freud and Weber give critical insight into the relationship between human consciousness and society. However, the themes that characterise their works – tragedy, conflict, disenchantment – are not wildly optimistic. Indeed, there is a shared sense across these authors that the repressive cultural forces of modernity, alongside technological advances, will eventuate in humanity's downfall. In response, scholars have begun to explore the 'enchanting' aspects of modern life, which bring magic and emotion back into an otherwise cold, bureaucratic world. For example, Jane Bennett (2001, p. 111), in *The Enchantment of Modern Life*, argues that Weber's concern with instrumentality overlooks the affective (emotional, spiritual, aesthetic) attachments in people's lives (see also Chapter 10). Bennett explains that social interaction, mainly through objects, brings a sense of 'liveliness' to social life that displaces instrumental reason. Bennett gives the example of the 1998 GAP 'Khakis swing' advert as an expression of this enchantment, suggesting that the dancing to American swing music from the 1930s and 1940s reveals the energy, exhilaration and playfulness that accompanies commodity culture. The ad takes place in an ample space where 20 young people, in beige trousers, dance to Louis Prima's 'Jump, Jive and Wail'. At multiple points in the video, as the music continues uninterrupted, the camera freezes and pans across an image of a dancer in midflight. Bennett (2001, p. 112) suggests that this camera technique captures the vitality of the scene and the mobility and expression of social dance: 'I position this GAP ad … in a tradition of works of art that explore the phenomenon of animation – of dead things coming alive, of objects revealing a secret capacity for self-propulsion'. Bennett's point is that the mood of the advert is enchanting, inducing a sense of the lively and intense engagements that characterise interactions between people and materials. Bennett (2001, p. 118) concludes that Weber's notion of rationalisation cannot account for this 'fantastic realm' of experience. Indeed, what enchants human life is the often wondrous, magical experiences that come from the emotional attachments that people develop with objects.

Michael Saler (2012) takes a similar perspective in *As If: Modern Enchantment and the Literary Prehistory of Virtual Reality*. Saler too challenges Weber's analysis of modernity, suggesting that '[t]he modern West has been called "disenchanted", but this is a half-truth'. We are familiar with fans of *Harry Potter*, *The Lord of the Rings*, *Star Trek* and Marvel Comics forming online communities and attending conventions in cosplay. Saler shows that this phenomenon of creating 'virtual reality' began in the late nineteenth century, bringing enchantment back to a disenchanted world. He illustrates this argument by examining adult immersion in fictional novels, particularly those of Arthur Conan Doyle (Sherlock Holmes), H.P. Lovecraft (Cthulhu Mythos) and J.R.R. Tolkien (*The Hobbit*; *The Lord of the Rings*). Saler asserts that these texts, which feature wildly imaginative plots, also incorporate realism into their storylines through reference to historical and scientific ideas. Indeed, the Sherlock Holmes stories are a detective fiction that mixes fantasy with the science of observation, deduction, forensics and logical reasoning. Saler argues that these texts reveal how 'enchanting' reason can be as fans embrace these

(Continued)

virtual worlds 'as if' they were real places with real people. This immersion is not an escape from the real world, argues Saler, but a magical space where readers can consider alternative possibilities. As such, 'virtual reality' helps readers question modernity's more instrumental, disenchanting aspects.

Summary

- Friedrich Nietzsche, Sigmund Freud and Max Weber offer critical perspectives on modernity, paying particular attention to the power of social institutions to control people's thoughts, feelings and actions.
- A key concept here is repression: the idea that moral values and social norms come to dominate people's beliefs and (un)conscious practices.
- Nietzsche provides existential insight into the power of religion and the dangers of nihilism.
- Freud offers new tools to describe the mind and identifies antagonisms between human nature and social conduct.
- Weber generates a critique of modernity by examining the expansion of rationalisation and bureaucracy in capitalist societies.
- Each theorist foreshadows the development of critical theory and remains relevant to contemporary social analyses.

Review Questions

- What are the strengths and weaknesses of Nietzsche's perspective on religion and secularism?
- Freud claims that modern civilisation is a paradox that we create to protect ourselves from unhappiness. Do you agree?
- Is Weber's 'rationalisation thesis' still relevant today? What examples can you think of?

Annotated Reading

Nietzsche can be a challenging read. Michael Tanner's (2000) *Nietzsche: A Very Short Introduction* (Oxford: Oxford University Press) makes his ideas much more accessible.

For a companion to Nietzsche that captures his influence on social thought, see Keith A. Pearson's (2006) *A Companion to Nietzsche* (Oxford: Blackwell).

Peter Gay's (1995) introduction and chronology in *The Freud Reader* (New York: W.W. Norton) gives a helpful overview of Freud's work and insight into his biography.

For those interested in learning more about hysteria, especially within contemporary life, see Christopher Bollas's (2000) *Hysteria* (London: Routledge).

Nicholas Gane's (2012) *Max Weber and Contemporary Capitalism* (London: Palgrave) revisits and reworks key concepts within Weber's writings to explain the social and cultural dynamics of contemporary capitalism.

R. Bruce Douglas (2018) questions whether contemporary society has escaped Weber's 'iron cage' in *The Iron Cage Revisited: Max Weber in the Neoliberal Era* (London: Routledge).

4

Durkheim and Functionalism

Chapter Objectives

This chapter will:

- Introduce Émile Durkheim's sociological vision and impact on social research methods.
- Describe key concepts, including social facts, social solidarity, collective conscience, and functionalism.
- Explore Durkheim's ongoing relevance through studying crime, culture, play and games.

Keywords

Social facts, suicide, anomie, the enlightenment, individualism, functionalism, socialisation, structure, agency, culture

Introduction

Alongside Karl Marx and Max Weber, Émile Durkheim ranks as an essential theorist of modernity whose work represents a contrasting perspective on its crises and opportunities. Unlike critical theory, which focuses on economic or psychological contradictions, Durkheim focuses on social functioning and moral order. His work draws from influential philosophers of the **Enlightenment** to consider social cohesion in times of economic, political and cultural upheaval. In particular, Durkheim's work considers the progressive evolution of societies from traditional to modern settings. This perspective allows him to identify the elementary forms of social interaction needed to maintain stable, moral societies and question what causes social breakdown. As such, Durkheim sets out to establish a discipline – sociology – that provides scientific guidance on how to research social functioning by examining the relationship between **social structure** and **agency**. This chapter begins by considering Durkheim's *Rules of Sociological Method* (2014/1895) and his conception of sociological research, before dealing with his substantive arguments about the origins and nature of modern society in *The Division of Labour in Society* (2014/1893) and *Suicide* (2006/1897). Notably, the chapter also introduces Durkheim's *The Elementary Forms of Religious Life* (2008/1912), where Durkheim discusses the importance of religion and communal living for emotional security and social stability. This work has had a lasting impact, given its influence on the development of cultural sociology and theories of play and games.

Sociology as a Science

Born in France, Émile Durkheim spent his intellectual career trying to legitimate the idea that researchers can study society scientifically. Indeed, perhaps he is the first 'sociologist' in so far as a significant theme of his work is that sociology has a distinct object of study – social facts. In *The Rules of Sociological Method* (2014/1895), Durkheim proposes a scientific, empirically minded research programme that moves forward ideas within Enlightenment philosophy to give sociology a clear and separate identity.

Social facts are social structures and cultural norms external to and coercive of people – from religious beliefs, legal codes and moral rules to pedagogical activities and economic and political institutions. Durkheim argues that such phenomena are social rather than individual. They are social because they originate from and are characteristic of the group: they constitute a shared or collective reality. To say they are facts means that they have an objective reality outside the individual's mind; they possess a nature of their own, no less substantial than physical phenomena (see **realism**). Durkheim insists that social facts are external to individual consciousness, studied by acquiring data through observation, experimentation and comparison. Indeed, the shared, objective quality of group behaviour allows social facts to be studied sociologically. For example, he writes:

> When I perform my duties as a brother, a husband or a citizen and carry out the commitments I have entered into, I fulfil obligations which are defined in law and custom and which are external to myself and my actions. Even when they conform to my own sentiments and when I feel their reality within me, that reality does not cease to be objective, for it is not I who have prescribed these duties; I have received them through education. (Durkheim, 2014/1895, p. 50)

Durkheim's point here is that social facts are not individual intentions, motivations or desires. Instead, they are the general structures and norms that create a level of conformity within groups of people. Such facts, Durkheim argues, are not reducible to individuals but have an objective reality because they are social. Indeed, he uses the Latin term *sui generis*, which means 'unique', to claim that social facts exist above and beyond individual consciousness.

To support his argument, Durkheim identifies three traits of social facts which make them unique to sociology and, therefore, distinct from other disciplines, like psychology or biology. The first trait is 'externality'. Durkheim argues that we are born into a world of existing institutions, ideas and practices. As members of any society, we are accustomed to some form of legal rules, moral obligations and social conventions. For example, as students, teachers, friends, partners, or siblings, we adhere to social conventions that guide the rules and responsibilities of these roles. While we might act more or less freely within these positions, we subscribe to a general system of values and beliefs guiding how we should act in these positions. These systems are not expressions of individual intention but representations of collective conduct that we endorse and enforce.

To give another example, Durkheim argues that language is a social fact, of which externality is a crucial trait (see Quine, 1972 in Ritzer, 2008, p. 190). People cannot communicate with one another without a set of shared rules through which to reach a mutual understanding. Indeed, every language has logic regarding syntax, spelling and diction, structuring how people communicate by creating shared parameters of expression (see also Chapters 5 and 6). Durkheim's point, then, is that language is a 'thing' external to the individual because it is a collective phenomenon that establishes shared practices. No individual can create a language without explaining the rules governing permissible speech or gestures.

The second trait of social facts is their coercive power to compel people to act. Again, consider language as an example. We often use language to reason, urge or even pressure people into acting in 'appropriate' ways. A typical example is the regulation of speech and gestures that purposively promote hate, prejudice and social inequality. Durkheim broadens this argument beyond language to suggest that social facts exist anywhere that the power of public opinion, religious belief, or laws establish social obligations. These obligations, much like language, cannot be explained by an individual's intentions, though people do internalise and routinely confirm them through habitual behaviour. On the contrary, these obligations exist as part of a system of social facts, the force of which becomes apparent when we deviate from the norm. This idea anticipates Durkheim's theory of crime and deviance (see below).

The third trait of social facts is that they are widespread within a social group. This feature may sound like common sense, but Durkheim makes an essential point about the functioning of ideas. He argues that social facts are a collective phenomenon because we share them to meet a group's needs. In other words, social facts exert power and influence on people's behaviours and beliefs because these facts are a condition of existing within a given social group. So, for example, to be able to participate in a work or sports team, many of us would have to endorse and enforce certain norms, such as treating one another with dignity, respect, honesty and humility. These norms are not merely common sense. They are critical to the cohesiveness and performance of the team, shaping its rhythm, communication and decision-making.

Social facts, then, are a means for Durkheim to establish a subject matter for sociology. He uses the term to affirm the idea that there is a collective reality external to the consciousness of individuals. Later, Durkheim will introduce the term **collective conscience** to refer to this characteristically social phenomenon. From this perspective, Durkheim insists on the scientific status of sociology, which concerns itself with studying social surroundings rather than individual actions. Social facts are also a means for Durkheim to distinguish sociology from common sense. He insists that everyday views, typically formed through opinions about politics, morality and society, lack the scientific validity required to explain social phenomena. Indeed, Durkheim argues that our everyday conceptions 'are as a veil interposed between the things and ourselves', a world filtered through 'traditional prejudices' and 'accepted opinions' (Durkheim, 1982, cited in Royce, 2015, p. 62). As such, Durkheim guards against social research based on first impressions and recommends that sociology be the enemy of conventional wisdom (Royce, 2015, p. 62).

Causality

Shaping Durkheim's view of sociology as a science is his philosophical assumptions about the reality of the social world and the role of causal explanation in making sense of it. Durkheim is a realist (see realism), which means that he thinks that society's rules, roles and responsibilities take on an objective status, irreducible to people's feelings or beliefs. To put it another way, Durkheim reasons that social institutions *structure* human behaviour, a process with reality and truth to it, allowing researchers to study the causes of social phenomena. As such, realists maintain that sociology, as a science, is a means of explaining how society transmits ideas from the past, structuring future social action.

This philosophical position is essential to understanding the role of causality within Durkheim's thesis. As a realist, Durkheim recognises that individuals contribute to the emergence of social phenomena, mainly as they create new laws, norms and rules as 'historical actors' (Royce, 2015, p. 66). These actors are typically unaware of the complex and contingent effects of their activities, making it difficult to reduce the cause of any social change to one individual. In other words, social change is a collective phenomenon which plays out through the (re)structuring of social action. For Durkheim, individuals perform only a small role in shaping the course of this process as many accept and live within pre-existing social conditions.

This reasoning brings us to an essential distinction that Durkheim makes between investigating the causes of social phenomena and explaining their effects. Durkheim argues that causal explanation aims to discover the origins of social facts and investigate how collective behaviour emerges. A causal explanation is about tracing the evolution of social systems and identifying the social forces that govern human behaviour. By contrast, Durkheim argues that a functional analysis (see below) seeks to explain the role of social phenomena and their purposes (Royce, 2015, pp. 65–66). For example, a sociologist might trace the history of the UK's judiciary to explain how it has evolved since the twelfth century. This investigation is quite different from trying to identify the function of the criminal justice system and explain why it persists, albeit in an elaborated form, today. Durkheim argues that the sociological method can do both. However, it is logical to identify causes before considering their effects – a rationale that guides Durkheim's investigation in his book *The Division of Labour in Society* (1893).

In sum, Durkheim argues that our societies exist because of the structures – rules, roles and responsibilities – that emerge from collective behaviour rather than individual preferences. He calls these social facts and makes a case for sociology as a discipline that reveals the causes at work beneath the surface of social life.

Focus on Facts

It is important to note that Durkheim's interest in social causality emerges from the writings of the philosopher Auguste Comte. Comte is known as the writer who coined the terms *sociologie* ('sociology') and 'positive philosophy' ('positivism'). Comte argues that the study of society should be scientific: it should rely on testable hypotheses through which researchers can create new knowledge about 'social laws'. Comte uses the phrase 'positive philosophy' to refer to this vision of social science, arguing that we need a new social epistemology that produces knowledge through empirical testing and data, rather than speculation and common sense.

Figure 4.1 Social facts

Think about the 'weight' of social facts – how, in many ways, legal rules, social conventions and moral obligations are a constant presence in our lives, constantly influencing our beliefs and practices.

Society in Transition

In *The Division of Labour*, Durkheim analyses social life by tracing the development of modern relations between individuals and society. In particular, he compares and contrasts features of the modern and pre-modern world to reflect on the causes of social change and their impact on social cohesion. As Ritzer (2008, p. 196) notes, *The Division of Labour* was Durkheim's first attempt at using his new science of society – sociology – to examine what many at the time had come to see as a crisis of morality. In the 100 years preceding, France had been through a series of violent revolutions causing social unrest and political turmoil. Values associated with the Enlightenment, such as **individualism**, were blamed for undermining traditional authority and religious belief. As such, Durkheim's starting point was to diagnose the problems inherent within the evolution of societies and, later, to prescribe a cure through moral education (Durkheim, 2002/1925).

Durkheim proceeds by examining the earliest forms of social life, from marauding factions and tribal groups to more advanced forms of social organisation, such as those present within industrial and urban societies. Holding pre-modern groups together, Durkheim argues, are the similarities between people whose comparable working roles replicate social positions, values and strong social bonds ('mechanical solidarity'). This view contrasts with modern societies, where an advanced division of labour has the potential to erode feelings of **social solidarity** (Ritzer, 2008, p. 197). Durkheim argues that the specialisation of work within modern societies makes it difficult for people to find common ground ('organic solidarity'). Indeed, how many of us get to know the bus or train driver during our daily commute? As such, Durkheim signals that the interdependent nature of work roles in modern societies is changing social morality.

Informing this perspective is Durkheim's view of the structure of pre-modern and modern societies. He argues that the earliest social groups were relatively small, functioning independently of one another but sharing the same building blocks, such as performing basic survival tasks like hunting or gathering. These groups cease to be viable, Durkheim suggests, when the level of contact and social interaction between them prompts a change in structure. Durkheim refers to this process of interaction as 'dynamic' or 'moral' density, arguing that an increase in the density of social groups can weaken their independent functioning (see Royce, 2015, p. 71). In other words, social organisations become more complex as more people join and interact.

As these populations grow, Durkheim argues that the density of social groups affects competition, as rivalries emerge for scarce resources and opportunities. As Royce (2015, p. 71) notes, the resulting intensification compels individuals to seek new ways to earn a livelihood as a matter of survival. From this perspective, this division of labour develops as individuals attempt to manage increasingly challenging circumstances. Indeed, Durkheim argues that the specialisation of work roles represents an amicable way of managing conflict over resources, especially as individuals take on different occupational roles – farmer, baker, blacksmith – to coexist peacefully (Royce, 2015, p. 72).

Collective Conscience

A crucial concept of Durkheim's is that of the collective conscience, which refers to 'the totality of beliefs and sentiments common to average citizens' (Durkheim, 1964/1893, cited in Ritzer, 2008, p. 193). Durkheim argues that the collective conscience changes as the structures of societies transition towards modernity. In the pre-modern world, the collective conscience is a universal or omnipresent social force that impresses itself on every aspect of an individual's life, steering them towards a collective effort. Consider, for example, the beliefs and sentiments common to members of the armed forces. The collective conscience here is powerful, consisting of exact rules of behaviour, which prioritise military effectiveness and, as such, restrain individual opinion or discretion. From this perspective, Durkheim argues that, in pre-modern societies, the 'individual consciousness is almost indistinct from the collective consciousness' as 'every consciousness beats as one' (Durkheim, 1984, cited in Royce, 2015, p. 72).

The specialisation of work changes how the collective conscience operates in modern societies. Durkheim recognises that the collective conscience adapts as people's interactions and circumstances change. In particular, he argues that the division of labour makes it very difficult to unify modern societies through a single set of beliefs or sentiments. Consider, for example, the idea of choosing a career today. One of the benefits of living within a liberal democracy is the freedom to choose a career path. As such, the collective conscience is more flexible in modern societies, permitting diversity and variation in people's thoughts and actions. Durkheim notes that the process of modernisation, then, entails not only a specialisation of working roles but also individualism as people experience autonomy from the rule of the collective (see Royce, 2015, p. 73).

It is crucial to recognise that Durkheim is not arguing that the collective conscience disappears as societies transition towards modernity. Instead, he claims that the collective conscience changes, organising itself around the values we place on individuality. Indeed, today, many of us respect the sanctity of human life and an individual's right to express themselves through their beliefs and sentiments. Individualism, then, has become the rallying point for the modern mind (Royce, 2015, p. 73).

Repressive and Restitutive Law

An essential point for Durkheim is that as societies develop, so do their laws. He argues that pre-modern societies have repressive laws as the legal code reflects a rigid collective conscience, insistent on severe sanctions for individual rule breakers. As Ritzer (2008, p. 199) argues, mechanical societies tend to share a common morality, any offence against which is significant to the collective. As such, wrongdoers will expect strict punishments, including imprisonment, bodily torture, mutilation or death. Even minor offences draw harsh penalties, if only as a deterrent against offending against the collective moral system. Legal interventions, such as removing the tongues of blasphemers, or cutting off the hands of thieves, bolster the collective conscience and reaffirm the authority of traditions (Ritzer, 2008, p. 199; Royce, 2015, p. 74).

In contrast, modern societies, with a weaker collective conscience, adopt restitutive laws, where offenders make amends for the harms of their crimes by some act of restoration or

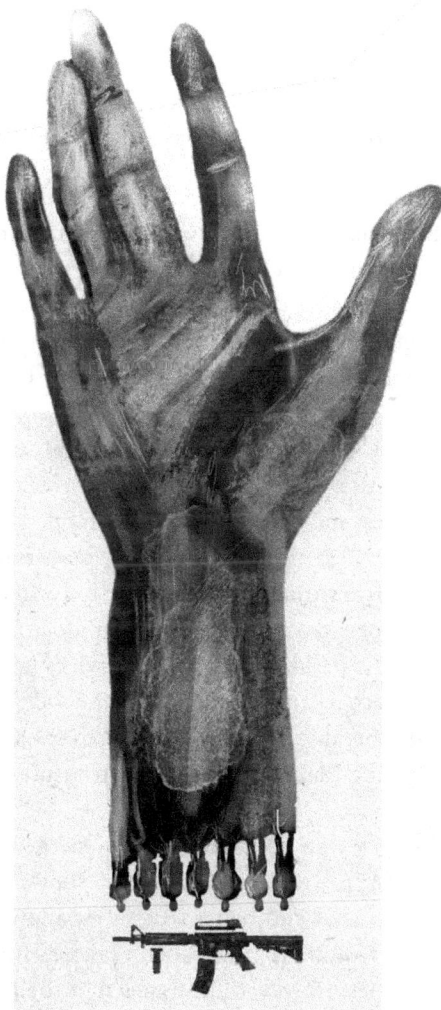

Figure 4.2 Collective conscience

Reflect on what life is like in the military as an example of collective conscience. Soldiers are disciplined by sharing rules, beliefs and practices to act together as a unit rather than as a collection of individuals.

repayment to their victims. In such societies, wrongdoing is not an attack or offence against the collective but a matter to resolve between individuals. As such, legal systems emerge to resolve conflicts between parties, whether those be the crimes of thieves, adulterous couples, or exploitative business owners. From this perspective, the modern legal system works to maintain social order rather than policing collective morality. Its purpose is to maintain social interdependency by achieving restitution between individuals.

Mechanical and Organic Solidarity

In *The Division of Labour*, Durkheim focuses on how social solidarity changes as societies transition towards this modern, restitutive world. In particular, he refers to two types of solidarity – mechanical and organic – as a means to consider the different ways in which societies stick together. The characteristics of a mechanical society are that they produce social bonds through shared activities and similar belief structures. In contrast, organic societies produce social bonds through interdependence, as different duties and obligations draw people together.

In the pre-modern era, Durkheim argues that mechanical solidarity emerges as people replicate and resemble one another. Individuals form cohesive communities based on primitive functions, such as creating shelter or hunting for food. These groups are practically self-sufficient (Ritzer, 2008, p. 197) and, as such, develop a robust collective conscience that guides them towards survival through collective activity. In contrast, the modern family, for example, needs access to a grocer, baker, butcher, doctor, teacher and mechanic to survive (Ritzer, 2008, p. 197). Shared access to these services becomes the pivot on which modern society operates as people understand that others depend on them to function adequately. Indeed, the term 'organic solidarity' describes the essential needs that people address in one another. This interdependency is why restitutive law is necessary to keep society functioning.

Altogether, then, Durkheim's work draws attention to the moral significance of *The Division of Labour* (Royce, 2015, p. 76). In particular, he shows that as societies transition towards modernity, so do their laws and belief structures, allowing us to account for new working patterns. It is easy to assume that Durkheim favours the collective morality present in these pre-modern societies. However, he argues that the modern world can produce strong social bonds, mainly as people connect through their different social positions. As such, the division of labour becomes a foundation for less competitive and coercive relationships, especially as people recognise that each individual contributes to the overall functioning of societies. Durkheim views the modern collective conscience as something that appraises individual thoughts and actions, making it difficult to establish a shared or collective morality.

Functionalism

Durkheim was one of the first social theorists to offer what is known as a functionalist explanation of society, comparing the structuring of social life to the workings of biological organisms. In particular, functionalists suggest that the survival of society, much like the natural body, depends on the integrated functioning of various 'parts' into the 'whole'. From this perspective, social stability is a question of how well individuals and institutions combine to form a 'healthy' society. Indeed, Durkheim recognises that the division of labour may create 'unhealthy' societies, especially as outdated norms and expectations force people into roles and responsibilities for which they are ill-suited (Ritzer, 2008, p. 200). Nevertheless, using a biological analogy helps us trace the causal interactions within **social systems**.

The analogy starts from the idea that a biological organism is a living entity whose existence and health are interdependent on the operations of other organs (Jones and Bradbury, 2018, p. 89). For example, the workings of the circulatory system are dependent upon the heart and lungs to pump oxygen-rich blood throughout the body. Similarly, the digestive system works in parallel with the excretory system (kidneys and urination) to remove bodily waste. In each case, a particular *part* of the body exists to ensure the overall functioning of the *whole*. Indeed, the body has evolved to create such part–whole relationships to survive. According to this approach, we can refer to these integrated wholes as systems, which describes the interdependent working of part–whole relationships.

Durkheim and other functionalists, like Talcott Parsons (Parsons and Bales, 1956), argue that social systems work similarly: that social rules, roles and responsibilities structure social behaviour according to societal needs. Sociologists often describe this established way of thinking or acting as **socialisation**, which functionalists see as a process necessary for maintaining society. Talcott Parsons is a sociologist well known for developing this idea. He argues that socialisation helps parts of society integrate into the whole. So, for example, the family helps integrate children and young people into society by teaching them basic norms, values and beliefs. Education also gives young people learning experiences that promote social belonging and the construction of local and national identities. Indeed, Parsons argues that teaching a shared history and language is vital in promoting 'value consensus' – agreement around shared values and practices (Parsons and Bales, 1956; see also Giddens, 1968).

Perhaps two of the most significant values in modern societies concern work ethic and meritocracy. Parsons argues that these values integrate individuals into society by providing a dedicated workforce. So, for example, through education, we learn that society rewards those who work hard and punishes those who are lazy. Better pay and lifestyle opportunities await an excellent work ethic; idleness leads to social humiliation and financial hardship. While there is no doubt that these societal norms produce **stigma** (see Tyler, 2020), Parson's view is that they are necessary for the overall functioning of social systems. Society only survives if its members remain productive and controlled by stable social arrangements. Indeed, functionalists agree that modern societies work for most people as socialisation resolves conflicts around the distribution of resources and work roles.

Suicide

Durkheim continues his efforts to authenticate the discipline of sociology in his work *Suicide*. Although suicide is an individual act that we typically consider a 'problem', Durkheim argues that it is a social phenomenon 'normal' to societies worldwide. Every society, Durkheim suggests, has a specific rate of suicide, which is indicative of varying levels of social integration and regulation. Durkheim (2006/1897, p. 167) analyses suicide rates from across western Europe to conclude that:

> suicide varies inversely with the degree of integration of the social groups of which
> the individual forms a part … The more weakened the groups to which he belongs,
> the less he depends on them, the more he consequently depends only on himself and
> recognises no other rules of conduct than what are founded on his private interests.

His point here is that suicide rates increase in societies where social groups fail to exercise a constraining force upon the individual. He argues that integrated societies hold individuals under social control, forbidding them to self-destroy by promoting a strong sense of group belonging and duty. In particular, Durkheim explains that some religious groups (e.g., Catholics) have a collective tendency to stop suicidal acts. This tendency is because Catholics have strict penalties for suicide, viewing it as a mortal sin and an act of blasphemy. As such, the community has created common bonds and systems of mutual support, which Durkheim (2006/1897, p. 168) suggests, enable people to 'cling to life', even during times of profound personal struggle.

So while we might think of suicide in psychological terms, Durkheim views it as a social fact that emerges from collective conduct and experiences of social cohesion. He argues that the rate of suicide is always a product of social forces external to individuals and, as such, of interest to sociological study. Durkheim is not dismissing the role that individual circumstances, motives and experiences play in acts of suicide. Instead, he acknowledges that the 'moral constitution' of people's social environments structures the patterns exhibited in the character and number of suicidal acts.

To better understand the character of suicide rates across different societies, Durkheim develops a typology that describes the distinct conditions leading to suicide. In particular, he draws on critical themes concerning social solidarity to categorise suicide in terms of mechanical or organic societies. He identifies four types of suicide: 'altruistic', 'fatalistic', 'egoistic' and 'anomic'. These social types name varieties of irregular social environments, each referring to a particular context where there is an imbalance between individuals and the group. Indeed, Durkheim distinguishes between 'healthy' and 'pathological' societies by attributing higher rates of suicide to irregularities within social milieus (Royce, 2015, p. 80).

Durkheim assesses the 'health' of societies by examining the relationship between the individual and the group. He suggests that societies are 'unhealthy' whenever the presence of the group is either too strong or too weak within an individual's life. As such, he measures the group's presence across two dimensions: social integration and social regulation. Integration refers to group attachment; regulation refers to social control. Regarding integration, a healthy social environment exists where individuals have a life in common with others, where they are active participants in the social world and oriented to collective goals and ideals (Royce, 2015, p. 80). Regarding regulation, a healthy social environment exists where the passions and desires of individuals have attainable outlets and clearly defined limits such that people experience congruity between their aspirations and resources, between their needs and desires.

Durkheim argues that a stable and harmonious social order requires social integration and regulation. Too much or too little creates a situation where individuals are vulnerable to suicide. Durkheim's four types of suicide emerge from this proposition. Altruistic suicide stems from excessive integration, fatalistic from excessive regulation, egoistic from insufficient integration, and anomic from insufficient regulation. These social types denote pathological conditions that shape the minds of individuals (Royce, 2015, p. 80).

Altruistic Suicide

Altruistic suicide occurs in traditional societies or communities where social integration is excessive. In these contexts, individuals must orientate themselves to fulfil social expectations. A failure to do so leaves suicide as an obligatory or honourable option (Stack, 2004). For example, consider the act of *seppuku* (or *hara-kiri*) within Japanese culture. *Seppuku* is a form of ritual suicide by disembowelment, once reserved for Japanese samurai as a means to restore honour following defeat in battle. Later, it became a means for Japanese people to atone for the shame of committing crimes. In each case, the act of *seppuku* is met with cultural approval as the Japanese recognise its role in maintaining social order through a strong sense of duty and honour.

Egoistic Suicide

Egoistic suicide, the opposite of altruistic suicide, arises from a social environment characterised by insufficient social integration. It refers to suicide under conditions in which individuals are excessively self-oriented and, as such, have loose social ties with other individuals and social groups. Durkheim argues that the specialisation of labour contributes to this process by creating a self-centred culture in which individualism threatens social bonds. For example, consider the impact of an individual's ambitions and aspirations on social attachments with family and friends. Research shows that the freedoms that Western societies associate with individual success come at the cost of weakened social ties (Boltanski and Chiapello, 2007). For Durkheim, it is these ties that bind and protect people against suicide.

Anomic Suicide

Where an egoistic culture can weaken social ties, dramatic social changes can produce the anomic conditions necessary to disrupt an individual's bond with society – and this can lead to what Durkheim calls anomic suicide. Anomic suicide occurs when societies can no longer provide the conditions for the social regulation of an individual's behaviour. This process leaves individuals vulnerable to the disruptions of social life and, thus, more likely to commit suicide. For example, consider the 2007–2008 global financial crisis. Research shows that the crises caused at least 10,000 additional suicides between 2008 and 2010, with job losses, debt worries and home and business foreclosure increasing the risks of suicidal thinking (Reeves et al., 2014). For Durkheim, such economic crises aggravate suicide by disturbing the collective order and leaving many people cut adrift from traditional support structures (Holligan and McLean, 2019).

Fatalistic Suicide

Fatalistic suicide results from excessive social regulation, such as when people's futures are blocked, their aspirations denied, or their lives are lived in highly controlled political situations. For example, research shows that people who emigrate from oppressive political regimes have higher rates of suicide than those within democratic societies (Bergen et al., 2009). For Durkheim, too much regulation unleashes a tide of despair that causes a rise in the rate of fatalistic suicide.

Summary

Durkheim uses these typologies to evidence his argument that the rate of suicide is an index of the effectiveness (or not) of social bonding. As he sees it, social bonds regulate individual desires and aspirations as well as provide a culture of discipline that wards off anomie and egoism. Such bonds serve a vital moral purpose: to provide attachment to social groups and equip individuals with essential teachings, ideas and purposes.

Focus on Facts

Before Durkheim, early in the nineteenth century, Harriet Martineau, one of the first female sociologists, had recognised suicide as a social fact. Martineau (1838, cited in Dillon, 2009, p. 99) states: 'Every society has its suicides, and much may be learned from the character and number, both as to the notions on morals which prevail and the religious sentiment which ... controls the act'.

┤Case Study 4.1├

Anomie and Crime

As discussed above, Durkheim uses the term 'anomie' to capture the idea of moral uncertainty at times of dramatic social or economic change. In Durkheim's view, the transition from mechanical to organic solidarity leads to individualism which produces a change in norms, such as the lessening of social controls over the individual. As such, Durkheim recognises that individualism, while resulting in greater freedoms for people, also produces the possibility of deviant behaviour. This idea has had a significant impact on the early study of crime through the field of criminology, which examines the origins of crime in society and its associated social processes.

Merton's Theory of Anomie

Robert Merton (1938) develops Durkheim's concept of anomie in his account of social structure and its relationship to deviant behaviour. He argues that anomie is a social condition that occurs when discrepancies exist between societal goals and the means to accomplish them (see Hagan and Daigle, 2020). Merton argues that most people strive to achieve culturally situated goals, such as the 'American Dream', in which people's social worth is based on their apparent hard work and material success. However, a state of anomie emerges as access to these goals is blocked to individuals or broader parts of the population. Merton calls this discrepancy 'strain', and it results in deviant behaviour, as people rebel against the values and social rules that limit their ambitions and aspirations. As such, crime results from innovative attempts to circumvent inconsistencies within modern social structures, though such attempts contribute to psychological stress and social conflict.

Steven Messner and Richard Rosenfeld (2013) extend Merton's theory of anomie in their book *Crime and the American Dream*. Here, they argue that the hunger for wealth within contemporary American society has become insatiable, so much so that all social institutions now serve economic interests. The result is the institutionalisation of anomie as cultural pressures to accumulate material rewards produce weak controls on any deviant means to secure economic success (Messner and Rosenfeld, 2013, cited in Hagan and Daigle, 2020). As such, we see examples of banking fraud and financial misconduct in the years leading up to financial crises, both in the 1980s and in 2007–2008.

Merton's modification of Durkheim's concept of anomie also influenced the 'anomie tradition' in US criminology. Writers like Albert Cohen directed the notion of anomie to better explain types of crime due to delinquent subcultures. For example, Cohen presents a theory about lower-class subcultural delinquency in his book *Delinquent Boys* (1955). He argues that lower-class youths use delinquent subcultures to react against dominant (middle-class) value systems. These systems, which typically discriminate against lower-class lifestyles, tastes and values, become the target of disdain. Cohen suggests that acts of juvenile crime emerge because lower-class youths seek self-esteem by rejecting dominant value systems. As such, they would perform criminal acts, such as theft, to gain status within the gang, instead of out of need or desire (Cohen, 1955, cited in Hagan and Daigle, 2020).

Religion and Society

The perspective on society that Durkheim develops in *The Elementary Forms of Religious Life* (1912) differs from his other major works. Durkheim moves away from the comparative statistics and number-crunching associated with his vision of sociology as a science. Instead, he focuses on the crucial role that religious ideas, beliefs, symbols and customs have on social behaviour. Durkheim begins by examining a totemic religion in a clan-based society, the Arunta, arguing that this religious group represents the most elementary form of social organisation. Durkheim suggests that if he can identify the essence of religion within this group, then sociology has the principles to examine the origins of ideology in other aspects of life (see Thompson, 2002, p. 98).

Contra Nietzsche and Freud (see Chapter 3), Durkheim views religious beliefs as a 'symbol' of social reality, not as an error of fantasy or manipulation. He writes: 'The most barbarous and the most fantastic rites and the strangest myths translate some human need, some aspect of life, either individual or social' (Durkheim, 1965, cited in Thompson, 2002, p. 99). From this perspective, it is the job of sociologists to use the tools of science to discover the conditions that give rise to these religious practices. Indeed, Durkheim argues that sociologists need to identify religion's essential characteristics and functions to explain why people become faithful.

To do this, Durkheim argues that societies, through individuals, create religion by defining certain phenomena as sacred or profane. He defines the sacred as those rituals that inspire feelings of reverence, awe and obligation. These ritualistic experiences then bind individuals to social groups, often through the power of religious symbols and institutions. Durkheim argues that this bond is moral and cognitive in that religious rituals and symbols become the lens through which people make sense of and act within society. The profane is set apart from the sacred due to its practical or secular worldview. It refers to the commonplace or practical aspects of everyday life that cannot reproduce the transcendent experiences of the social.

From this perspective, Durkheim argues that the source of sacred exists within society. It is not God that inspires religious belief but the power of moral communities to offer sacred experiences. Durkheim calls these communities a 'Church', an overarching moral authority that brings followers together through sanctioned beliefs and rituals. For example, consider the Catholic Church. Followers of Catholicism will kneel when receiving bread and wine, following the rules and procedures of Holy Communion. Holy Communion is a sacred ritual with a symbolic gesture towards Jesus's Last Supper with his disciples. As such, Durkheim argues that the function of the Church is to connect the individual to society through these kinds of social practices. Indeed, through such meaningful acts, individuals learn to participate and serve within moral communities, thereby producing social solidarity.

The Arunta

It is essential to understand Durkheim's case study in *The Elementary Forms of Religious Life*. His primary data source was studies of a clan-based Australian tribe called the Arunta. Durkheim saw the Arunta as an example of a 'primitive' civilisation, arguing that their religious systems were less developed than those of modern societies (a perspective criticised by postcolonial theorists; see Chapter 9). Durkheim believed that within these more 'straightforward' groupings, the fundamental elements and relations of social life were closer and more apparent (as if akin to mechanical solidarity). In studying the Arunta, he notes that this tribe established strong bonds of kinship through the use of totems. Members of the groups attach through a shared name, the inspiration of which came from particular animals to which the clan had an affinity. For example, clan members would create the image of an emu through head-dresses made of twigs, human hair and bird down. Durkheim argues that the function of this totemism was to bind clan members together through symbolic unity.

These primitive tribes also held ritual gatherings of extraordinary social energy. Members would literally 'play with fire' as their participation in a larger group would affirm the superior moral force and protection afforded by their collectivity (Thompson, 2002, p. 106). A range of positive and negative rituals would help strengthen the group's bond, some of which celebrated communion and sacred unity, while others dealt with taboo and superstition. In each case, Durkheim argues that the clans would transition between the sacred and profane by marking the rituals through acts of abstinence, physical ordeal, and the donning of unique clothes and ornaments (Thompson, 2002, p. 106).

Modern Morality

In studying primitive cultures, then, Durkheim moves to cast a light on religion in modern societies. Where totemism was once a means of ensuring a robust collective conscience, Durkheim recognises that social practices under modernity are different. Indeed, he notes that religion is coming to occupy an increasingly narrow domain as the specialisation of labour gives rise to new ways of expressing morality. In particular, Durkheim argues that what we see in modern societies is the emergence of other moral institutions, such as the law, science and education. Each of these institutions offer a vision of morality that is quite distinct from that of the Church. Indeed, the Church is no longer the only moral binding force in modern societies as these non-religious systems source people with new understandings about the moral significance of the individual.

For Durkheim, the social transition to organic solidarity brings a corresponding shift towards individualism. He argues that modern organic societies now give people a sense of individuality rarely present in primitive cultures. This sense of individuality develops alongside the specialisation of labour as a function of more sweeping changes in the collective conscience.

For example, today, many laws and teachings respect individual liberty and personal freedoms as well as individual rights to social and economic equality. As such, modern societies increasingly integrate around the individual.

One aspect of this change in conscience, which Durkheim questions, is the role of egoism in modern morality. He argues that the selfish pursuit of personal interests may lead individuals to sacrifice the principles that keep societies functioning. For example, Durkheim suggests that egoism undermines the social discipline needed to resist personal impulses, which is essential when negotiating conflict between group and individual interests. Society cannot function if we only ever act to make ourselves happy at the expense of how others think and feel. Similarly, if we only act for ourselves, then egoism will also weaken group commitment, and the sense of belonging that follows from secure social attachments. As such, Durkheim suggests that egoism, if left unchecked, threatens the autonomy that accompanies the transition to organic solidarity. In other words, what keeps modern societies together is the freedom to exercise self-discipline, as this is what is needed to cultivate social attachments.

One final point. In response to these concerns, Durkheim recommends reform in society through the notion of moral education. Durkheim believed that education could help children develop a moral attitude towards society that would oppose egoistic expressions of the self. He viewed the classroom as an example of a small society and concluded that it was powerful enough to impress moral attitudes on children. First, the classroom provides individuals with the discipline needed to restrain individual passions and impulses. Second, education could give students a sense of attachment to society through learning about its moral systems (Ritzer, 2008, pp. 217–218). Together, education promised to nurture self-discipline and collective responsibility at a time when **secularism** was challenging the moral authority of the Church and religion (see also Chapter 3).

After Émile Durkheim

Durkheim's examination of religion has significantly impacted sociology and further research into religious cultures. For example, Robert Bellah's (1967) article 'Civil Religion in America' considers how Americans embrace fundamental beliefs, values, holidays and rituals that often run parallel to or independent of their chosen religion. Bellah calls this 'civil religion' and suggests that holidays, such as Thanksgiving, exemplify how Americans keep the nation functioning by integrating through shared practices. American civil religion, Bellah suggests, is a force for social solidarity, setting out what Americans should believe in and how they should act in society. Indeed, Americans of all backgrounds recite the Pledge of Allegiance to affirm their commitment to the United States.

Peter Berger and Thomas Luckmann (cited in Thompson, 2002, p. 110) also develop Durkheim's work by arguing that moral individualism has become commonplace in modern societies. They argue that no matter how similar belief systems may be, sacred things no longer unite individuals into a single community. Instead, Berger (cited in Thompson, 2002, p. 110) likens the modern religious scene to an economic marketplace where individuals shop around for whatever brand suits their needs. For example, today, we are very familiar with the commercialisation of spirituality. Many smartphone apps available for purchase offer a wide range of spiritual experiences, from yoga and meditation masterclasses to breathing exercises and reflective prayer. Berger (cited in Thompson, 2002, p. 110) argues that spiritual consumerism means that people feel no particular commitment to others holding similar beliefs. As such, the very content of modern belief systems has become individualistic, focused on concepts like self-enhancement and personal well-being.

Robert Bellah considers this issue in his book *Habits of the Heart* (Bellah et al., 1985), where he argues that individualism has become a core value of (American) culture and is reshaping how members of society make sense of religion in their lives. One of his participants, Sheila Larson, identifies her faith in terms of her own identity, saying:

> I believe in God. I am not a religious fanatic. I can't remember the last time I went to church. My faith has carried me a long way. It's Sheilaism. Just my own little voice. (Bellah et al., 1985, p. 221)

Bellah argues that this new value system stands in stark contrast to the biblical and republican traditions that precede it in the USA. Both systems recognise that there is a social dimension to human individuality, which is necessary for creating a moral foundation through which to engage in public life. What troubles Bellah is the erosion of these traditions, which he argues allows for 'a strident and ultimately destructive individualism to flourish' (Bellah et al., 1985, p. x). Bellah's key point is that, when carried to excess, individualism leads to an empty, materialistic life marked by personal ambition and consumerism. He writes:

> Many of those with whom we talked were locked into a split between a public world of competitive striving and a private world supposed to provide the meaning and love that make competitive striving bearable. (Bellah et al., 1985, p. 292)

As such, Bellah defends the idea that social stability requires a common culture in which most people participate. As people turn to their individual concerns, religious authority wanes, and people now feel less constrained by those values which extend beyond their own self-interest.

Cultural Sociology

A student of Robert Bellah, the sociologist Jeffrey C. Alexander, has been the pioneer of an influential sociological approach known as 'cultural sociology'. A central principle of this approach is that research analyses culture as a variable which shapes the nature and structure of social life. Like Durkheim, Alexander argues that cultural meanings are a significant site for sociological analysis. Indeed, Alexander argues that the sacred infuses contemporary life through symbolic meanings, moralities and affective rituals that draw people together.

Perhaps his most famous example is the Watergate scandal in the USA, where President Richard Nixon conspired to cover up his administration's involvement in the break-in at the Democratic National Committee's headquarters in Washington, DC. Alexander (2003, p. 155) argues that news of this political espionage did not generate a real sense of outrage at the time in June 1972. In the words of Durkheim, it remained part of the profane world. However, two years later, the same incident, still called 'Watergate', initiated a severe political crisis in American history. Alexander (2003) argues that what changed was how Nixon's political opponents created 'rituals' out of the scandal. For example, he suggests that Nixon's opponents pushed for constant trials of Watergate conspirators, former cabinet officers, and high-ranking aides. Through these rituals, Nixon became a source of pollution in politics (Alexander, 2003, p. 175). Indeed, Americans mobilised around this intensely moral issue, shunning and booing Nixon at crowd events and sending angry letters to be read to him whenever he appeared on television. Alexander (2003, p. 195) argues that the result was a collective attempt to protect American democracy against Nixon, who had come to personify a dangerous evil.

Neo-Tribes

Michel Maffesoli (1996) was also interested in Durkheim's notion of collective conscience, writing about it in his book *The Time of the Tribes*. Here, Maffesoli coins the term 'neo-tribe' as he theorises society in terms of many affinity-based groups with overlapping membership. When many writers were concerned about individualism and the decline of the community, Maffesoli suggests neo-tribes are emerging, primarily in urban contexts, as sources of informal cultural expression. He argues that these tribal-like groups emerge from opportunities provided by fleeting physical contact, emotional frenzy, and collective frameworks of memory and lived experience (Maffesoli, 1996). For example, today, we might consider the many informal cultures and identities that emerge around leisure, sporting or gaming commitments. Here, social identities are relatively unfixed or fluid, as participants move effortlessly between multiple groups or 'tribes' of people that share similar interests. An individual could, for instance, have different tribes for playing video games online during the week and then have other tribes for yoga and spinning class on the weekend. Maffesoli's point is that we hold temporary roles and identities within these groups as we only come together to share a particular passion.

Case Study 4.2

Play and the Sacred

Durkheim's *Elementary Forms of Religious Life* argues for more than just understanding religious meaning. His work shows the importance of understanding culture more broadly. Culture is how people construct and reconstruct the sacred in social life. Influenced by Durkheim, one sociologist who understood this well was Roger Caillois (2001/1961). His writings on playful activities give us insight into how they generate culture and take on a symbolic, if not sacred, quality. Caillois begins by arguing that the realm of play parallels that of the sacred. Following Durkheim, the sacred is defined by the transcendence of ordinary experience, typically through ritualised acts intended to represent symbolic truths about the world. Caillois notes that playful activities, from carnivals to games, characterise a mixture of dramatic rituals, ecstatic abandon and sober attention to symbolic rules (Riley, 2005).

Consider, for example, the experience of going to a carnival (Burke, 1978, cited in Riley, 2005, p. 105). Historically, carnivals were select times of the year that authorised mass transgressions. People would come together to experience playful performances, whether by wearing costumes, singing and dancing, or competing in games, such as jousting or football. The euphoric nature of these events captured the freedom they afforded people. Carnivals were spaces where people could transcend the inhibitions of everyday life while preparing to observe more stringent religious rituals, such as Lent. The carnival became a template for how the secular world and, later, popular culture would enact sacred experiences.

Today, the realm of popular music has become a powerful site for the enactment of the sacred in Western society (Riley, 2005, pp. 110–111). Large groups regularly gather around shared symbols, languages, customs and meanings attributed to particular forms of music, such as indie, rock and roll, rap and hip-hop. Equally, raves and other musical festivals draw on communal experiences, including intoxication and substance misuse, to create moments of what Caillois (2001/1961, p. 23) refers to as 'ilinx' – times of surrender, whereby people try to inflict a kind of rush or panic upon an otherwise clear mind. Here, music experiences are marked by an element of collective ecstatic pursuit as bodies play dangerously to find spiritual-like states (see Riley, 2005, p. 111).

Finally, in an echo of Durkheim, the sociologist Randall Collins considers how games, and other kinds of leisure pursuits, create sacredness. Collins (2004, cited in Riley, 2005, p. 112) argues that games are rituals that produce situations of dramatic tension, victory and collective emotion. Sports games, such as football, are rituals of shared passion, anxiety and conflict. Collins argues that such games are sacred objects because people must respect their rules, symbols, signs and practices if they are to participate. Indeed, among fans, it is often taboo to pretend to support a team, unmindful of the time, energy, passion and knowledge it takes. As such, Collins (2004, cited in Riley, 2005, p. 112) concludes that the sacred power of games comes from a human desire to associate with highly successful rituals and the sacred experiences that result. Perhaps this is why we revere sports players as celebrities.

Figure 4.3 Games and collective rituals

Consider how games bring people together through acts of collective participation and collective emotion. What kinds of ritualistic practices surround play, and how might these reflect examples of Durkheim's collective conscience?

Summary

- Émile Durkheim envisioned sociology as a science that explains social change. His particular interest was in explaining shifts in the moral constitution of society as a result of the division of labour.
- Durkheim offers the sociological method to identify the social facts that structure social change in complex ways.
- Durkheim's primary case study was in his book *Suicide*, in which he identifies the effects of social change on social and moral bonds. His concepts of social solidarity and anomie are particularly influential in studies of crime and culture.
- The role of religion and sacred rituals is also an essential part of Durkheim's cultural sociology, revealing how people participate in secular activities to help draw societies together. Sports, leisure and other playful activities are examples of the sacred in action today.

Review Questions

- What do you think are the strengths and weaknesses of Durkheim's method?
- Do you agree with Durkheim's perspective on morality? Are there tensions between individual and social needs?
- What examples of the 'sacred' can you think of?

Annotated Reading

For a companion to Durkheim's arguments and relevance in social thinking, see Jeffrey Alexander and Philip Smith's (2005) *The Cambridge Companion to Durkheim* (Cambridge: Cambridge University Press).

Steven Lukes's (1982) introduction to Émile Durkheim's *The Rules of Sociological Method* (New York: Free Press) gives a helpful overview of Durkheim's vision for social research and realist philosophy.

For those interested in the emergence of French sociology, notably through the Collège de Sociologie, see Michèle Richman's (2002) *Sacred Revolutions* (Minneapolis: University of Minnesota Press).

W.S.F. Pickering and Geoffrey Walford's (2000) edited collection, *Durkheim's Suicide: A Century of Research and Debate* (London: Routledge) offers a selection of studies that engage with Durkheim's sociological method.

5

Phenomenology and Symbolic Interactions

Chapter Objectives

This chapter will:

- Introduce critical thinkers in the interpretive tradition, from Edmund Husserl and Alfred Schütz to Martin Heidegger, Maurice Merleau-Ponty and Erving Goffman.
- Familiarise essential concepts, including phenomenology, pragmatism, ethnomethodology and stigma.
- Provide contemporary examples of research that applies phenomenological thinking.

Keywords

Phenomenology, phenomenological sociology, symbolic interactionism, self, identity, ethnomethodology, pragmatism, stigma

Introduction

Qualitative research owes a great deal to the interpretive tradition, which can be traced back to Edmund Husserl's phenomenology of the mind and Alfred Schütz's phenomenological sociology. Indeed, many microsociological accounts of social life, including symbolic interactionism, owe a debt to these early thinkers. This chapter will introduce students to these concepts and invite them to consider contemporary examples that show why everyday experiences are an essential departure point for understanding social life. Students will question the idea that people are passive agents of **social structure** (as Marxism or functionalism might have it) and why it is crucial to view individuals as *subjectively engaged social actors* whose experiences help them order and make sense of their realities. Importantly, this understanding will foreground the concepts of **self** and identity and how individuals use language and symbols to form social bonds and groupings. **Ethnomethodology** offers a practical approach to researching these processes.

Phenomenology

While Max Weber's injunction is to interpret social action (see Chapter 3), phenomenology takes the nature of meaning seriously. Phenomenology is the science or study of *phenomena*, an approach to understanding how people conceive and experience things. It is distinct from those social theories that attempt to explain the cause and effect of social structures. Phenomenologists study human consciousness to describe how people perceive the world and try to live within it. It is a philosophy about everyday life that reveals the richness of human existence within otherwise mundane or ordinary circumstances.

Dan Zahavi (2018, p. 10) provides a welcome example of phenomenology in action by considering the experience of buying an antique alarm clock for a friend. Zahavi suggests that the experience is far from one-dimensional, asking a simple question: how does an alarm clock *appear*? Zahavi contends that there is no straightforward answer to this question because the alarm clock can appear in several ways – one can see, touch, hear, imagine, and use this object – changing its perception. Zahavi pushes the point further, asking us to reflect on how easily our perception of an object changes depending on our perspective. For example, when looking at an alarm clock from the front, we can see its face, top, and sides but not its back side or bottom or inner workings. As we change position, this reveals new aspects to the clock as former perspectives disappear from view. Zahavi's point is that, for the phenomenologist, the experience of an object (or person) is far more complex than the initial perception. Indeed, perception never occurs in isolation – it is situated within a horizon that affects the meaning of what we see. Phenomenologists study this situatedness to grapple with objects' *apparent* nature. This departure point contrasts with the scientific goal of grasping objects as they 'truly' are.

Immanuel Kant

Strictly speaking, phenomenology has its origins within the philosophical ideas of Immanuel Kant. In his *Critique of Pure Reason*, Kant (1998/1781) argues that we do not simply and directly perceive the external world. Instead, the intrinsic faculties of the human mind structure and order the world around us. Kant gives us the example of space and time, suggesting that they are not 'things-in-themselves' that exist independently of us but are features of how we perceive objects. Indeed, many of us are familiar with the phrase 'time flies when you're having fun', which points to its subjective and situated nature. Kant argues that this subjective quality is necessary to how people experience the world. Objects cannot exist independently of our perceptions, for their 'reality' is a product of human consciousness. Indeed, the human mind perceives and creates what is understood to be 'objective reality'. Phenomenology then elaborates on this position, seeking out ways to conceptualise how consciousness creates this sense of reality for us.

Edmund Husserl

The German philosopher Edmund Husserl first develops phenomenology as a form of investigation into the experiences of thinking and knowing. In *Logical Investigations* (1900–1901), Husserl critiques psychology within the natural sciences, suggesting that one cannot reduce human meaning to principles of psychological explanation. In other words, Husserl argues that psychology cannot 'explain away' the nature of human experience in terms of general or universal laws. Instead, Husserl wants a philosophy that does not impose such constructions on experience in advance. He seeks to return experience to the living human (Husserl, 1900–1901, cited in Moran, 2000, p. 5). In practice, phenomenologists pay close attention to the nature of consciousness as the experiencer experiences it.

An important concept here is **intentionality**. For Husserl, consciousness is always intentional; we direct our thoughts towards particular objects and things. For example, in love, something is loved; in hate, something is hated; in desire, something is desired. Husserl's point is that when the mind becomes conscious *of* something, it reaches out to it and brings it into conscious experience. This idea proposes a very active relationship between the conscious subject and the object of the subject's consciousness (Crotty, 1998, p. 44). Indeed, intentionality is a way of understanding the various ways the mind actively relates to subjects and objects.

Phenomenological Sociology

Husserl's student Alfred Schütz, develops phenomenology into a form of sociology that studies social life as manifested through descriptions of people's intentional consciousness. In particular, Schütz argues that humans experience the world not as an 'objective reality' but as made up of meaningful objects and relations. It is the sociologist's task to pay careful attention to the meaningful structures that underscore how individuals perceive the world.

To begin, Schütz extends Husserl's view that people, as socialised members of society, operate within a **lifeworld** – the mundane, everyday world of social and cultural structures. Schütz argues that people create their lifeworld through their daily activities but that, in turn, the lifeworld comes to structure (enable and constrain) their choices. This structuring is particularly apparent in the taken-for-granted assumptions – or **typifications** – that people use to navigate their everyday lives. As Schütz (1970, p. 111) comments:

> What is taken for granted is, until invalidation, believed to be simply 'given' and 'given-as-it-appears-to-me'... It is this zone of things taken for granted within which we have to find our bearings. All our possible questioning for the unknown arises only within such a world of supposedly preknown things, and presupposes its existence.

Schütz's point here is that the lifeworld is the unproblematic ground for the emergence of practical concerns and solutions. In other words, guiding a person's everyday existence is the practical task of living and with this comes the need to take certain phenomena for granted. For instance, we rarely question how to brush our teeth, dress in the morning or prepare breakfast. These practical activities form part of our lifeworld – a backdrop on which we measure and attribute meaning to social life.

Notably, the lifeworld is an intersubjective world, always known and experienced by others. **Intersubjectivity** refers to the intersection between people's consciousnesses. For instance, how do people attribute intentionality, feelings, and beliefs towards one another? Schütz argues that phenomenological sociology details intersubjective occurrences, revealing the essential characteristics of human understanding and cooperation. Initially inspired by Max Weber's interpretive sociology (see Chapter 3), Schütz is less interested in how different historical and cultural contexts (e.g., Calvinism) thematise the meaning actors attribute to their actions. Instead, Schütz is concerned with describing and analysing how people grasp others' consciousness while living with their own perspectives. In other words, Schütz is interested in how intersubjectivity allows humans from various personal and social backgrounds to function and interact. Pushing Weber's concept of **Verstehen** further, Schütz (1972/1967, p. 8) writes:

> Weber makes no distinction between the *action*, considered as something in progress, and the completed *act* ... He does not ask how an actor's meaning is constituted or

what modifications this meaning undergoes ... He does not try to identify the unique and fundamental relation existing between the self and the other self, that relation whose clarification is essential to a precise understanding of what it is to know another person ... there are radical differences in the meaning-structure of my own behaviour, the behaviour of my consociates, which I immediately experience, and the behaviour of those who are merely my *contemporaries* or even my *predecessors*, which is known to me quite indirectly.

Schütz's point here is that the social world, far from being homogeneous, is a complex system with many perspectives that emerge through living. He suggests that actions and situations become meaningful through intersubjective agreement. As such, the phenomenologist's task is to describe and interpret social action with a view towards human understanding. Schütz sets out a few concepts to clarify where to begin.

The first is 'stocks of knowledge'. Schütz suggests that everyone has stocks of knowledge that provide them with the rules for interpreting physical and social interactions. This knowledge exists at a highly pragmatic level of consciousness, which does not receive much critical reflection – even from those most engaged with (or 'wide awake' to) practical concerns. Instead, stocks of knowledge are the storehouses of lived experience, from which one readily draws to interact and negotiate with physical and cultural phenomena daily. When new situations occur, Schütz recognises that people may question this taken-for-granted knowledge and consider alternative frames of reference (Appelrouth and Edles, 2021, p. 1127).

The second is 'recipe knowledge', which Schütz refers to as those implicit instructions that help people complete their daily activities, from morning to evening routines, and which 'are performed by following recipes reduced to automatic habits or unquestioned platitudes' (Schütz, 1970, cited in Appelrouth and Edles, 2021, p. 1127).

What phenomenologists have to investigate is how people act in taken-for-granted ways, describing and analysing the detail and particularities of any given lifeworld. Phenomenologists examine how lifeworlds make action and interaction possible and, in turn, how such actions come to shape and reinforce the structures of a person's social existence.

Peter Berger and Thomas Luckmann

Berger and Luckmann (1991/1966) extend Schütz's phenomenological sociology by arguing that society is a social construction, a process that begins at birth. Human infants, they suggest, lack the basic biological or instinctual drives required to survive early periods of childhood development. Instead, humans construct social arrangements and institutions that provide infants protection and stability from an early age. Following Schütz, Berger and Luckmann emphasise the intersubjective nature of these arrangements, suggesting that human survival depends on our capacity to apprehend one another's thoughts and actions. Indeed, like Schütz, they argue that common-sense knowledge functions as a 'natural attitude' to ensure that humans engage with life's practical concerns.

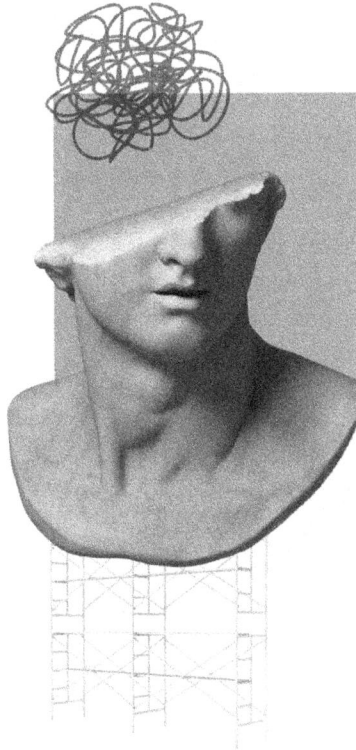

Figure 5.1 Conceptual schemes

Think about how our experiences help us to construct a mental scaffold or framework that we use to inform our daily perceptions and understandings of the world. We can think of this scaffold as a conceptual scheme, a way of organising reality to support us in living within it.

One of Berger and Luckmann's key concepts is 'habitualisation', which refers to how routine behaviours produce habits that shape human action. They suggest that social interactions, over time, become a typical means of telling people how to act within a given lifeworld (Appelrouth and Edles, 2021, pp. 1150–1151). Like Schütz, they refer to recipe knowledge as an excellent example of this habituated thinking. Consider, for example, how cooking recipes often narrow our choices by giving clear instructions about what ingredients to use and what preparatory methods to follow. Berger and Luckmann suggest that the same is true of our daily routines practices such as commuting or food shopping – which become so prescriptive that we think of them as a natural part of life. For instance, we rarely question why we shower before work, prepare our lunch, refuel the car or walk the dog. These practices have become habituated to the extent that we follow them like a script that gives us direction.

Language, too, is an example of habitualisation. Many of us will be familiar with phrases like 'please' and 'thank you' – which we use as part of a script to maintain the order and meaning of interaction. For example, 'please' initiates conversation (e.g., 'Please can I purchase this item?') and 'thank you' concludes it (e.g., 'Thank you for your help'). Yet, consider the expectations these phrases create as they become a typical means of expressing civility and gratitude. What happens when someone does not say 'please' and 'thank you'? Or feels compelled to use these phrases in less than ideal circumstances? The point is that, as language becomes habitual, it creates an almost inescapable reality as each time we speak, gesture, or communicate symbolically, we affirm routine ways of interacting.

This idea of habit relates closely to another of Berger and Luckmann's concepts: 'institutionalisation'. They argue that habitual action sets the stage for the construction of social institutions as habits become the groundwork for a shared history and knowledge between people (Appelrouth and Edles, 2021, p. 1151). For example, we seldom question things like getting a good education, working, paying taxes, or raising a family. Berger and Luckmann suggest that, as people's actions generate shared practices, they become fixed objectives, generating the social institutions we see today. Only when our lifeworlds change (e.g., through social exclusion, unemployment or excessive taxation) does this disrupt our perception of the objectivity of these institutions. Indeed, such change may initiate questions about the control institutions have over human conduct through the extent to which they provide coherency and meaningfulness.

Here, Berger and Luckmann share some affinity with Marx's ideas (see Chapter 2). They, too, recognise that social institutions can confront individuals as inescapable facts. They recognise that social constructs can limit people's actions, forcing them to act in specific ways. Marxists refer to this as **reification**: that social constructs, such as money, have become fetishised to the extent that they now control their very producers – people. Yet, Berger and Luckmann do not consider social institutions to be alienating. Instead, in keeping with phenomenology, they are concerned with how people produce and order the world. They view Marxist concepts, such as ideology and freedom, as speaking to an ideal world rather than one that people actively produce.

In several ways, Berger and Luckmann are also indebted to Durkheim (see Chapter 4). First, they share his view on social facts: that general ways of acting throughout society come to confront the individual as something objective or outside of their behaviour. For example, through participating in society, we learn about the etiquette of greeting one another and yet, as we participate, we also affirm these rules for others and ourselves. Second, Berger and Luckmann agree with Durkheim's position on culture as a means to share a history and encode collective sentiments. For example, social institutions such as religion tie people together into an objective social existence by sharing signs, symbols, rituals and experiences. This is not to say that Berger and Luckmann view agents as passive 'dupes' of cultural contexts. Instead, they emphasise the active role that individuals play in maintaining their lifeworlds.

Ethnomethodology

Berger and Luckmann were not the only researchers to develop Schütz's phenomenological sociology. Another perspective emerges – ethnomethodology – which originates in Harold

Garfinkel's (1967) writings. Garfinkel proposes that ethnomethodology is interested in how people create, order and accomplish their everyday lives. Like Schütz, ethnomethodologists see the world as an ongoing practical accomplishment: people use their reasoning and practices to perceive and act upon the worlds they live in. Garfinkel argues that this perspective is distinct from the classical sociology of Émile Durkheim (see Chapter 4). Indeed, he argues that the point of social inquiry is not to *explain* society through social facts but, instead, to interpret how people's activities and accomplishments produce such facts.

For example, consider how an ethnomethodologist might approach Durkheim's study *Suicide*. Instead of explaining the 'causes' of suicide through reference to variations in social integration, an ethnomethodologist might explicate how social scientists collect data and use statistical analyses to construct such causal explanations. Alternatively, an ethnomethodologist might investigate how members of the professional services come to define and understand sudden death cases as suicide – drawing attention to the factuality of such definitions (see ten Have, 2004).

Two core notions within Garfinkel's programme for ethnomethodology are 'accounting' and **reflexivity**. Here is how he describes them:

> Ethnomethodological studies analyse everyday activities as members' methods for making those same activities visibly-rational-and-reportable-for-all-practical-purposes, i.e., 'accountable', as organizations of commonplace everyday activities. The reflexivity of that phenomenon is a singular feature of practical actions, of practical circumstances, of commonsense knowledge of social structures, and of practical sociological reasoning. By permitting us to locate and examine their occurrence, the reflexivity of that phenomenon establishes their study. (Garfinkel, 1967, cited in ten Have, 2004, p. 19)

Garfinkel's point is that ethnomethodology is interested in how people produce reflexively accountable acts. In other words, what are the methods by which people design their actions so that their sense is immediately apparent to others? Consider, for example, how they might position themselves in a queue or ask questions like 'are you next in line?' to express their intentionality. By focusing on people's accounts, ethnomethodologists can illustrate how people describe (or explain or criticise or idealise) certain situations, thereby gaining insight into their practical reasoning. This focus is why ethnomethodologists analyse conversations (see below); they are interested in how people reflexively account for their practices.

Relatedly, Garfinkel prefers to speak of 'members' when conceptualising social behaviour rather than individuals. Ethnomethodologists focus their attention on cohorts of people who populate particular social scenes. They are less interested in a single person's norms, values and intentions, preferring to capture the contextual, intersubjective and practical nature of people's activities. This perspective means that ethnomethodology can abstract away from a given individual's inner thoughts or raw emotions, focusing on people's accounts (ten Have,

2004). To put it another way, ethnomethodologists favour neither structures nor agents when conceptualising social action. They view people as members of organisational and personal structures, neither overly determined nor endlessly reflexive.

This situated nature of social action brings ethnomethodologists to reckon with 'indexical expressions', that is, how a person's utterances depend on the local circumstances in which they emerge and to whom they apply (ten Have, 2004, pp. 20–21). Indexical expressions are phrases like 'you', 'I', 'here' and 'that', which may refer to different things for different people simultaneously. For example, consider the phrase, 'let's meet next weekend!' For one person, this phrase could mean meeting at the weekend that is currently approaching. For another, it could mean meeting at the weekend following the next. For Garfinkel, such 'gaps' in our understanding are common when our utterances are abstract or inexact (e.g., 'next'). Indeed, people often try to bridge these gaps by giving more explicit details, such as confirming the date of when to meet next. Ethnomethodology offers a means to interpret how people problem-solve these tensions in language by describing the situated and instructional basis of human expression.

Finally, this brings us to 'conversation analysis': an essential part of ethnomethodology that originates in the ideas of Harvey Sacks, a contemporary of Garfinkel (see Peräkylä, 2004). Sacks seeks to describe the hidden rules, meanings and structures that make conversations an orderly thing. He proposes conversation analysis as a method to analyse 'talk-in-interaction', which refers to how participants (in a natural conversation) understand and respond to one another when it is their time to talk. Conversation analysts describe how action sequences are generated by forming requests, advice, plans and complaints. Indeed, they seek to unpack the subtle meanings within conversations to show how hard people work to keep a shared sense of reality going. When conversations fail, analysts describe what people do to try to repair this breakdown.

What ethnomethodology offers is a theory and method to investigate the social situations people create and sustain, often through conversations. Ethnomethodologists are interested in describing how social situations come into being, paying particular attention to people's knowledge and meanings to establish social interaction patterns.

Existential Phenomenology

Existential phenomenology describes subjective human experiences by reflecting on people's actions, intentions, emotions, ideals and purposes. It differs from phenomenological sociology as it concerns individual experiences and actions rather than how people create and conform to social situations. Indeed, existential phenomenologists treat people as active and creative subjects whose inner experiences generate the meaning that makes social existence possible (Thorpe and Holt, 2008).

The German philosopher Martin Heidegger, influences this perspective in his book *Being and Time* (1996/1927). Like Husserl, Heidegger wishes philosophy to return to the living subject's life and so asks a fundamental question: 'what is being?' Heidegger's response is to suggest that being *is* time. That is, what it means for a human being to *be* is to exist temporally in the interval between birth and death. Heidegger suggests that if people want to understand what it means to be an authentic human being, they must project their lives onto the horizon of death, thereby contending with the fragility of human existence. From this perspective, Heidegger questions how people are 'thrown' into daily life, suggesting that everyday distractions, such as jobs, are designed to keep them from asking these scary existential questions (see **existentialism**). The phenomenologist is interested in this existential 'angst' and how it shapes lived experience.

Maurice Merleau-Ponty, a French philosopher, also influences existential phenomenology through his book the *Phenomenology of Perception* (2012/1945). Here, Merleau-Ponty challenges the idea (within some Western philosophy) that human thought and action are discrete entities (mind–body **dualism**). In contrast, he argues that the mind and body are indissociable – two aspects of the same human being. This connection becomes particularly apparent when considering the nature of human perception. Merleau-Ponty argues that perception is not merely a representation of a given phenomenon but an embodied and subjective experience. For example, consider what happens when we perceive a painting. We do not merely reproduce a picture within our heads. Instead, we project our tastes, intentions, and values towards this object, perhaps expressing curiosity, wonder, or indifference. This interaction is evidence of what Merleau-Ponty terms 'body subjects': that people perceive and organise phenomena according to *their* embodied and subjective meaning systems.

Importantly, Merleau-Ponty suggests that the body-subject is a form of *practical* consciousness rather than reflective contemplation. Perception is in the 'doing' of the body-subject as something that comes before the 'thinking' or 'knowing' person. Consider, for example, the critical role of touch (and the hand) in human perception. Rarely do people contemplate how the hand grasps a glass of water, holds a partner's hand or points out something of significance. These acts are fundamental to how people give phenomena meaning and express creativity, agency and a sense of control over the world (Tallis, 2003). The phenomenologist, then, is interested in people's practical engagement with the world and how this configures human bodies and experiences in meaningful ways.

Finally, the sociological work of Pierre Bourdieu (2013/1977) is also influential here (see also Chapter 7), particularly his theory of **habitus**. Habitus refers to the socially inscribed habits, skills and dispositions that shape how individuals perceive and act within the social world around them. Influenced by Merleau-Ponty, Bourdieu focuses on the power of culture to shape people's bodies and minds. He argues that similar social backgrounds (such as class, religion or ethnicity) socialise people into sharing bodily practices that reproduce a given social order. From this perspective, a person's tastes, attitudes, mannerisms and habits may limit their social position, life experiences and opportunities. As such, Bourdieu reminds us that even the most inner experiences are environmentally bound as we learn about the world through contextual and bodily engagement.

Case Study 5.1

The Phenomenology of Coffee Tasting

Kenneth Liberman's (2013) extensive ethnography of the practices of professional coffee tasters is an excellent example of phenomenology in action. The study begins with Liberman (2013, p. 215) posing a phenomenological problem: 'if the perfect cup of coffee were something strictly subjective, then purveyors of coffee worldwide would probably not invest as much energy and as many resources … as they do'. Liberman suggests that no one denies that drinking coffee is a subjective experience. Yet, there must be something objective about the 'perfect cup', given the effort that often goes into identifying, locating, purchasing, processing and marketing coffees. What interests Liberman mainly is how purveyors of coffee establish this objective meaning. Indeed, he writes that much of the practical work of the coffee industry seems to focus on taming and stabilising 'the intelligibility of the objective tastes that they market' (Liberman, 2013, p. 215).

To explore this point further, Liberman undertakes a study of coffee tasters in Italy, Brazil, Central America, India and the Pacific Northwest. Coffee companies often rely upon coffee tasters to identify elements within the taste of coffee and search worldwide for new flavours. Liberman argues that coffee tasters rely heavily upon 'taste descriptors' to earn their trade, and he undertakes a conversation analysis of tape recordings with them as part of his inquiry. He points out that because 'the taste of coffee is never quite capable of evading subjective differences in palates, these taste descriptors are interesting social objects' (Liberman, 2013, p. 215). For example, existing tastes differ from person to person, but the same taster's taste can differ from day to day. There are also differences in terms of 'taste domains' (e.g., acidity, sweetness, fruitiness and nuttiness) and the ever-present possibility of new tastes emerging. As such, Liberman argues that the stability of the taste palette becomes problematic within the profession, especially when you add in regional variances in terminology, and that coffee tasters may violate limited taste descriptors when searching for answers.

Interestingly, Liberman also alerts us to the 'semantic lability' of taste descriptors, particularly as coffee tasters begin conducting their business. Consider, for example, what happens when someone tells you that a Caribbean coffee you just bought is well known for its chocolate tones. Liberman argues that you will naturally use that information to interrogate the taste that you find in your cup. 'Even if you don't find chocolate, you will find yourself oriented to tastes that work in that region or flavour' (Liberman, 2013, p. 218). In other words, there is a subjective orientation to taste – we use language to help us discover it, even though the taste is also objectively there. Liberman's point, then, is that by hearing a taste descriptor, you can explore more extensively that region of taste while at the same time necessarily closing off others. As such, language and conceptualisation affect the experience of how coffee tastes and tasters must work with these complications.

To show how, Liberman presents analyses of transcripts of professional tasters participating in what is called a 'cupping': cupping is a method of evaluating different characteristics of a particular coffee as tasters compare and contrast coffee against each other, allowing them to get a better understanding of each coffee. Liberman suggests that most tasters work collaboratively as

(Continued)

their accounts help one another search and locate the relevant region(s) of taste. For example, Liberman (2013, p. 218) presents two tasters talking about what they are tasting though they are still struggling to name it:

A: I had a very distinct retro-nasal cinnamon aroma.

B: I got more of a dry cocoa powder.

A: Yeah, it's kind of in that range.

Some may find this account puzzling: how are cinnamon and cocoa considered closely related flavours? Liberman suggests that the tasters learn from each other about where to search and locate taste. By naming 'cinnamon' and 'cocoa', the tasters give a taste range to reflect and refine further. The two tasters continue with their interrogation:

A: It could be Kenyan.

B: It doesn't have a Kenyan berry to it.

A: It doesn't have the spice.

Here, Liberman suggests that the tasters begin to direct themselves to something real – the 'Kenyan' – which suggests a range of typical flavours. In denying that the coffee does not have the right spice to be Kenyan, the tasters further narrow their search criteria. This investigation continues for some time as the tasters keep refining their descriptors until they reach an agreement.

Liberman argues that reaching an agreement is an accomplishment of intersubjective communication. Professional tasters must not only share in the meaning of descriptors but also use differences between them to open up (or close) the scope of tastes under discussion. At one moment or another, the work of a coffee taster is to both settle and stabilise the sense of the categories of taste they are using and remain authentic to their experience of the coffee. This balancing act is no easy task, and Liberman reveals that coffee tasters often battle over formalising their practice descriptions. 'The coffee has to speak for itself', says one of Liberman's (2013, p. 232) participants, capturing the sense by which the taster's aim is not simply to produce a consistent methodology for assessing coffee but also to *taste* it. As such, coffee tasters have a natural resistance to capitulating too quickly to any particular taste descriptor. Indeed, they seek to describe the coffee as authentically as possible and recognise that formal descriptions can distract or even restrain this process.

Liberman's ethnography shows, then, that the objectivity and subjectivity of social phenomena are deeply intertwined. It is the phenomenologist's task to unpack this process, paying particular attention to how people create knowledge through shared social practices and meanings.

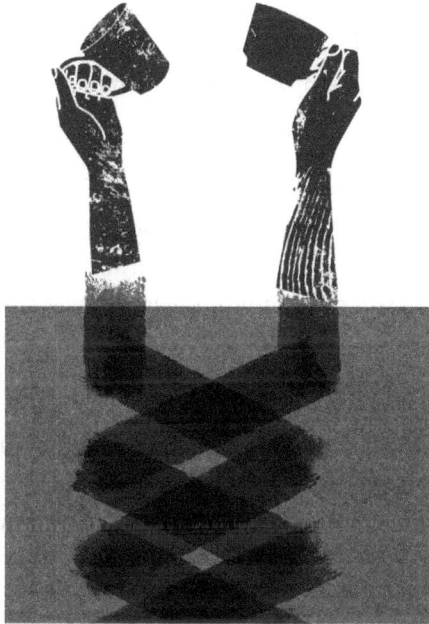

Figure 5.2 Phenomenology of coffee tasting

Reflect on how processes of objectivity and subjectivity come together through the experience of tasting coffee.

Symbolic Interactions

Where phenomenology emphasises the subjective meaning of reality, symbolic interactionism proposes a social theory of the self. It mainly focuses on the micro-interactions between individuals, suggesting that language, symbols and signs mediate the construction of self-image and personhood. Symbolic interactionists examine all forms of human signification (e.g., body posture, gestures, emotional expressions, ways of talking) to reveal the self's dynamic and evolving nature. Importantly, symbolic interaction has its origins in **pragmatism**, particularly the philosophical thoughts of George Herbert Mead (1934) and, later, Herbert Blumer (1969), who enunciates two basic interactionist assumptions:

- That people employ symbols to communicate to one another what they mean
- That the interpretation of these symbols affects how people behave.

These assumptions emphasise that social interaction is a two-way interpretive process. People not only interpret one another's behaviour. *The interpretation itself impacts how people behave.*

As such, symbolic interactionists describe and explain the different effects that these interpretations have on self-image and personhood. Indeed, they study how people become objects of others' interpretations (e.g., through concepts like **stigma**) and how this shapes people's behaviour.

Pragmatism

Symbolic interactionism has its roots in a philosophy known as pragmatism, which claims that a proposition or idea is valid if it works satisfactorily or if there are practical consequences to accepting it. Pragmatists like to reject impractical ideas, suggesting that the effectiveness of an idea is what constitutes 'truth'. Pragmatism derives from the work of Charles Sander Pierce and, later, William James, who sought to understand how people problem-solve by creating practical knowledge through purposive action. James, in particular, contributes to the development of symbolic interaction as he contends with how people use their experiences to impose structures upon their 'stream of consciousness' – that multitude of thoughts that flow through the conscious mind as people think. James argues that people structure their consciousness by a process known as 'select interest'. Select interest enables people to direct their attention towards aspects of experience relevant to achieving a particular course of action (Inglis with Thorpe, 2019, p. 102). This process is vital for human cognition, argues James, because various stimuli and potential courses of action bombard people constantly. As such, select interest is a method by which people construct reality and bring a sense of determinacy to an otherwise busy and unpredictable world (Inglis with Thorpe, 2019, p. 102).

James also provides an account of perception that influences how symbolic interactionists view individual subjectivity. He distinguishes between the 'I' and the 'Me': two aspects of what James refers to as the 'dialogical self'. The 'I' is the individual subject to whom consciousness reveals reality. James argues that, during experiences, the 'I' engages in constant interaction with the 'Me', which names that part of the self we contemplate as an object (Inglis with Thorpe, 2019, p. 103). Consider, for example, how we talk to ourselves when contemplating, reasoning through or evaluating our actions. We use self-talk to consider issues on our minds, perhaps by making internal lists of the things we would like to accomplish. We also use inner speech to reason through any challenges that we encounter or as a means of providing positive (or negative) judgement of our person (e.g., 'I am kind'). For James, these forms of self-communication evidence how we orientate our thoughts to shape our perception of the world and our place within it.

Self and Society

George Herbert Mead develops pragmatism into a social psychological account of human interaction. Mead makes two crucial points:

- that language is central to human interaction by providing a shared system of symbols and signs needed for interpersonal communication
- that social interaction brings the self into realisation.

Mead's central contention is that human self-image is a product of how other people think of us – it is a profoundly social entity. Mead attributes personhood to the social forces that shape people's behaviour, arguing that '[a] person … is a personality because he belongs to a community, because he takes over the institutions of that community into his own conduct' (Mead, 1934, cited in Crotty, 1998, p. 74). In other words, Mead argues that social and cultural practices are the source of personhood. We owe society our very being as conscious and self-conscious entities because our identities arise through social gesturing and symbolic interactions. Going further, Mead writes:

> Only in terms of gestures as significant symbols is the existence of mind or intelligence possible; for only in terms of gestures which are significant symbols can thinking – which is simply an internalised or implicit conversation of the individual with himself by means of such gestures – take place. (Mead, 1934, cited in Crotty, 1998, p. 74)

Mead's point here is that socialisation is the outcome of an interpretive process by which people allocate meanings to themselves through others – 'I am what I think *you* think I am'. This process is especially apparent, Mead argues, when people enter into the 'attitudes of the community'; that is, when people take on others' roles, adopt their standpoints, and see themselves as social objects. Through this process, we learn to construct an image of how the community sees us and adapt our behaviour accordingly. Language is crucial to this, a means to describe not merely the world but also the existence and appearance of people.

By referring to this process, Mead develops James's distinction between the 'I' and 'Me' (Inglis with Thorpe, 2019, p. 104). The 'I' is the reality as we experience it from the inside, the source from which all consciously directed and creative action springs. The 'Me' is the socialised aspect of the person, representing what is learnt and internalised through social interaction (such as other people's attitudes or social roles). Both are enabling and regulating. Mead also identifies the 'generalised other' as that collection of social roles and attitudes that people use to make sense of how to behave in a particular situation. From this perspective, Mead argues that the 'self' is not a fixed or static structure but rather an ongoing interpretation of these aspects of personhood. Indeed, selves develop in social contexts as people learn to take on others' roles and begin to predict the kind of response (or expectations) these actions will generate with a fair degree of accuracy. Without doing so, people would be unable to engage in complex and intricate social processes.

Mead gives the example of role-playing and games in childhood to evidence the generalised other. He argues that children at first imitate their parents and other adults and cannot improvise or form responses based on the adult's role. As they develop, they begin role-playing, developing the language and understanding needed to play the adult and guess what their responses to situations might be. For example, a child might take on a nurse's role, helping support a patient. As they play, they take on the nurse's role of understanding their expectations. These expectations might be showing acts of kindness, care and treating people with politeness and respect. Without this context, it would be hard for a child to create a dialogue that fits the nurse's persona. Mead believed that reaching the stage of forming and understanding a generalised other was evidence of a child's new level of maturity.

Herbert Blumer's (1969) ideas are also vital to developing symbolic interactionism. Blumer develops Mead's psychological model of interaction by focusing on how individuals create a social reality through individual and collective action. Blumer identifies a process he terms 'self-indication' as the basis for autonomous acts and social interaction. Self-indication refers to how people notate events, objects and interactions with other people as they enter their consciousness (Inglis with Thorpe, 2019, p. 108). Blumer suggests that self-indication is pivotal to how people attribute subjective meaning to social objects, including other people or situations, symbolically. He argues that people regulate their behaviour based on the relevant meaning that they assign to objects.

The process of attributing symbolic meaning to objects is twofold. First, objects have situational meanings that people identify; second, people decide which meaningful objects to respond to through internal communication. Blumer notes that people use their interpretations of others to predict the outcome of social actions. People use these predictive insights to make decisions about their behaviour, hoping to reach a practical goal. Blumer refers to this process as a 'social act' and suggests that it is pivotal in social coordination and consensus-building. Indeed, he argues that society consists of social acts between individuals and that these collective activities construct potential paths for meaningful behaviour. From this perspective, Blumer is critical of positivist social science, which attempts to reduce human decision-making to cultural norms or social roles (see Chapter 4). Instead, Blumer argues that symbolic interactionism affords a way to understand the subjective nature of social interaction as people attach symbolic meaning to objects, situations and behaviours.

Erving Goffman

One of the most influential figures within symbolic interactionism is Erving Goffman, whose work advances our understanding of microsociology. In particular, Goffman focuses on the essential elements involved in face-to-face interactions and how they contribute to everyday behaviour. He is mainly known for the **dramaturgical** analysis that he develops in *The Presentation of Self in Everyday Life* (1959), as well as his account of 'total institutions' in *Asylums* (1961) and stigma in *Stigma: Notes on the Management of Spoiled Identity* (1963)

Goffman's work begins by considering how people influence, even manipulate, social interaction to shape the interpretive process. In *The Presentation of Self in Everyday Life*, Goffman suggests that people quickly learn that others interpret our social behaviour and that our capacity to self-reflect allows us to influence these interpretations to suit a vision of ourselves. In particular, Goffman argues that people find ways to elicit the responses they desire from others. He uses the concept of 'impression management' to capture how people take control of others' perceptions of them or events relating to them. Consider, for example, how people might provide explanations to escape disapproval or justify negative actions. Goffman suggests that this is an example of how people seek to satisfy their needs and goals but in a way that is also consistent with how they wish to present themselves to others.

Goffman's notion of impression management builds into his broader dramaturgical analysis of social interaction. Dramaturgy is about offering the theatre as a metaphor for society. Goffman argues that social life is a stage on which people are actors, preparing, writing and delivering their lines. Dramaturgical analysis is a way for sociologists to study these social performances, notably how actors ensure their success or what happens when they fail. Indeed, Goffman writes about how people carefully conduct their social performances, including the stages of planning and preparation needed for the performance to be believable. To this end, consider the different 'masks' that people wear, depending on the social roles that they perform and the audiences with whom they expect to interact. A waiter, for example, acts differently depending on whether they are working the restaurant floor or performing a different role such as parenting. Indeed, the waiter might pick out different clothing or 'costumes' consistent with their identity as a waiter for diners. They also may enlist the support of colleagues to help successfully stage their performance. Goffman differentiates between the front stage and backstage of these social performances, noting that when people need to make adjustments to their performances that they typically do it out of sight of their intended audience. Indeed, waiters might use the kitchen as a backstage, where they can relax until another order is ready and they resume their performance.

'Labelling theory' takes up this conception of social life as a stage. Labelling theorists suggest that people can be victims of the interpretive process, having negative identities imposed on them, such as 'deviant'. One consequence of labelling people as deviant is to increase the likelihood of future deviant behaviour and interventions by other social institutions, such as medicine, law enforcement or religion. Goffman provides an excellent example of labelling in his book, *Asylums*, where he considers the process of psychiatric assessment and incarceration in the United States. He writes:

> The process of examining a person psychiatrically and then altering or reducing his status in consequence is known in hospital and prison parlance as bugging, the assumption being that once you come to the attention of the testers you either will automatically be labeled crazy or the process of testing itself will make you crazy. Thus, psychiatric staff are sometimes seen not as discovering whether you are sick, but as making you sick. (Goffman, 1961, p. 154)

Goffman's account of bugging highlights the power of labels to construct alternative images of people for social control purposes. Indeed, the use of labels by psychiatrists can justify interventions, such as medical tests, which produce psychiatric labels based on the psychiatrists opinion or record of a patient's character or past. Goffman argues that the overwhelming nature of labels can make it difficult for patients to resist them, even coming to embrace them as the foundation for a new self image.

In his account of total institutions, Goffman advances this view, examining how official treatment of deviant behaviour is a conscious effort to alter the deviant's self-image through resocialisation. Goffman argues that establishments like mental hospitals, prisons and concentration camps are spaces that incarcerate deviants for long periods and subject them to practices that strip them of their former self-image. He writes:

> The inmate, then, finds certain roles are lost to him by virtue of the barrier that separates him from the outside world. The process of entrance typically brings other kinds of loss and mortification as well. We very generally find staff employing what are called admission procedures, such as ... disinfecting, haircutting, issuing institutional clothing, instructing as to rules, and assigning to quarters. Admission procedures might better be called 'trimming' or 'programming' because in thus being squared away the new arrival allows himself to be shaped and coded into an object that can be fed into the administrative machinery of the establishment, to be worked on smoothly by routine operations. (Goffman, 1961, p. 16)

Goffman's point here is that the administrative procedures within institutions seek to control deviant behaviour by creating barriers that separate them from the outside world. He argues that inmates undergo a process of 'civil death', losing many of the rights and liberties afforded citizens, such as voting, as well as having previous bases of self-identification ignored and replaced. Through these practices, Goffman concludes that total institutions attempt to assign inmates new self-images that are acceptable to the institution's ethos (and the social and cultural norms of society more widely).

Why is it that certain people become labelled and not others? Goffman (1963) addresses this question in his book *Stigma* where he describes stigma as a consequence of labelling a person with a quality or attribute to discredit them within social interactions. He writes:

> Society establishes the means of categorising persons and the complement of attributes felt to be ordinary and natural for members of each of these categories ... While the stranger is present before us, evidence can arise of his possessing an attribute that makes him different from others in the categories of persons available for him to be ... He is thus reduced in our minds from a whole and usual person to a tainted, discounted one. (Goffman, 1963, pp. 2–3)

Goffman (1963, p. 3) suggests that not only is such a tainted attribute a 'stigma', but also it constitutes a 'special discrepancy between virtual and actual social identity', which allows members of society to reclassify others downward. Goffman identifies three different types of stigmas:

1   The stigma of physical deformities (e.g., amputees, scars, blindness)
2   The stigma of character traits (e.g., records of imprisonment, unemployment, mental illness, radical political behaviour)
3   The stigma of group identity (e.g., race, religion, ethnicity, nationality).

Goffman (1963, p. 5) suggests that what these stigmas have in common is that they refer to 'undesired differentness' attributes that allow 'normals' to attach damaging labels to others. For example, Goffman (1963, p. 131) comments on the stigma of mental illness and how employers attach labels, such as 'work-shy' or 'unemployable', to ex-patients whose anxieties make working evening shifts difficult. He also talks about the stigmatisation of deviants, through labels like 'criminal' or 'prostitute', as a means of social control and the use of religious and ethnic slurs as a justification for genocide and slavery (Goffman, 1963, pp. 46, 73).

Importantly, Goffman recognises the power of these labels to become a 'self-fulfilling prophecy' – that people come to see themselves as the labels forced upon them. Goffman (1963, pp. 8–9) writes:

> The central feature of the stigmatized individual's situation in life can now be stated. It is a question of what is often, if vaguely, called 'acceptance'. Those who have dealings with him fail to accord him the respect and regard which the uncontaminated aspects of his social identity have led them to anticipate extending, and have led him to anticipate receiving; he echoes this denial by finding that some of his own attributes warrant it.

Goffman's point here is that the labelling process obliges stigmatised people to accept their stigmatised position. He notes that there is an expectation that stigmatised peoples try to 'correct' their particular blemishes or to celebrate their 'secondary gains' by identifying the benefits of their condition or circumstance. For example, Goffman (1963, pp. 11–12) reflects on patients who consider their blindness and other physical disabilities as a 'blessing in disguise' that opens up the self to new experiences and identities. Goffman draws attention to these practices, which he calls 'stigma management', to suggest that they hide the impact of the labelling process and, ultimately, protect 'normals' from the fear of a contaminated social identity.

In summary, Goffman provides insight into the essential principles of structuring face-to-face interactions and brings to light the micro-dimensions of interpersonal communication, particularly for social control purposes.

Figure 5.3 Stigma

Consider the effects of stigma. How might negative labels start to fracture or 'discredit' an individual's sense of self?

Focus on Facts

- The sociologist Howard Becker (1963) is exceptionally influential in developing labelling theory through his book *Outsiders: Studies in the Sociology of Deviance*. Becker argues that deviance is not an intrinsic feature of behaviour. Instead, individuals are not inherently deviant until some groups can successfully define them that way, often by projecting rules and definitions onto their behaviour.
- Many develop Goffman's work – of particular note is Arlie Hochschild's (2003/1983) book *The Managed Heart*, which develops the concept of 'emotional labour' to discuss how workers manage their outer expressions in professional settings, inducing or suppressing feelings of love, envy and anger as part of their daily routines. Hochschild notes the estrangement element that comes from working within occupations where one needs to manage one's personal feelings daily.

Case Study 5.2

Stigma Today

We can consider the continuing relevance of Goffman's concept of stigma by examining the issue of racism and migration in recent years. Imogen Tyler's (2020) book *Stigma: The Machinery of Inequality* develops Goffman's concept of stigma by (re)connecting it with notions of power. In particular, Tyler reads Goffman's stigma concept through the lens of Black sociology and activist writings to develop an account of racial stigma that reflects the microaggressions of everyday social interactions and the larger structural and structuring power relations that shape contemporary societies. From this perspective, Tyler argues that stigma is a concept for thinking more deeply about how power etches itself into society by connecting people to social experiences that dehumanise and control.

One example that Tyler provides is the European migrant crisis in 2015. Tyler suggests that during 2015, an unprecedented 1.3 million people applied for asylum in the European Union. Many sought protection in Europe, fleeing wars, conflicts and political oppression in Syria, Iraq, Afghanistan and Eritrea. Tyler notes that some arrived via Balkan land routes, but many of these routes were blocked, forcing the vast majority to cross via the treacherous Mediterranean Sea. An estimated 3,771 people drowned in the Mediterranean in 2015 alone.

Tyler argues that it is within this context that one can begin to identify the use of stigma to justify the inhumane treatment of migrants at this time, as well as the mass breaching of international law and human rights regimes. Tyler pays particular attention to the resurgence of public racism through the right-wing tabloid press, suggesting that newspapers like the *Daily Mail*, and semi-anonymous comment sections like MailOnline, became spaces for stigmatisation practices

(Continued)

and the incitement of racial hatred. In one example, Tyler discusses the public's response to a news story titled: 'Fury as Czech police write numbers on arms of migrants "like concentration camp prisoners"'. Tyler notes that the story drew comments from 4,000 readers across the UK, Ireland, USA, Australia and elsewhere. Tyler suggests that some readers responded with outrage at the suggestion of an analogy between the inking of refugees' hands and concentration camp regimes, insisting that 'it's no different than having your hand stamped as you enter a night club'. Tyler notes that others were offering a more permanent and graphic form of penal stigmatisation:

> They should write the id numbers on the forehead instead!

> You could inject them with an RFID tag, at least you could track them!

> Rubber stamp their foreheads instead!

> They should be made to wear a yellow badge so that members of the public know who they are and know to stay well away from them. (Tyler, 2020, p. 149)

Tyler argues that our task as sociologists is to develop an attentiveness to this type of racist speech and recognise the power of such sentiments to stigmatise and dehumanise. Tyler suggests that the resurgence of public racism on the scale witnessed in Europe during the 2015 migrant crisis did not emerge from nowhere. Instead, Tyler argues that racism is historical: its energy comes from existing grids of associations and discourses within the collective memories of people and places. As such, Tyler argues that word choices and phrases have power. People mobilise them as a deliberate attempt to stigmatise others by invoking (previous) dehumanisation rituals, such as 'inking' as a precursor to ethnic and racial genocide. Tyler concludes by arguing that racism is a system of 'marks' – a stigma that assigns deviancy to exclude those whose identities are deliberately spoilt.

Summary

- Phenomenology plays a crucial role in developing qualitative research because it emphasises the importance of studying how phenomena appear to us and how people direct consciousness intentionally.
- Phenomenological sociology develops this perspective by examining everyday life and the behaviours that order and maintain a sense of social reality.
- A key idea within phenomenology (and phenomenological sociology) is that people achieve social reality through intersubjective communication.
- Ethnomethodology offers a practical way to research everyday life.

- Symbolic interactionism focuses on self-image and identity. It has its origins in pragmatism and the psychology of decision-making.
- Symbolic interactionists are particularly interested in how the community (or group relations) shape self-image, identifying concepts like impression management and stigma to describe the power of social and cultural contexts.

Review Questions

- Schütz describes recipe knowledge as implicit instructions that help people complete their daily activities. What examples can you think of where people script their daily routines? What knowledge do they create? How does it help them complete their daily lives?
- If you were an ethnomethodologist, what aspect of everyday life would you research? What conversations would you begin to analyse?
- Are Goffman's concepts of impression management, total institutions or stigma relevant today? What examples can you think of?

Annotated Reading

Dan Zahavi (2018) provides an accessible introduction to and intellectual history of phenomenology in *Phenomenology: The Basics* (Abingdon: Routledge).

Students interested in a classic ethnomethodological study should turn to D.L. Wieder's (1974) study of a parole house in *Language and Reality* (The Hague: Mouton).

Ken Liberman (2004) has also done extensive ethnomethodological work on Tibetan monks in *Dialectical Practice in Tibetan Philosophical Culture: An Ethnomethodological Inquiry into Formal Reasoning* (Lanham, MD: Rowman and Littlefield Publishers).

Howard Becker's (1963) classic study of cannabis users in *Outsiders* (New York: Free Press) provides a thorough exploration of social deviance and labelling theory.

For a detailed historical account of symbolic interactionism, see Paul Rock's (1979) *The Making of Symbolic Interactionism* (London: Palgrave Macmillan).

6

Language, Discourse and Postmodernity

Chapter Objectives

This chapter will:

- Introduce the role that language plays in social theory, mainly through Ferdinand de Saussure, Michel Foucault, Jean-François Lyotard and Jean Baudrillard.
- Describe key concepts, including structuralism, poststructuralism, discourse and postmodernity.
- Show the relevance of language and discourse through reference to contemporary arguments and case studies.

Keywords

Structuralism, semiotics, poststructuralism, discourse, power, deconstruction, surveillance, hyperreality, postmodernity

Introduction

A fundamental development in social theory comes in the form of questioning the very notion of 'truth', particularly as it relates to the possibility of creating a social 'science' of society. This chapter reflects on the works of a broad range of thinkers, from Ferdinand de Saussure and Louis Althusser to Jacques Derrida, Michel Foucault and others, to consider the implications that language and **discourse** have on our understanding of society, power and truth. The chapter will draw on examples from gender and sexuality studies and cultural studies to consider the importance of discourse in social theory and how its deconstruction can reveal the power relations in language and discourse. It will also reflect on the relationship between language and postmodernism, which, as the name suggests, represents the end of modernity. This chapter will argue that postmodernism represents a marked shift in social theory towards **pluralism** and the recognition that there are no stable definitions within language and, by extension, truths about social life.

Language and Structure

In the history of social theory, a fundamental shift has occurred concerning the central importance of language in understanding social life. In the social sciences, this is known as the 'linguistic turn', which refers to the idea that communication and meaning are conditional on the structures of language in which we think. From this perspective, no communicable thought is possible independent of language. Indeed, early advocates argue that it is misleading to assume the existence of some kind of world 'beyond' the language through which we gain access (Sturrock, 2008).

Within this context, a philosophy and method known as structuralism emerges, which has its origins in the works of the Swiss linguist Ferdinand de Saussure. Saussure is particularly interested in language structures and the consequences that these have for communication. Like Durkheim's functionalism (see Chapter 4), Saussure sees structuralism as a means of unearthing the underlying causes hidden deep within language, generating the laws that govern linguistic systems. Indeed, Saussure argues that it is the structure of language, rather than individual sayings or words, that is most significant. As such, Saussure makes an essential distinction between two aspects of language: *langue* and *parole*. *Langue* is the formal language system that governs the lexicon of acceptable words, rules concerning grammar, phonetics, morphology, etc. *Parole* is actual speech and concerns how speakers use language to express themselves. Thus, for example, when a speaker makes an utterance, such as writing down or saying the word 'hello' (*parole*), it is only understandable to another person because they use the same linguistic system and obey its rules concerning word use. On the other hand, if the speaker pronounces something random, like 'xcsgsd', this construct would exist outside the 'totality' of the *langue*, rendering it meaningless. Thus, Saussure argues that while people might use language in subjective ways, the structure of words, rather than their content (or meaning), is what is of interest to the linguist. Indeed, he argues that it is the existence of *langue* that makes *parole* possible.

Saussure continues his examination by suggesting that *langue* is a system in which relations of difference constitute the meanings we attribute to experiences through words and phrases. He uses the image of a chess game to clarify his point (Lechte, 2007, p. 179). Saussure argues that what constitutes the game's viability is the differential relationship between the pieces as constituted by the rules or structure of the game. Thus, it is not the intrinsic value of the materials that determines whether a chess piece is a 'king'. Instead, what makes a 'king' in chess is its relationship to the other pieces on the board at a given moment. Saussure argues that language operates similarly. For example, we recognise the word 'happy' not because of some intrinsic property of the word but because of its relationship to other words, such as 'unhappy' and 'sad'. As such, Saussure highlights the need to understand the rules by which language begins to structure meaning.

To elaborate on this point, a key idea within Saussure's *Course in General Linguistics* (2011/1916) is that a system of signs makes up language and that each sign is composed of two parts: a 'signifier' and 'signified'. The signifier refers to the sound-image or expression of an underlying concept or meaning. The signified is that concept or meaning that a sign denotes. Saussure uses this analysis to make a vital point: that the relationship that a word has to a real object or thing does not determine the meaning of that word. Instead, Saussure argues that it is the internal relationships between signifiers and signifieds that concern meaning. This point is essential. Saussure suggests that language is relatively autonomous from reality because our configurations of words only combine to refer to ideas rather than reality itself. So, when we use written or spoken language to describe something, like a 'tree', we are not referring to a real tree but, instead, the idea of a tree that our *langue* recognises.

The significance of this point becomes even more apparent if we consider that many of us typically use language (or 'discourse' as later authors call it) *as if* we are talking about something real. Saussure argues that language only ever refers to signifieds (or ideas), not reality itself. As such, structuralists stress that language users are often unaware of how deeply *langue* shapes their thinking and behaviour, even to the extent that they become captives of their discourse, treating it as a natural part of social life.

This is not to suggest that all language systems are the same. On the contrary, Saussure recognises the arbitrary nature of signs and that discourses are free to construct ideas about the world differently. Indeed, not all phrases or words convey the same meaning about objects or actions. Equally, many linguistic expressions for social activities do not necessarily translate across cultures. As such, we can say that language is not fixed in a reality of objects but nevertheless can structure behaviour through relations of words and ideas.

Semiotics

Saussure's interest in language structure plays a vital role in the development of 'semiotics': a field that studies signs and their processes beyond language to include other symbolic systems, such as facial expressions, body language, literary texts and other audible and visual information. Roland Barthes is seen as a founder of semiotics, extending Saussure's ideas by suggesting that social life is full of 'codes' (Hawkes, 1977). Barthes argues that we 'encode' our experiences of the world through signs and symbols so that we may experience it. From this perspective, Barthes suggests that we invent the world we inhabit, using signs and symbols to modify and reconstruct its presentation. Indeed, he argues that we cannot claim access to an 'uncoded', 'pure' or 'objective' experience of a real, permanently existing world. Instead, we all participate in a collaborative yet covert enterprise of coding social behaviour through representations or signs. Following Saussure, Barthes argues that semiotics can decode the significance of signs to reveal how they generate meaning.

One key issue for Barthes is that the codes we use are often presumed to be innocent or neutral when, in fact, semiotic analysis reveals the complex ways in which language imposes its meaning, shaping patterns of what we think of as an objective world 'out there' (Hawkes, 1977, p. 110). In his book, *Mythologies* (1991/1957), Barthes attempts to 'demystify' these codes by revealing how the French ruling class uses mass media to covertly manipulate language and images for their purposes. Drawing on Marx, Barthes argues that it is necessary to 'demystify' the 'myths' that French media create through images and messages within advertising, entertainment, consumer goods and popular culture.

In one critical analysis, Barthes decodes French toys, suggesting that they are a microcosm of adulthood and prefigure ruling-class relations in childhood development. Barthes argues that 'French toys *always mean something*, and this something is always entirely socialised, constituted by the myths or techniques of modern adult life' (1991/1957, p. 53). In other words, Barthes argues that French toys prepare children to accept the roles of conventional French society. For example, he suggests that toy dolls, which wet their nappies and require regular feeding, prepare 'the little girl for the causality of housekeeping, to 'condition' her to her future role as mother' (1991/1957, p. 53). He also questions the myth that children who play with toys exercise some fundamental creativity, arguing that 'French toys rely on imitation; they produce children who are users, not creators' (1991/1957, p. 54). From this perspective, Barthes attempts to subtly reveal how toys (but other examples too, such as cooking, fashion, and television shows) generate, confirm and reinforce a particular view in which bourgeois values emerge as the inevitable and 'right' way of organising social life. More pointedly, Barthes sees French media as carrying messages and intentions that confer capitalism's power by creating docile consumers.

Barthes' argument points to how semiotic analysis has a political dimension, exposing forms of power contained within and reproduced by codes. Semiotics helps expose the hidden meanings at 'depth' behind everyday messages, which supposedly communicate common-sense views. Indeed, Barthes shows that such views may be the products of ruling-class ideologies, which seek to express and promote 'myths' concerning capitalism as the best form of social organisation.

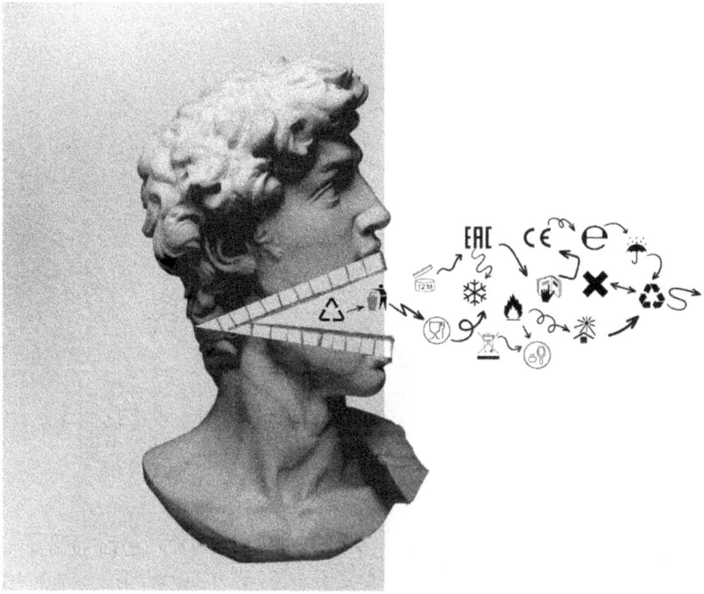

Figure 6.1 Signs and semiotics

Consider how human language is not only profoundly encoded but can obscure expression and meaning through various signs, symbols and myths.

Structural Marxism

Barthes' position is similar to that of another crucial French structuralist, the Marxist philosopher Louis Althusser (2001/1971). Althusser was vital in refocusing the Marxian account of how ruling-class ideology exercises social control over the masses. Althusser reconceptualises Marxist ideology (see Chapter 2), rejecting the idea that it is 'false consciousness' and suggesting that it is a 'system of representations' that subjects individuals to particular conditions (Boucher, 2012, p. 147). Moreover, Althusser argues that the ruling class does not achieve power over society through physical force alone (which he terms 'repressive state apparatus'). Instead, ruling-class ideas become habituated perceptions through the socialising of the ego (or mind). Althusser speaks at length about how particular social institutions (or what he calls 'ideological state apparatuses') generate social subjects by fitting them into functional roles, such as the family, the education system or religion. Importantly, Althusser argues that much of an individual's learnt perception of the world is unconscious as the ego conforms to social norms.

A key concept within Althusser's thinking is **interpellation**, which refers to how language (and social practices, more broadly) socialise individuals into the ideologies that institutions propagate. Althusser suggests that language plays a vital role in constituting individuals as 'subjects' of the capitalist state, such that they readily identify with the social practices necessary for its functioning.

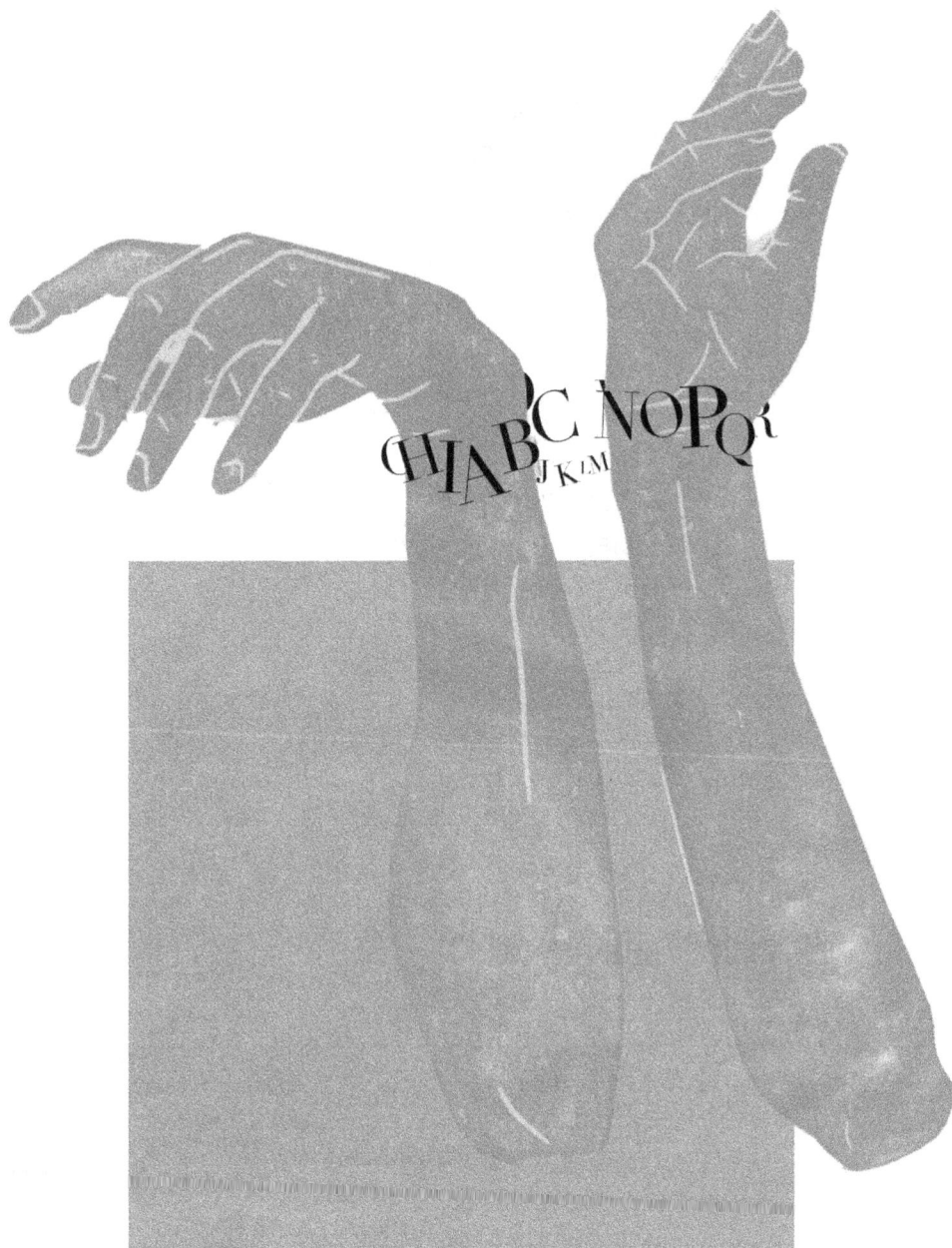

Figure 6.2 Interpellation

We often perceive language as a form of self-expression and (potentially) freedom. But is it? Consider how language, when rooted in capitalist ideology, acts as a set of chains, suppressing and controlling the things we do.

Indeed, he argues that language provides the means by which individuals have a sense of themselves as created by the system and reconfirmed by their ongoing exposure to it. In one example, Althusser likens this process to the hailing of a person by the police ('hey, you!'): as the person spins around and 'recognises' themselves as hailed, they at once become an individual citizen but also subject themselves to the discipline of the state (Boucher, 2012, p. 149). From this perspective, the objective features of social structures, such as the competitive logic of capitalism, become part of the very language that people use to think about themselves and the world around them.

Focus on Facts

Taking a different perspective on language, the critical theorist Jürgen Habermas argues that language can be a means to reveal covert forms of power and provide the theoretical foundations for furthering social enlightenment and democracy. In the first volume of *The Theory of Communicative Action*, Habermas (1984/1981) argues that language provides the resources to construct emancipatory communicative acts – a kind of 'ideal speech' – through which societies establish progressive norms and values. Habermas establishes this argument in defence of modernity, suggesting that the possibility of achieving progress through reason remains a relevant project for our times. This argument puts Habermas at odds with postmodern theorising (see below) and the Frankfurt School (Chapter 2).

Poststructuralism

In response to these arguments, an alternative perspective on language emerges in France in the 1960s known as 'poststructuralism' ('post' means 'after'). Poststructuralism describes a set of ideas by theorists who question structuralism for its preoccupation with studying the structure and patterns of language. Poststructuralists reject the idea that there can be an objective or scientific account of language, arguing that language holds no single or unified meaning. Instead, poststructuralists point to the instability and plurality of meaning (particularly in written texts) as evidence of the multiple, unruly nature of discourse and its ongoing capacity to shape different subjectivities. From this view, poststructuralism shares an affinity with the arguments of Friedrich Nietzsche (see Chapter 3) as it questions the capacity of metanarratives (or grand theories, such as Marxism or functionalism) to offer truths about social life.

Derrida

One way into poststructuralism is through the work of Jacques Derrida and his concept of *sous rature*, a term which translates as 'under erasure'. Sarup (1993, p. 33) argues that to put a term *sous rature* is to write out a word, cross it out, and then print both word and deletion.

The idea is to signify that words may be inadequate yet necessary. A particular signifier is not entirely suitable for the concept that it represents. Yet, it is the only word that is legible. So, for example, we might put the word ~~love~~ under erasure because we feel that the word does not adequately represent our feelings, yet it is the only word we know.

Derrida's concept of *sous rature* comes from his view of language, which contrasts with that of Saussure. Saussure sees language as a unifying system with an internal logic of relations that create meaningful wholes (or signs). Derrida does not view language in this way. He suggests that there is no fixed correspondence between signifier and signified, such that words and thoughts never come together to form a singular meaning. Instead, Derrida talks of language as chains of **signification** within which signifiers and signs continually break apart and reattach in new combinations to momentarily reveal (some sense of) meaning. From this perspective, language or a single word is not rooted in anything real or that guarantees truth. Instead, signs only ever point to more signs, which point to more signs and so on. Put simply, Derrida recognises that language is polysemic – that words can have multiple meanings or interpretations. This argument implies that we must study language under erasure precisely because there is always the possibility that another sign (or word) may appear to produce different meanings and interpretations (Sarup, 1993, pp. 33–34).

This argument led Derrida to develop a procedure called **deconstruction**. Deconstruction is a method of reading a written text very closely, such that the author's conceptual distinctions, on which the text relies, are shown to be faulty on account of the inconsistent or paradoxical use of the very concepts within the text as a whole (Sarup, 1993, p. 50). This method shares some affinity with Nietzsche's attempt to show the inadequacies and irrationalities within Christian teachings (see Chapter 3). Indeed, deconstruction shows how texts fail according to their own criteria: that the standards or definitions that texts set up are unreliable or contradictory, thus unsettling their original distinctions (Sarup, 1993, p. 52). From this perspective, Derrida argues that deconstruction reveals the arbitrary nature of signs within writing. Writing does not represent a singular or authorial truth. Indeed, deconstruction reveals the multiple meanings and shifting interpretations that texts convey. For example, consider religious scripture within the Bible. There are many different ways to derive meaning from these texts, such as whether to take the teachings within them literally, allegorically or metaphorically.

Finally, Derrida applies this thinking to **social ontology**. He argues that social ontology depends on a foundation or first principle (see also Chapter 1) that is often defined by what it excludes. For example, within social theory, there are many binary oppositions, such as mind–body, subject–object, nature–culture and reason–emotion, which operate as a form of ideology, privileging one perspective over the other. Derrida suggests that we should try to deconstruct these oppositions and challenge the orthodoxy of this dualistic thinking. Indeed, he sees deconstruction as a means to dislodge these dichotomies and reveal their interdependent and related nature. This perspective is particularly influential on new materialist thinkers (see Chapter 10).

Focus on Facts

Derrida draws on the main characteristics of Nietzsche's **scepticism** (see Chapter 3), such as a mistrust of ontology and a suspicion of 'truth' and 'meaning'. Like Nietzsche, Derrida believes that there is no single reality beyond our interpretations. Therefore, our use of language is rooted only in different perspectives, not a single experience of the world.

Lacan

Derrida's account of signification – boundless, shifting and unpredictable – shares an affinity with the poststructuralist thinking of Jacques Lacan. Lacan was a psychoanalyst who developed Freud's ideas (see Chapter 3) to explore the social and linguistic construction of the self and how the individual relates to society. Lacan's theory begins from the premise that individuals become social by appropriating language into the human psyche. It is language that constitutes us as a subject of society, argues Lacan, as it is through language that society comes to inhabit each individual. Lacan views language as the precondition for self-awareness and the vehicle through which individuals recognise social norms and develop a knowledge of the world. Indeed, Lacan argues that language structures our conscious and unconscious minds, shaping how we represent ourselves to the world.

A key idea within Lacan is that multiple discourses shape our unconscious mind, of which our self-identity is only ever a representation. Like Derrida, Lacan insists that meaning emerges along a chain of signification that is constantly fluctuating, unsettled and transient. Lacan uses this view to highlight the transitory nature of identity, arguing that the human psyche is often the site of contending discourses, many of which have multiple meanings and contradictory dispositions. Indeed, Lacan challenges the cultural claim that the self is a rational and coherent project, suggesting that any attempt to define or describe the subject (with any completeness) is impossible. What emerges is Lacan's critique of the idea of intersubjectivity (see also Chapter 5), within which he queries our capacity for full mutual recognition, arguing that the ambiguity of signifiers highlights how difficult it is to get inside the minds of others (Sarup, 1993, pp. 8–13). From this perspective, the modern subject is not unified; instead, there is something lacking in self-identity – our capacity to be fully understood by another. Lacan uses this position to argue that the subject seeks out recognition in an attempt to achieve a secure and coherent identity, but one which will never be found or achieved.

Foucault

Michel Foucault emerged among these developments to establish a very influential body of ideas, making him a significant source of poststructuralist and postmodern thought. Generally speaking, Foucault's work draws upon an anti-Enlightenment tradition that rejects any equivalency between reason, emancipation and progress, arguing that modern forms of knowledge create discourses of power and domination (Best and Kellner, 1991). Through a series of historical and philosophical studies, Foucault problematises modern forms of knowledge as they are built into various social institutions such as the prison, medicine, psychiatry and the human sciences. Foucault argues that systems of social organisation may appear natural but are, in fact, contingent sociohistorical constructs of power and domination (Best and Kellner, 1991). Foucault exposes this power by paying critical attention to the discursive practices (see discourse) that establish knowledge and construct particular meanings about reality and the self. From this perspective, Foucault's work draws on a range of theoretical influences, notably Nietzsche's account of the will to power and Weber's understanding of power and domination (see Chapter 3).

Foucault's (2002/1969) earliest work is associated with structuralist thinking. However, he adopts a distinct methodology known as an 'archaeology of knowledge'; a historical method whereby discursive practices are 'excavated' much like artefacts from the past. Foucault argues that this method is a means of examining the evolution of modern Western societies through successful layers of knowledge or 'epistemes'. An episteme is a knowledge framework, such as science or religion, that shapes discourse. Foucault uses the term 'episteme' in a manner that resembles Saussure's concept of *langue*; it is a structure or a set of rules that determines the conditions of possibility for all that can be said and understood. However, Foucault argues that epistemes are not universal but relate to a particular period of history. They also can account for what is 'not there' – in other words, 'repressed' or impossible to think. As such, Foucault considers the episteme a means of establishing the boundaries of what is 'true' or 'false' at a given moment and the practices or procedures for arriving at these decisions. The implication is that Foucault questions the idea that the historical record is an example of 'truth' or 'progress'. Instead, he seeks to uncover the development of epistemes and the discursive practices they set into motion.

One example of how an episteme organises thought is medicine. As Danaher et al. (2000, p. 17) argue, most people accept, without thinking, that medicine is useful, valuable and good for us. Why? For Foucault, it is because all kinds of institutions, such as hospitals, medical colleges, schools and the media, tell us that this is so. These institutions also tell us what is 'real' medicine (e.g., antibiotics), compared with what is not (e.g., homoeopathy). Foucault argues that this 'order of things' is based on the relation between the idea of scientific principles, methods and reason on the one hand and a body of discursive practices undertaken by doctors and nurses on the other. Thus, things (people, ideas, materials, approaches) are classed as either medicine – valuable and scientific – or folk remedies, which are not to be taken seriously (Danaher et al., 2000, p. 17). Consider, for example, the controversy that would occur if government medical advisors began recommending spiritual healing for severe medical conditions instead of the 'standard' medical practices. It is as if the episteme speaks for itself, establishing what is acceptable or not based on a series of discursive formations that legitimate or exclude particular ideas, practices and objects of knowledge.

Significantly, Foucault goes to great lengths to draw attention to the experts behind these discourses. In *Madness and Civilization*, Foucault (2001/1961) explores how disciplines, such as psychology, psychoanalysis and psychiatry, exercise power over people's minds by creating discourses that define mental health. In particular, Foucault reflects on the designation of 'madness', suggesting that these disciplines (and the institutions and practitioners associated with them) produce the 'object of madness' through their discursive practices. Such practices include becoming familiar with the episteme through access to the right texts (books, articles, policy documents) or participating in the appropriate institutional practices (a relevant degree) that test their 'fit' with that particular discipline. Other examples also include offering up 'expert testimony' to evaluate or judge someone's behaviour, such as in the context of a court of law or being able to identify or accept as legitimate the arguments of various disciplinary authors, such as Freud (Danaher et al., 2000, p. 22). Finally, Foucault argues that the combination of these practices constitutes an authority that produces the so-called 'truth of madness', which edits out or censures anything that does not fit within its discursive formation (Danaher et al., 2000, p. 23).

Foucault's excavation of knowledge offers us a way of conceptualising power that is different from previous examples in history and social thought. For Foucault, power is not something held solely by individuals or groups, such as how a medieval jailer exercises physical control over the bodies of his prisoners in a dungeon. Instead, Foucault sees power as a complex flow of relations between different groups and areas of society. Like the discipline of psychiatry, the discourses of scientific authorities evidence this flow of power as they establish an episteme that effectively exercises control over the minds of those they examine. Foucault sees this as a far more productive power than that of the jailer, especially as these scientific discourses create new locations or sites through which to exercise new forms of social control. So, for example, new medical clinics, mental asylums or new types of prisons emerge as sites where disciplinary authorities can exercise their expertise to institutionalise 'unhealthy' behaviour.

Perhaps the best example of this new form of power comes from Foucault's (2020/1975) book *Discipline and Punish: The Birth of the Prison*. Here, Foucault considers the power of prison surveillance as a distinctive feature of modern disciplinary control. In particular, Foucault refers to the building of modern prisons to normalise judgements over the prison population. Foucault's argument begins by referring to Jeremy Bentham's model of the panopticon, in which a prison locates a surveillance tower in a central position between the cells. From this tower, the guards can watch every cell and the prisoners inside them. A characteristic design feature of this tower is that the prisoners cannot see if the guards are there (perhaps due to tinted windows or an elevated viewing position). Foucault argues that the power of the panopticon resides in this imbalance of perceptibility between groups. Prisoners have to assume that they are under constant observation and, therefore, must adjust their behaviour according to the normalising judgements of the institution and its associated discourses. For example, prisoners must self-regulate concerning rules about inmate contact, the use of banned substances or the damaging of private or personal property. Foucault argues that this 'normalising gaze' of the panopticon soon spreads out from prisons to hospitals, schools and the military, each with expert discourses and procedures for producing distinct subjects.

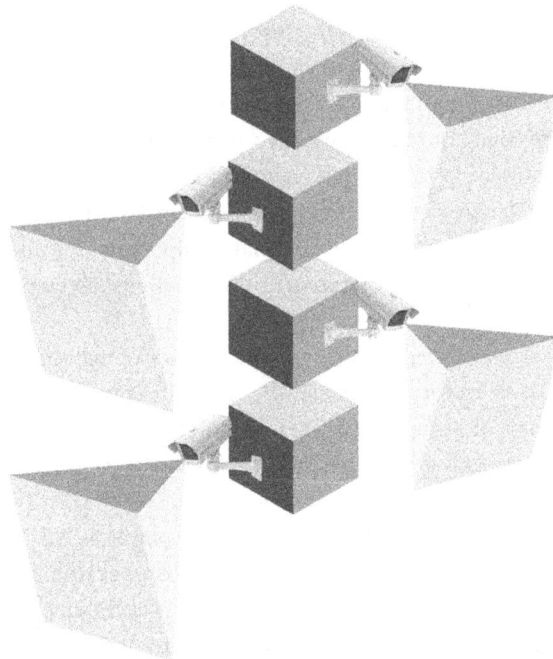

Figure 6.3 Surveillance

What does the panopticon look like today? What are the modern forms of surveillance, and how do they monitor and modify social behaviour?

Later in his work, Foucault shifts towards poststructuralism, with Nietzsche's concept of **genealogy** guiding his ideas. Unlike archaeology, which concentrates on marking out how discourse orders and excludes through the construction of particular discursive formations, genealogy conveys the dependence of knowledge on power relations. For example, Nietzsche uses the term 'genealogy' to investigate the historical origins of social institutions, such as religion, whose discourses concerning faith, morality and forgiveness claim to be universal and eternal. Nietzsche reveals the power behind these ethical and moral claims to take hold over people's experiences but also the fact that they are social constructs specific to particular historical and cultural contexts. Foucault similarly uses the method of genealogy, drawing attention to ideas within history only to examine their beginnings as social constructions, made up of many different sources with multiple understandings. Like Derrida's account of signification, Foucault shows history as heterogeneous and contingent, full of incoherent layers of knowledge and practices, some of which often emerge by accident or randomly. The historical archive, then, cannot guarantee what we think of as truth or reality. Instead, Foucault reveals history to be full of ideas and discourses, which we accept as natural but which the genealogical method can deconstruct.

In *The History of Sexuality* (Vol. 1), Foucault (2020/1976) demonstrates this method by applying it to the 'sciences of sexuality' – various bodies of knowledge about sexuality, which Foucault reveals to have intimate associations with power. Foucault's discussion focuses on what he calls the 'repressive hypothesis', the idea that the primary attitude of modern society towards sex is negative. For example, the 'Victorian Age' is often thought of as a period of history with puritanical views on sex, opposing and silencing sexuality, except in the closely restricted boundaries of marriage. Foucault challenges this idea by suggesting that, at this time, various institutions and disciplines were also producing vast amounts of knowledge about sex as part of an exhaustive search for the 'truth' about human sexuality. Foucault speaks of the creation of new social categories, such as the 'homosexual', 'the frigid woman', 'the nymphomaniac' or the 'hysteric', as examples of the power of scientific disciplines to create subjects with symptoms that require treatment and monitoring (Danaher et al., 2000, p. 25). Indeed, Foucault argues that, through these interventions, science not only comes to define the possibilities of one's sexual nature but also the practices of self-knowledge. In other words, to make sense of our sexuality, Foucault argues that we begin to examine ourselves through the discursive frameworks that science demarcates. Thus, our sexual nature is not self-chosen but constructed by authorities within the sexual sciences.

An important concept to emerge from Foucault's thinking here is **biopower**, which refers to how modern nation-states regulate and control subjects through various techniques and technologies of the body. The term links biological processes with examples of economic and political power which attempt the task of 'administering life'. In other words, biopower is about those technologies which try to manage humans, often through discourses like public health or practices like risk assessments. Foucault argues that biopower operates on two levels. The first is through an 'anatomo-politics of the human body'; the second is through the 'biopolitics of population'. The first concerns how medical norms become encoded into social practices, so subjects gradually accept regulations, permissions and expectations into their lives. The second concerns the focus of the modern nation-state on protecting, supervising and improving its population. So, for example, consider how discourses concerning health and well-being nudge people into regimes of exercise, calorie-counting or special diets. Foucault's point is that such activities reflect the biopolitics of the nation-state, which must produce a healthy and productive workforce. Indeed, Foucault suggests that biopower plays an essential role in developing modern capitalist economies.

What Foucault offers social theory, then, is a new way of looking at history and ideas. Where we might think of history (or modernity) as a particular tradition or one set of ideas, values and principles, Foucault brings this into question by showing that people make sense of their world through context-specific discourses. There is no such thing as 'essential' knowledge. Instead, we each exist within an episteme that acts as 'truth'. From this perspective, Foucault deconstructs the role that power plays in bringing particular 'truths' to light, such as how science frames the subject and the relationship this has to the biopolitics of the nation-state.

Focus on Facts

Foucault uses the term **governmentality** to convey the idea that the discursive power of the modern state spreads through various political, economic and technical institutions. These institutions increasingly manage people's conduct by organising their practices through various mentalities, rationalities and techniques. Thus, the purpose of governmentality is to subject people to ever more efficient modes of social control. Miller and Rose (2008) give an example of governmentality when discussing the 'psy disciplines'; professions linked with psychology, such as GPs, therapists and health visitors. They argue that these disciplines encourage patients to self-govern through a range of practices and strategies by which individuals represent to themselves what the state considers 'healthy' behaviour. As such, the concept grasps the dramatic expansion in the scope of government into private life.

Case Study 6.1

Sexuality and Promiscuity

Perhaps one of the most important ideas to emerge from Foucault's thinking about sexuality is his 'history of the subject'; the suggestion that we are not only objects of disciplinary control (through expert knowledge) but also control ourselves through self-scrutinising and self-forming behaviour. For Foucault, we become *subjects* of our own knowledge as we internalise norms and monitor our behaviour in keeping with them. This perspective informs not only Foucault's understanding of sexuality but also his view on sexual liberation. Foucault recognises that sexuality is integral to our identity or selves as subjects. For example, he argues that we discover our sexual nature by scrutinising our sexual fixations and anxieties, thereby overcoming them. Yet, he also queries whether this process is genuinely freeing or simply an opportunity to reshape our lives according to a new set of rules and customs. Indeed, Foucault recognises that the very idea of a 'liberated sexuality' is a discursive formation that comes with new norms and practices that demand acceptance and internalisation. So, for example, consider the anxieties and insecurities that magazines and other erotic media create around sexual performance through disciplinary techniques such as 'sex tips'. Foucault, then, sees the irony of becoming too focused on sexual liberation, such that we might assume a new identity just to end up governed by a different set of knowledge and power relations.

Christian Klesse's (2007) book *The Spectre of Promiscuity* draws attention to Foucault's concerns by examining the relationship styles and attitudes towards monogamy and promiscuity among bisexual men and women. In particular, Klesse investigates these relationships through the concept of power to show how discursive formations shape bisexual practices. For example, Klesse argues that part of the framing of bisexuality is the belief that bisexuals *must* have sexual relationships with both men and women. This discourse, Klesse suggests, necessitates the idea that bisexuals must also be non-monogamous and promiscuous. Indeed, Klesse points to an element of biphobia in those who draw this equivalency, suggesting that an anti-promiscuity discourse guides the assumption that bisexuals cannot have committed, monogamous relationships. From this perspective, Klesse (2007, p. 78) shows that specific ideas around promiscuity and non-monogamy come to control (or 'hegemonise') bisexuality, writing:

> Non-monogamy is a troubling issue for many bisexuals because dominant discourse constructs bisexuals as non-monogamous *by necessity* … Monogamy with a partner of either sex tends to destabilise (certain) bisexual identity narratives.

Klesse extends this discussion into areas such as marriage, noting that the issue of who is the 'primary partner' often triggers particular interpersonal dynamics in non-monogamous relationship networks. Klesse suggests that the decision to marry is often the subject of intense negotiation and conflict, partly because the act of marriage reinforces hierarchies about who is the primary or secondary partner. From this perspective, Klesse (2007, pp. 94–95) reflects on some of the limitations of same-sex marriage rights, suggesting that, for bisexuals in non-monogamous contexts, such rights inevitably feed into heteronormative discourses, such as valorising the idea of monogamy itself.

Another relevant example is Klesse's account of the discursive formations around polyamory. Klesse (2007, p. 97) argues that many interviewees use the term 'polyamory' as a positive alternative to 'non-monogamy', suggesting that it emphasises love over sex. In particular, Klesse notes how love becomes a central feature of the discourse around polyamory and that some use this framing to rescript their sexual identities and relationship orientations. Indeed, Klesse (2007, pp. 106–107) provides an account of the ethical dimension of polyamory, suggesting that people attempt to secure an understanding of 'responsible non-monogamy' by mobilising concepts such as honesty and consensus. Ironically, these framings, Klesse argues, also become a way for polyamorous communities to 'other' some forms of relationships and sexual practices, such as 'wife swapping', 'swinging' (and other forms of 'casual sex'). Klesse (2007, p. 112) writes:

> these modes of representation correlate with processes of 'othering' that primarily work through the discursive distinction between 'good homosexuals' and 'dangerous queers' … established in polyamory discourses are 'the good polyamorist'/'the bad swinger' or the 'responsible non-monogamist'/'the promiscuous queer'.

(Continued)

From this perspective, Klesse suggests that while polyamory offers new ways to understand love and relationships, it also deploys discourses that ostracise the non-conforming. This argument resonates with Foucault's claim that sexuality always operates through disciplinary techniques, despite efforts to break with previous epistemes and frameworks of knowledge and power.

Postmodern theory

Instead of the certainty of progress, whether associated with the Enlightenment project (see Chapter 1) or the arguments of early sociological theorists, there is now an awareness that social life is far too ambiguous to search for single truths or fixed meanings of things. This scepticism towards truth (and the authorities who present knowledge claims as true) characterises postmodern social theory. Postmodern social thought attempts to transgress and reject established parameters and boundaries of knowledge, suggesting that any claim to 'know' something comprehensively and objectively is fiction. Instead, things and their meanings are shown to be chaotic and often refuse the simplistic definitions that science attributes to them. Indeed, it is crucial to understand that postmodern social theory rejects the goals of the social sciences, which seek to identify properties or patterns that enable analytical distinctions between people or social structures. Postmodern thought is suspicious of these procedures for the binary oppositions they create (see **dualism**), suggesting that reality is plural and open to many diverse, heterogeneous perspectives. Indeed, they suggest that any attempt to impose order or categorise social life will likely reflect the political motivations of dominant social groups, similar to Foucault's critique of the disciplinary power of science. From this perspective, postmodern theorists often set out to destabilise existing understandings of the world by questioning the assumptions and authority of particular knowledge claims.

One of the leading figures in this regard was Jean-François Lyotard (1984/1979), whose book *The Postmodern Condition* is a powerful expression of postmodern theorising. In the book, Lyotard draws on the ideas of Friedrich Nietzsche (see Chapter 3) and Ludwig Wittgenstein to argue that no one perspective or method of generating knowledge has a monopoly on truth, despite claims to the contrary. Instead, Lyotard argues that truths are plural and relative to particular contexts. Thus, what counts as 'true' in one place or time might count as 'false' in another. From this perspective, Lyotard defines the postmodern as an 'incredulity towards metanarratives', where metanarratives are totalising stories that purport to explain the reasons behind social life (Sarup, 1993, pp. 133–137).

Lyotard argues that metanarratives are fiction for two reasons. First, they reflect the ideas and interests of particular groups, with each group claiming that *their* perspective is of universal significance and applicability. Lyotard insists that there is no way of deciding which group's truth is more valid than others, making it impossible to establish the certainty of any truth claim. Second, Lyotard argues that each group's knowledge is subjective and increasingly fragmented, particularly as members within each group begin to *contest* the metanarrative. So, for example, post-Marxist philosophies reject Marx's view that the economy plays a foundational role in the state's politics as a reflection of ruling-class interests. Lyotard's point is that as different factions and movements emerge around particular ideas, they also develop their own 'mini-narratives', which challenge what the metanarrative considers valid or not. This insecurity around knowledge makes it impossible to confidently announce that any metanarrative has access to the truth.

For Lyotard, this inability to form universal or totalising truth characterises the postmodern condition. Instead, knowledge increasingly takes on a localised form, with minimal possibilities for consensual understanding. No longer does knowledge accumulate into universal truths, validated by scientific discovery. Instead, science takes the form of a **language game** in which scientists deploy contesting narratives as 'moves' (like on a chessboard) to certify their authority on a given subject matter. Lyotard argues that power is deeply entwined with such moves. Indeed, today, science does not derive its legitimacy from its search for the truth but rather its support from the state or corporations, which saturate the public with 'epic narratives' and 'heroic storylines' to affirm its usefulness.

Jean Baudrillard's work is also another vital expression of postmodern theorising. Baudrillard characterises postmodern society as a form of what he calls 'hyperreality' – a world in which the distinction between 'reality' and simulation completely dissolves. In this world, Baudrillard argues that simulations stand in for – or are more real than – reality itself. This is particularly apparent in the twentieth century, which Baudrillard characterises in terms of **simulacra**, whereby layers of symbolic meaning sever our connection to reality. Drawing on poststructuralism, Baudrillard describes simulacra as signs that no longer connect to material reality and are completely liberated from any signifieds. From this perspective, meaning emerges not from material objects but from semantic codes with no grounding in reality. Put simply, reality is a total fabrication as meaning no longer represents – or has any grounding in – anything 'real'.

Baudrillard offers television as an example of the simulacra he describes. Television invites viewers into fantasy worlds that imitate the intimate details and personal lives of 'fictional' and 'non-fictional' characters. Baudrillard argues that these imitations encourage viewers to delve deep into imaginary worlds, making it impossible to distinguish between what is real and what is spectacle. He suggests that we can see the power of these simulations in examples where viewers confuse television characters with actors, extending offers of marriage or sending get-well-soon cards to characters on a show. In addition, it is not uncommon for television doctors, lawyers and therapists to receive requests for advice from members of the public. From this perspective, Baudrillard argues that television dissolves into life and that life dissolves into television as fiction becomes reality.

For Baudrillard, mass media has an endless ability to create and produce the images and signs that drive this process. Indeed, there are many examples of simulations in our contemporary world – interactive video games, IMAX films, artificial intelligence, digital celebrity and computer-generated animation. What's critical is that these simulations and imitations of the real provide a new source of fulfilment and satisfaction. Indeed, consider how ready people are to escape the real world to their virtual reality 'oasis' – see, for example, Ernest Cline's (2011) science fiction novel *Ready Player One*.

Case Study 6.2

Metric Power

In his book, *Metric Power*, the sociologist Dave Beer (2016) draws on the work of Michel Foucault to examine the intensifying role that systems of measurement and calculation play in ordering and shaping everyday life. Drawing on various examples from Apple Watch, Facebook, Google Scholar, and altmetrics, Beer argues that metrics interweave contemporary forms of neoliberal governance into our lives (see **neoliberalism**). Beer's argument begins from the simple premise that metrics are often used to judge our performances and create mechanisms that compare, rank and display our victories and failures. Apple Watch is an obvious example: its systems continuously measure and evaluate our bodily routines against a set of performative goals, telling us what to eat, when to sleep, how much to walk, and so on. Beer suggests that these devices are an excellent example of biopower in operation, linking our biological processes to the matter of administering life or, more specifically, managing our health. As such, Beer notes how each device ranks successful or failed performances, encouraging users through positive or corrective feedback in the form of a 'score'. These quantifiable judgements, Beer argues, are what align our bodily performances towards the values of neoliberalism.

What is meant by 'neoliberal' here? Beer argues that neoliberalism refers to attitudes and logics that support free market capitalism, often by encouraging competitive behaviour by establishing an individualised, entrepreneurial point of view. Beer argues that metrics like 'personal bests' or 'top scores', which display information through competitive leaderboards, reward the kind of competitive self-interest and entrepreneurial spirit required of neoliberal capitalism. Specifically, Beer argues that metrics normalise the idea that the market is the principal organising feature of social life. By attaching metrics to our wrists or accepting rankings into everything we say and do, Beer follows Foucault in warning against the anatomo-politics of the human body; that is, the gradual acceptance of regulations, permissions and expectations into our lives.

Of particular interest is Beer's analysis of the affective or emotional capacity of metrics to entangle our bodies into neoliberal forms of governance. Beer argues that the power of metrics extends beyond surveillance and discipline into *structuring how we feel*. He argues that metrics entangle our bodies into self-governance processes by provoking emotions of anticipation, expectation, worry, fear, anxiety and concern. So, for example, metrics motivate expectations concerning success or failure, which drive anxieties that encourage further engagement with systems of measurement and calculation. Brock (2021) draws out this irony in the context of video game cultures, suggesting that players often rely on metrics to position themselves as competitive yet quickly become anxious, insecure and uncertain about having their performances quantified. To manage these anxieties, Brock argues that players often develop strategies of self-regulation that rely on the very systems of measurement and calculation that are affectively responsible in the first instance. This irony, Brock suggests, speaks to the need for a critical attitude towards the discursive framings that metrics legitimate in the context of competitive video game cultures.

Summary

- Structuralist and poststructuralist accounts of language structure draw attention to different ways of conceptualising meaning and truth in social life.
- A key concept here is deconstruction: the idea of revealing the inconsistencies and paradoxes within a text.
- Foucault provides essential insight into the power of discourse to construct knowledge or epistemes that shape a normative understanding of the self.
- Foucault also offers tools to reckon with the disciplinary power of discourses, examining how people internalise the rationalities and techniques of surveillance.
- Poststructuralism contends with the ambiguities within language and meaning to give way to postmodern theories of social life.
- Lyotard critiques the very idea of metanarrative, asserting that 'truths' are plural and relative to particular contexts or mini-narratives.
- Baudrillard characterises the postmodern in terms of hyperreality, which refers to the breakdown between reality and fiction. Baudrillard offers a sceptical vision of society that only consumes and never engages with anything real.

Review Questions

- What are the significant differences between structuralist and poststructuralist perspectives on language and meaning?
- Foucault claims that scientific disciplines create subjects through techniques and technologies of the body. What examples can you think of?
- Do you agree with Baudrillard's assessment of society as postmodern? What evidence could support the concept of 'hyperreality'?

Annotated Reading

Structuralism has a long and detailed history, extending from language to the social sciences and literature. John Sturrock (2008) provides a detailed account in *Structuralism* (Oxford: Blackwell).

For a detailed yet accessible guide to poststructuralism and postmodern theory, see Madan Sarup's (1993) *An Introductory Guide to Post-Structuralism and Postmodernism* (London: Harvester Wheatsheaf).

Barry Smart's (2002) book *Michel Foucault* (London: Routledge) engages comprehensively with major Foucauldian themes and issues.

For those interested in accessing essential readings within postmodern social theory, see Steven Seidman's (1994) edited volume, *The Postmodern Turn: New Perspectives on Social Theory* (Cambridge: Cambridge University Press).

Richard Appignanesi and Chris Garratt's (1997) *Introducing Postmodernism* (Cambridge: Totem Books) offers an illustrative guide to the art, theory and history that foregrounds postmodern thinking, as well as structuralism, semiotics and deconstruction.

7

Structure, Agency and Reflexivity

Chapter Objectives

This chapter will:

- Introduce 'the problem of structure and agency' in social theory through theorists such as Pierre Bourdieu, Anthony Giddens and Margaret Archer.
- Familiarise essential concepts, including structuration, habitus, practices, reflexivity, objectivism and subjectivism.
- Provide contemporary examples of (post)structuration research.

Keywords

Social structure, agency, social system, social ontology, structuration, culture, habitus, practices, reflexivity, analytical dualism

Introduction

Not all social theory develops in parallel to poststructural and postmodern themes. This chapter introduces students to 'the problem of structure and agency' in social theory, a debate that goes to the very heart of social research. By asking how **social structure** shapes human behaviour or how agents reproduce or transform social structures, students will grasp the different ways that three prominent thinkers (Pierre Bourdieu, Anthony Giddens and Margaret Archer) conceptualise the relationship between the two. Drawing on examples from education, students will see the practical application of the debate through key concepts such as **habitus**, **analytical dualism** and **reflexivity**. Indeed, reflexivity – people's capacity to deliberate structural contexts – is a crucial point of contention between these thinkers, as is the suggestion that structure and **agency** are 'co-constitutive' of one another. Examples of existing research from education will help students grasp the issues at stake here, notably whether agents internalise their structural contexts or reflect upon them with relative autonomy.

The Problem of Structure and Agency

One of the central problems in social theory is whether we ascribe causal significance to social structures or the actions of social agents when explaining social behaviour. This problem has become the focus of intense debate within social theory, particularly as theorists disagree about the importance of 'structure' or 'agency' in shaping social behaviour. This section will briefly overview the different perspectives on structure and agency before detailing the arguments of three contributors who attempt to reconcile the debate: Pierre Bourdieu, Anthony Giddens and Margaret Archer.

As we saw in previous chapters, sociology begins with the belief that social factors causally determine human behaviour, whether in the form of social norms, cultural values or economic imperatives. Like Marx and Durkheim, classical social theorists account for these social factors in terms of the explanatory power of social structures. As discussed in Chapter 4, for example, Durkheim credits the functioning of modern societies to social structures that maintain social solidarity through shared norms and institutions. He argues that sociologists can identify these structures by pursuing a science of 'social facts', which involves determining how structures exert social forces external to and coercive of people (see also **realism**). An essential aspect of Durkheim's thesis is that these structures are crucial to the survival of society, akin to how the natural body depends on the integrated functioning of various organs and systems. Indeed, the term 'functionalism' comes from the idea that the stability of societies depends on the structures of socialisation to integrate people into functional roles and duties. One of the most important (if controversial) assumptions of functionalism is that social structures, like the family or education, have the causal power to ensure stable social arrangements by determining how people think and act. This assumption is particularly evident in the work of Talcott Parsons (see Chapter 4), who argues that societies will only function if people meet the needs of structures with predetermined ends.

One of the significant criticisms of functionalism is how it overemphasises the causal significance of structure while downplaying the autonomy of human agents. Its primary interest in the integration of a functioning social order leads to a vision of society in which people are 'dupes', simply required to satisfy the expectations of specific roles based on assumptions about societal needs. Here, there is very little sense of people as capable of self-direction and intentionality, nor as historically significant actors, with the capacity to influence social change. Instead, people are 'functionaries', acting as a resource for the structural prerequisites that the **social system** determines are necessary (Parker, 2000, p. 20). This overly determined view of structure makes it difficult to account for the many contradictions and social ills that exist within societies and the capacity of individuals and social groups to resist collective pressures.

Of course, Durkheim and Parsons were not the only theorists to stress the importance of structure in explaining the development of societies and the effects that these have on social agents. As discussed in Chapter 2, Marx also argues that structure plays a critical role in modern capitalist societies. In particular, Marx argues that the structures that organise modern labour production, such as wage labour, coerce workers into exploitative working conditions that have social effects, such as alienation. Marx argues that a social revolution that targets these structures can cause the supporting institutions to change. Indeed, by workers withdrawing their labour through strikes, Marx argues that they can remove the power of employment structures to generate value.

Some critics argue that Marx's theory is a form of structural determinism: it suggests that economic structures (e.g., wage-labour relations between a capitalist and worker) are the foundation upon which society bases all other social and political arrangements. From this perspective, Marx's theory overemphasises the division of societies into competing economic classes, characterised by class antagonisms, which resolve through inevitable revolution. While some maintain that this is a misreading of Marx (Eagleton, 2011), others argue that structuralist versions of Marxism (e.g., Althusser) often overstate the objective nature of class structures and the extent to which these determine people's actions and lived experience. Indeed, structuralist Marxists downplay the idea that human agents are makers of history, viewing them only as bearers of structural functions ('ideological state apparatuses'; see Chapter 6) that ensure the viability of capitalism. This structural determinism is the subject of intense debate within Marxist political theory and social history (see Thompson, 2008/1978).

By stressing the causal importance of social structures, these classical theories explain social behaviour in terms of social factors that exist independently of, yet shape, human agency. Some criticise this view as **objectivism**: the idea that we can determine the nature of truth or reality by appealing to permanent structures that shape social being (see Parker, 2000, p. 32). The problem with objectivism is that it downplays the capacity of agents to act independently of social structures. Indeed, it overlooks the role of meaning in constructing knowledge, suggesting that truth exists 'out there' waiting on science and reason for its discovery. As a result, agents' choices are either ignored or reduced to components acting predictably within a predetermined system.

This charge against objectivism has led some to challenge the concept of social structure, questioning whether social factors can have a causal effect on social behaviour. As we saw in Chapter 5, phenomenologists and ethnomethodologists dispense with the idea that objective social structures can explain cause and effect in the social world. Instead, these theories focus on human **subjectivity**: the meanings implicit in social behaviour, particularly as people perceive and live within the world. These accounts deliberately privilege the role of human agency in explaining social behaviour. Take Merleau-Ponty, who argues that people perceive and organise social experiences according to *their own* embodied and subjective meaning systems. From this perspective, people's practical engagement with the world shapes social behaviour as humans configure their bodies and experiences in meaningful ways.

Despite the value in interpreting social action, some critics suggest that these theories overprivilege human subjectivity, failing to explain how broader social factors shape social behaviour. By focusing solely on 'individuals', 'actions' or 'experiences', interpretive theories rarely give a satisfactory account of how societies continue or change. As a result, some criticise the **subjectivism** of interpretive sociology – the idea that one can examine things from only an actor's point of view. The problem with subjectivism is that it reduces knowledge claims to subjective experiences, overlooking the structures independent of consciousness or perception that shape social behaviour. This position is apparent in the arguments of Husserl, who dismisses the objective world to make subjective experience the object of philosophical inquiry (see Chapter 5).

Many contemporary authors reject the suggestion that structure and agency represent a binary choice: that social behaviour is determined either by structural forces or by the free choices of individuals. Indeed, it is plausible that people make the societies they live in but not in ways that they entirely control. With this in mind, some theorists attempt to reconcile the roles of both structure and agency. The first two are known as 'structurationists' – Pierre Bourdieu and Anthony Giddens (Parker, 2000). These two theorists stress the importance of structure and agency but see structure as something that resides *within* human individuals through the concept of practice. Margaret Archer, alternatively, is known as a 'poststructurationist' (Parker, 2000). Archer stresses the importance of structure and agency but criticises the move to 'conflate' them together through practice. Instead, Archer argues that it is essential that social science keep structure and agency analytically distinct if it is to explain how structures enable or constrain social behaviour and how agents reproduce or change existing social structures. What will become clear is that the differences between these perspectives relate to questions of **social ontology**: the study of the nature and properties of the social world. In particular, while interpretive sociologies influence Bourdieu and Giddens, Archer is a critical realist (see **critical realism**) who insists on the objective existence of social reality and the possibility of studying its causal mechanisms.

Pierre Bourdieu

Pierre Bourdieu's interest in structure and agency comes from providing sociologists with a theoretical and empirical framework that explains what happens in the social world. As part of this practical endeavour, Bourdieu wishes to avoid the dangers of objectivism, which overemphasises the power of social structures to condition social behaviour, *and* subjectivism, which reduces the complexity of social phenomena to individual actions. In response, Bourdieu argues that it is possible to transcend the problem of structure and agency through a series of interrelated concepts, habitus, doxa, field and **cultural capital**.

As briefly discussed in Chapter 5, habitus is one of Bourdieu's most important concepts. It draws on a phenomenological understanding of human experience to explain how social environments shape people's practices (see Chapter 5). The notion of habitus is central to Bourdieu's analysis of the conditioning of class-based cultures. He writes:

> The conditionings associated with a particular class of conditions of existence produce *habitus*, systems of durable, transposable dispositions, structured structures predisposed to function as structuring structures, that is, as principles which generate and organise practices and representations that can be objectively adapted to their outcomes without presupposing a conscious aiming at ends or an express mastery of the operations necessary in order to attain them. Objectively 'regulated' and 'regular' without being in anyway the product of obedience to rules, they can be collectively orchestrated without being the product of the organising action of a conductor. (Bourdieu, 1992, p. 53)

Bourdieu's point here is that habitus refers to the conditioning effects of social (or class-based) positions. Inherent within these positions are specific logics (opportunities, necessities, constraints) which tend to generate dispositions or practices compatible with these conditioning effects. This process is particularly evident in early life, where the habitus generates stable attitudes to the world that motivate people to behave in ways structured by their early social position. Indeed, Bourdieu argues that those with similar social positions will develop a similar habitus due to similar opportunities and constraints. From this perspective, habitus is the mechanism produced by social conditioning, which encourages people to behave in ways that reproduce existing structures of society.

Again, it is essential to note the influence of phenomenology on Bourdieu here. Bourdieu argues that the conditioning effects of the habitus are so practical because they set forth dispositions written onto the body, embedded into physical and emotional being, yet operate below the level of consciousness. Bourdieu (1992, p. 56) writes:

> The *habitus* – embodied history, internalised as a second nature and so forgotten as history – is the active presence of the whole past of which it is the product. As such, it is what gives practices their relative autonomy with respect to external determinations of the immediate present.

In other words, social conditions can shape bodily practices in ways that do not require active consideration or reflection. They become 'second nature', inscribed cognitively and emotionally as structures in the body-subject. This process is seen, for example, in what Bourdieu refers to as the 'bodily hexis' of class language codes, that is, articulatory styles based on accent or dialect. Bourdieu argues that class and gender differences manifest in how people speak, with specific movements of the mouth reflecting social backgrounds and experiences (see Myles, 1999).

Bourdieu also illustrates the process of habitus by referring to the dynamics of games, observing that social conditioning works through what sports players call a 'feel for the game' (Bourdieu, 1992, p. 66) – the acquisition of practical mastery through experiences that operate outside of conscious control. Boxing, for example, involves the development of a body habitus – one that involves lessons about manners, customs, styles and postures, but also the conditioning of fighters through racialised cultural structures that exploit and subordinate (see Wacquant, 2001).

It is important to note that the habitus does not mandate specific actions or practices in a deterministic fashion; instead, it acts with a 'generative capacity' (Bourdieu, 1992, p. 55) to realise a range of different behaviours depending on the situation. Bourdieu notes that, much like artists, people can seek original inspiration but that, depending on the situation, this creativity is likely to fall within particular 'styles' (Bourdieu, 1992, p. 55). In other words, creativity is enabled and constrained by the habitus, as people pursue interests within the boundaries of social classes and cultural groupings (Parker, 2000, p. 46). From this perspective, Bourdieu (1992, p. 55) writes that the habitus helps reconcile the structure and agency problem. It has an infinite capacity to generate thoughts, perceptions, expressions and actions, set within the limits of historically and socially situated conditions.

A key point about the habitus is that it does not involve conscious deliberation. Indeed, few individuals fully know that everything they do is expressive of socialised dispositions. Bourdieu argues that people tend to accept their experiences of things as 'common sense' rather than critically reflecting upon their socially inscribed habits and practices. This taken-for-granted knowledge is called 'doxa', which refers to the 'undisputed' and 'pre-reflexive' ways of acting, which are foundational to a person's sense of being. Bourdieu (1992, p. 68) argues that doxa is about practical sense, about turning social conditions into automatic responses, such that specific ideas, beliefs and perceptions become part of a person's natural attitude. This attitude is integral to how people navigate their daily routines and what courses of action become part of 'the universe of the thinkable [and] unthinkable' (Bourdieu, 2013/1977, p. 170). For example, Bourdieu asks us to consider some common beliefs in school, such as the idea that educational achievement comes down to raw talent or gifted intelligence. Bourdieu argues that this idea reflects the doxa of those from lower social and economic backgrounds for whom their educational exclusion is often self-evident (see Bourdieu and Eagleton, 1992).

Figure 7.1 Habitus of a boxer

Think about the many pieces of a person's sense of self and how they come together to reflect a mixture of social circumstances and everyday (embodied) practices.

Related to Bourdieu's concept of habitus is his notion of 'field', which deals with the objective or structural aspects of the social world. We can think of various fields within society, from education, science and art to business, commerce and politics. Bourdieu argues that social life plays out across these fields, particularly as people (groups and institutions) find themselves in different positions, struggling for power. Indeed, Bourdieu sees fields as hierarchical settings within which people compete for social positions. For example, within education, people of different social and economic backgrounds, with better access to resources, can occupy advantageous positions, making them more competitive (e.g., in terms of access to scholarships or awards from prestigious schools). Importantly, Bourdieu also sees fields as hierarchical *between* themselves, often competing for power and class relations. So, for example, professions within law (judges) or politics (members of parliament) confer access to power and resources rarely afforded to artists or musicians. This enables specific fields (with particular class and power relations) to maintain dominant positions in social life.

Bourdieu makes sense of these struggles by discussing **capital** – the resources individuals or groups draw on to compete successfully within fields. Bourdieu identifies four types of capital, arguing that each one has the power to confer competitive advantages on people. The first is *economic* capital, which refers to the monetary resources that a person has available to them, such as income, land or other financial assets. The second is *social* capital, which refers to the valuable social relations and networks that a person has at their disposal. The third is *cultural* capital, which refers to the cultural resources that a person possesses, such as manners, taste, knowledge and skill. The fourth is *symbolic* capital, which refers to the award of honour, prestige and reputation. Bourdieu argues that those possessing the appropriate type and amount of capital can dominate a particular field. For example, those with advanced educational qualifications, such as degrees or titles, will acquire the cultural capital needed to signify competency and authority within an academic subject. Bourdieu argues that this capital can also become a 'currency' to access other fields and forms of capital. So, for example, obtaining a PhD can confer a reputation of expertise – symbolic capital – which an academic may trade for social, cultural or economic resources in other fields, such as business, politics or entertainment.

Notably, capital connects back to habitus. Bourdieu argues that having a particular habitus predisposes a person to possess varying amounts of each type of capital. Indeed, habitus is the physical embodiment of each type of capital as people develop their dispositions to compete effectively within fields. Bourdieu uses the metaphor of game playing to make sense of this relationship between capital, habitus and field. He argues that people develop a 'feel for the game' (Bourdieu, 1992, p. 66), in which their habitus allows them to successfully navigate their social circumstances (without consciously thinking about them). Like football players, people know when to deploy their skills and resources to play the 'game' as effectively as possible. From this perspective, each person's capital provides a distinct advantage in readying the habitus for social mobility. For example, a student from an upper-middle-class background may deploy their existing resources (private education, dialect, cultural knowledge, social networks) to excel in higher education. This action is because they are already familiar with the social and cultural practices required for success (reading, writing, referencing, networking). They would undoubtedly have a distinct positional advantage over a student from a lower-class background, whose habitus will likely need to adapt if they are to compete effectively.

In bringing these concepts together, we see that Bourdieu's response to the problem of structure and agency suggests that the habitus works to reproduce class-based social inequalities. Societies reproduce social inequalities because the habitus reproduces social hierarchies as people compete for capital within and between fields. Notably, much of this 'game playing' is done without conscious deliberation because the habitus is an embodied, practical phenomenon. In other words, the habitus produces an undisputed acceptance (or doxa) that **social stratification** is part of contemporary societies.

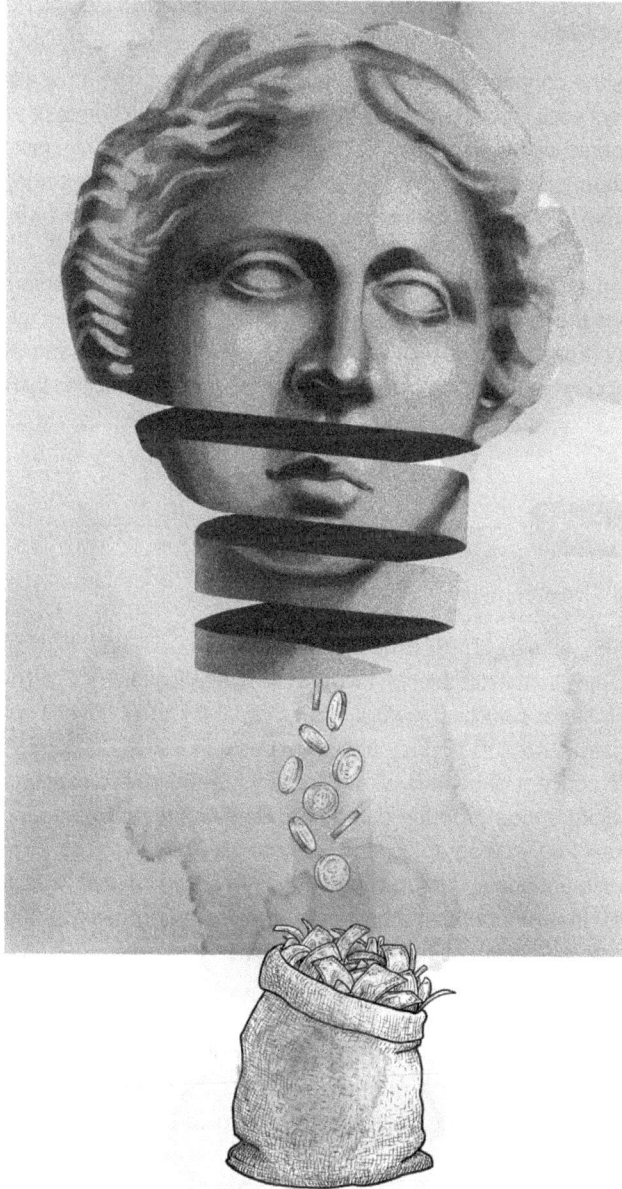

Figure 7.2 Capital

How do contemporary societies measure human value? Consider the role of economic, cultural and social capital and how it helps individuals 'cash out' in different ways to gain an advantage in society.

Focus on Facts

- Bourdieu uses the concept of 'symbolic violence' to convey the struggles for power between different social groups. It refers to non-physical or 'soft' forms of violence exercised upon social agents with their complicity. Bourdieu argues that social institutions, like the education system, practise symbolic violence by imposing the language, values and meaning of those in power on the rest of the population (see Bourdieu and Passeron, 1990/1977).
- 'Taste' is also an essential concept in Bourdieu's work. Bourdieu was interested in 'taste' as a social practice that gives individuals a sense of their place in the social order. Bourdieu argues that people use taste as a mark of distinction, classifying objects and differentiating between social classes based on preferences for art, food, sports and fashion.

Case Study 7.1

Habitus in the Classroom

Diane Reay's (1995) article, 'They Employ Cleaners to Do That: Habitus in the Primary Classroom', is an excellent example of the practical application of Bourdieu's ideas. Reay argues that the appeal of Bourdieu's work lies in its ability to uncover social inequalities by keeping issues of structure and agency simultaneously in focus. To support this point, Reay deploys Bourdieu's concept of habitus within primary classrooms to examine how school children of different backgrounds produce different understandings of gender, race and class. In particular, Reay draws on ethnographic and comparative observations of two urban primary schools with very different social compositions: the first, called 'Milner', with working-class children, predominantly from minoritised ethnic communities, and the second, called 'Oak Park', with mainly white middle-class children. Reay examines the peer-group interactions of these children, arguing that their habitus reveals the taken-for-granted inequalities embedded in their everyday practices and home lives.

In one notable example, Reay tells the story of four girls from Oak Park who were learning together about the Tudors through a computer program based on the life of a servant girl called Bess. Reay (1995, p. 362) recalls the unfolding of the peer-group interaction in the following terms:

> Negar was giving the instructions, Sarah was methodically typing them in, while Nancy and Sophie were providing ideas and suggestions. 'Tell her to go upstairs and hurry up.' 'OK I'll type in "go up", that's if she's not too stupid to understand.' Negar typed in 'go up' then started to tap in 'please' 'Don't be silly' said Sophie leaning over and putting her finger on the delete button. 'We don't have to say please or thank you. She's just a servant.'

Reay (1995, p. 362) continues with her observation, noting that:

A few minutes later Nancy mischievously said 'Make her run'. Bess was in her mistress' bedroom by now. 'Great idea' said Negar 'make her run downstairs' Sarah typed in 'run'. Sophie, who seemed to be getting heady on the prevailing sense of power and control became impatient with Sarah's typing speed, leaned over and typed in 'run quicker or else'. It was at that point that they noticed me scribbling away. Nancy beamed, noticed my bemused look and by way of explanation told me 'We have to give her orders and be a bit rude because she's the servant.'

Reay comments that these practices exemplify what Bourdieu calls a 'cultured habitus' in which access to particular goods, services and powers becomes the norm for some people. Reay argues that the responses of these children in Oak Park were very different to those in Milner, whom Reay also observed playing with the Tudor computer program. At Milner, the children did not position themselves as in charge of Bess (i.e., as Bess's mistress) but identified with Bess's subordinate role, commenting on the poor condition of her servant quarters. Reay suggests that the school children at Oak Park had naturally, unthinkingly, assumed a dominant role and entered into relations of ruling with Bess, demonstrating a particular understanding of the division of labour and their place within it. Indeed, Reay (1995, p. 362) argues that implicit within their dispositions was a sense of themselves as the kinds of people who can pay for the services of others.

In a related example, Reay recalls how the children responded differently to 'tidying up' in the classroom. In Milner, Reay (1995, p. 363) notes that there was always a 'good-natured scramble'– 'girls rushing around helpfully putting lids on felt tips, pushing chairs in, placing books back on shelves', etc. In Oak Park, however, the children did not want to tidy up. Reay (1995, p. 363) notes that some flatly refused, saying 'It's not our job' or 'They employ cleaners to do that'. Reay argues that such social distinctions were not part of the habitus of the girls at Milner, for whom these 'cleaners' were often their mothers. Instead, tidying up and generally helping out were working-class activities with which they felt at home. As such, Reay suggests that the habitus is both classed *and* gendered, as understandings about domestic labour become the grounds for the reproduction of social differences.

In the concluding example, Reay considers how race shapes habitus. In particular, Reay recalls the strategies of racial exclusion operating at Oak Park, which became apparent when a Black student named 'Temi' joined class 5S. Reay observes that most of the children in 5S simply ignored Temi. 'It was as if she did not exist', recalls Reay, 'there were no racist comments, no overt hostility, there was simply no recognition of Temi's presence at all' (Reay, 1995, p. 366). This treatment proceeded over nine months, with Reay noting that Temi's peer-group popularity never improved among Oak Park's white middle-class children. Reay (1995, p. 367) argues that this treatment of Temi reveals how habitus cultivates social distinction based on race:

the peer group habitus operated to keep Temi invisible through processes so subtle they were barely discernible … The racism of these middle-class children was not manifested in any action, rather it lay in the absences … in the lack of care, lack of contact, lack of recognition.

(Continued)

From this perspective, these children reinforced their understanding of social difference by rendering passive Temi's participation in peer-group activities. Reay argues that such practices reflect the prejudices and racial stereotypes ingrained in the habitus of these privileged white children.

Anthony Giddens

Anthony Giddens's interest in the problem of structure and agency comes from an attempt to resolve the endless oscillation between objectivist and subjectivist orientations in social thought. In *Central Problems in Social Theory*, Giddens (1979, p. 49) frames this concern as follows:

> 'Action' and 'structure' usually appear in both the sociological and philosophical literature as antinomies. It would be true to say that those schools of thought preoccupied with action have paid little attention to, or have found no way of coping with, conceptions of structural explanation or social causation.

Giddens (1979, p. 52) goes on to make the opposite remark about functionalism and Marxism, arguing that these theories overemphasise structure:

> The conduct of actors in society is treated as the outcome of a conjunction of social and psychological determinants, in which the former dominate the latter through the key influence attributed to normative elements. This effectively excludes certain essential components of the theory of action.

From this perspective, Giddens (1979, p. 53) argues that bringing structure and action together in a common process is possible. This process states that neither structure nor action has causal priority over the other. Instead, social structures become constituted through action, while action becomes constituted through social structures. Giddens refers to this process as **structuration**.

A fundamental building block within Giddens's structuration theory is the idea of the 'duality of structure', by which Giddens (1979, p. 5) means

> the essential recursiveness of social life, as constituted in social practices: structure is both medium and outcome of the reproduction of practices. Structure enters simultaneously into the constitution of the agent and social practices, and 'exists' in the generating moments of this constitution.

In other words, Giddens sees social structures as both the *medium* and *outcome* of agency. As Cruickshank (2003, p. 70) argues, instead of agency meaning free will and structures being conceptualised as external, determining forces on agents, Giddens sees structure and agency as definable only in relation to one another. Structure is the medium through which agents exercise their agency (Cruickshank, 2003, p. 70). From this perspective, agency does not exist in the form of the discrete acts of individuals, devoid of social and historical context. Instead, agency always exists within conditions of social life which continually rebound on the circumstances within which people make decisions (see Giddens, 1998, p. 115). Put simply, 'to understand agency is to understand the structures which act as the medium for the practices of agents' (Cruickshank, 2003, p. 70).

It is important to note that this perspective resonates with phenomenological sociology and ethnomethodology (see Chapter 5). Giddens argues for a social theory that makes sense of structure and agency in terms of people's situated practices. Like Schütz, Giddens is interested in agents' subjective and creative meaning and how these become part of the very methods by which agents practically accomplish their lives. Yet, Giddens seeks to emphasise the fundamentally 'recursive' character of social life: the idea that people are always drawing upon their knowledge of a given structural context when they engage in purposeful action, thereby reproducing patterns of social interactions through the 'situatedness' of their practices. This process has an essential temporal framing. Giddens (1979, p. 55) argues for a social theory that makes sense of the continuous flow of social conduct by which agents harness structures to achieve their projects.

Recognising that structure and agency presuppose one another in this 'duality', Giddens reworks the concept of structure. He begins by analytically dividing social structures into three different types: structures of *domination* (power), *signification* (meaning), and *legitimation* (norms) (Stones, 2005, p. 17). Structures of domination refer to the 'resources' that some agents have to exercise power over others or influence or transform their surroundings. These can be 'allocative resources', which constitute the power to control the distribution and use of materials and objects, such as capital, or they can be 'authoritative resources', which constitute the power to organise and control social behaviour, such as social status (Cruickshank, 2003, p. 71). Alternatively, structures of signification and legitimation refer to the 'rules' that ascribe meaning to action, such as the norms that commonly demarcate acceptable from unacceptable behaviour (Stones, 2005, p. 17; see also Cruickshank, 2003, p. 71).

In both cases, Giddens argues that these structures are not external to agents but similar to what Schütz calls 'stocks of knowledge' (see Chapter 5) – the repository of lived experience from which people draw to interact and negotiate everyday life. Through these stocks of knowledge agents perceive, understand and enact the distribution and configuration of power, meaning and norms within society (Stones, 2005, p. 17). Indeed, Giddens argues that to understand power in society is to examine what agents do rather than simply suggesting that power stems from material resources or rules (Cruikshank, 2003, pp. 71–72). '[P]ower is not a description of a state of affairs, but a capability,' writes Giddens (1979, p. 68), suggesting that power is not external to agency but the ability to be an agent: to engage in purposeful action and make a difference. From this perspective, all agents have power because they can draw on their rules and resources (or stocks of knowledge) as the medium through which to enact their intentions. For Giddens, this power does not necessarily result in social change. Instead, it speaks to the vital role that agency plays in the process of structuration: that society is not the result of objective structures determining social behaviour but of agents actively reproducing existing rules and resources through their social practices (Cruikshank, 2003, p. 72).

In reworking the concept of structure, then, Giddens rejects objectivism, arguing that structures exist only within human individuals. In particular, Giddens argues that structures have a 'virtual existence', becoming 'real' only as traces in people's memories as they draw upon their rules and resources (or stocks of knowledge) to interact. From this perspective, structures are only ever 'instantiated' through human action, forming the 'structural properties' of social systems. Put simply, Giddens argues that society is based on repeated social practices, which are themselves based on rules and resources that only have an existence when deployed in social interaction (Cruikshank, 2003, p. 76). For example, within the higher education system, the rules of the classroom, which constitute meaning and conduct for university students and teachers, are virtual until drawn upon through social interaction. Indeed, while some rules may change from class to class (e.g., seating arrangements, types of activity, formal/informal greetings), others become properties of the system through ongoing instantiation and repetitive practice (e.g., sitting quietly during lectures, raising a hand before asking a question, requesting permission to leave the room). It is the actions of agents that reproduce (or change) the 'reality' of higher education (as a social system).

Giddens's solution to the problem of structure and agency is to emphasise that external social structures do not determine social behaviour. Instead, agents acting recursively act to (re)produce social practices and social systems. Strictly speaking, this view is not the same as Bourdieu's concept of habitus. Social practices, for Giddens, do not solely reproduce class-based inequalities and positional struggles. Instead, Giddens argues that agents can transform their circumstances since social systems are nothing but 'instantiations' of rule-following behaviour.

Margaret Archer

Margaret Archer's (1982, 1988, 1995) interest in the problem of structure and agency is a response to three different errors of 'conflation' within social theory. These errors refer to theories which either overstate the extent to which structure or agency plays a primary role in shaping social behaviour ('downwards conflation' or 'upwards conflation') or those theories that merge structure and agency, making it difficult to examine their interplay ('central conflation'). A brief definition of each of these errors is as follows (see Layder, 2006, p. 264):

- 'Downwards conflation' refers to those theories that explain social activity in terms of the determinate results of structural factors. From this perspective, agency disappears into the imperatives of social norms, political economic arrangements, or the structures of language and **discourse**. Examples include functionalism, Marxism, and other structuralist accounts, which exaggerate the importance of social structure or social systems in setting the terms under which people play out their social lives.

- 'Upwards conflation' refers to those theories that view society as a free creation of social agency. From this perspective, social structure disappears into questions concerning human intentionality, self and identity. Examples include symbolic interactionism, ethnomethodology and phenomenology, which amplify subjective experience as the essential departure point for understanding social life.
- 'Central conflation' refers to those theories that attempt to transcend the problem of structure and agency by viewing the two as mutually constitutive, where structures are reproduced through agents whose actions are simultaneously constrained and enabled by structure. From this perspective, both structure and agency disappear into one another as their differences are 'explained away' through notions such as embodiment or rule-following practices. Examples include Bourdieu's concept of habitus and Giddens' structuration theory, which overlook the complex issues involved in adequately understanding how structure and agency interact.

In response, Archer offers analytical dualism as an approach that recognises the interplay of structure and agency but unpicks them analytically due to different time-scales, properties and powers. As Archer remarks:

> Because all structural properties found in any society are continuously activity-dependent, it is possible through analytical dualism to separate 'structure' and 'agency' and to examine their *interplay* in order to account for the structuring and re-structuring of social institutions such as education. (Archer and Morgan, 2020, p. 184)

Archer argues that this examination is possible for two reasons. First,

> 'structure' and 'agency' operate *diachronically* over different time periods because:
>
> 1 Structure necessarily pre-dates the action(s) that transform it and,
>
> 2 Structural elaboration necessarily post-dates those actions.

Second,

> 'structure' and 'agency' are *different kinds of emergent entities*, as is shown by the differences in their properties and powers, *despite* the fact that they are crucial for each other's formation, continuation and development. Thus, an educational system can be 'centralised', whilst a person cannot, and humans are 'reflexive', which cannot be the case for structures. (Archer and Morgan, 2020, p. 184)

Archer is making two crucial points here. The first is that, while structure and agency are related, they operate on *different time-scales*. Archer argues that, at any particular moment, pre-existing social structures enable and constrain agents, whose interactions then produce intended and unintended consequences. This process continues, with agents elaborating on these structures, providing the context for future action. Archer (1995) refers to this process as 'the morphogenetic sequence', a timeline we can visualise through the following formula:

structural conditioning → social interaction → structural elaboration.

Archer argues that this arrangement allows for an empirical account of the internal causal processes that link structural and agential phenomena over time (Brock et al., 2016, p. xvi).

The second point that Archer is making is that social structures and human agents have different causal properties and powers. When we talk of 'structures', for example, we do so because we wish to emphasise that a given structure has a particular property that endures over time and exerts influence over people, somewhat independent of given persons.

An important concept here is **emergence**. Archer argues that social structures, although the products of human action, have emergent properties that cannot be reduced to the power of those individuals. Consider, for example, organisations (see Elder-Vass, 2007a, pp. 31–32). An organisation is composed of a group of individuals, structured by social positions that people occupy. These positions implicitly or explicitly specify rules that define how incumbents must act, such as how to relate to other members of the organisation and how to relate to outsiders when acting on behalf of the organisation. In Archer's view, these rules cannot be reduced to any given person and their individual actions. Instead, they are emergent properties of the organisation of social behaviour into particular social positions (and other relations characteristic of an organisation). Put simply, if there were no organisation, then there would be no such causal properties via social positions to structure social behaviour in particular ways, leaving individuals to act differently. This is Archer's point: only by distinguishing structure from agency can social scientists begin to show how society takes on one form rather than another.

Archer makes a similar point about agency. When we talk of 'agency', we emphasise people's particular powers, such as their intentions to fulfil a specific wish, reach a particular goal, or reflect on and resist a particular challenge or dilemma. In Archer's view, it is not satisfactory to merely conflate these powers of agents with the causal properties of social structures (see Danermark et al., 2002, pp. 178–182). Indeed, Archer rails against any conflationist thinking that reduces a person to structural circumstances or argues that agents merely reproduce society through their unconscious social practices (including doxa or habitus). Instead, Archer argues that humans possess the power of reflexivity: consciously deliberating on their social circumstances, examining and evaluating their behaviour in light of personal concerns and structural conditions. From this perspective, Archer recovers agency from structure by suggesting that reflexivity plays a mediatory role: it allows people to monitor themselves in relation to their structural circumstances.

We must consider Archer's account of the 'internal conversation' to understand how this works. Archer (2003) argues that people exercise the power of reflexivity through the 'internal conversations' they conduct with and about themselves. This internal conversation is similar to William James's 'dialogical self' or what we might call 'self-talk' (see Chapter 5). It refers to people's inner speech to reason through their daily encounters and how people internally monitor their commitments and concerns. Archer argues that it is through internal conversation that people reflexively make their way through the world. Indeed, inner speech is what makes people 'active' as opposed to 'passive' agents. It involves delineating what a person cares about and relating this to their social context(s) to develop projects which guide the conduct of their lives. From this perspective, the internal conversation plays a fundamental role in shaping personhood and contributing to how people reflexively interact with the social world around them (Brock et al., 2016, p. xvii).

One final point. Archer argues that reflexivity is not a singular mode of deliberation practised more or less (as suggested by proponents of the concept of **reflexive modernisation**). Instead, Archer (2007, p. 93) distinguishes between four modalities of reflexivity that (begin to) account for the different strategies or capabilities that people use when making choices or evaluating their decisions:

- 'Communicative reflexivity' refers to people whose internal conversations require completion and confirmation by others before resulting in a course of action.
- 'Autonomous reflexivity' refers to people who sustain self-contained internal conversations leading directly to action.
- 'Meta-reflexivity' refers to people who are critically reflexive about their own internal conversations and critical too about effective action in society.
- 'Fractured reflexivity' refers to people whose internal conversations intensify their distress and disorientation rather than leading to purposeful courses of action.

Archer argues that these modalities reflect that the social influences the internal conversation, with each emerging to reflect aspects of an individual's biography, including their social background, vested interests, and personal concerns. At the same time, these modalities enable researchers to retain a sense of the diverse ways in which people (of similar backgrounds) deliberate over their social conduct. From this perspective, Archer recognises that people contemplate social structures *on their own terms*, exercising different modalities of reflexivity to mediate their causal properties.

Archer's response to the problem of structure and agency is to recognise that human beings and social structures have their own distinct existences and influences on social outcomes. What is critical for Archer is that these entities are not eliminated from the explanation of social behaviour nor conflated together, making it impossible to analyse their differences. Indeed, Archer suggests that we study the interaction of structure and agency over time to explain how social action reproduces or transforms pre-existing contexts. Archer strictly rejects any view of social action that denies the causal power of individual people and their reflexivity within this process. Equally, Archer (2000, p. 10) is critical of any theory that fails to recognise that 'our placement in society rebounds upon us, affecting the persons we become, but also more forcefully influencing the social identities which we can achieve'. Archer's four modalities of reflexivity conceptualise the internal and external consequences of the internal conversation for people and society (see also Brock et al., 2016, p. xviii).

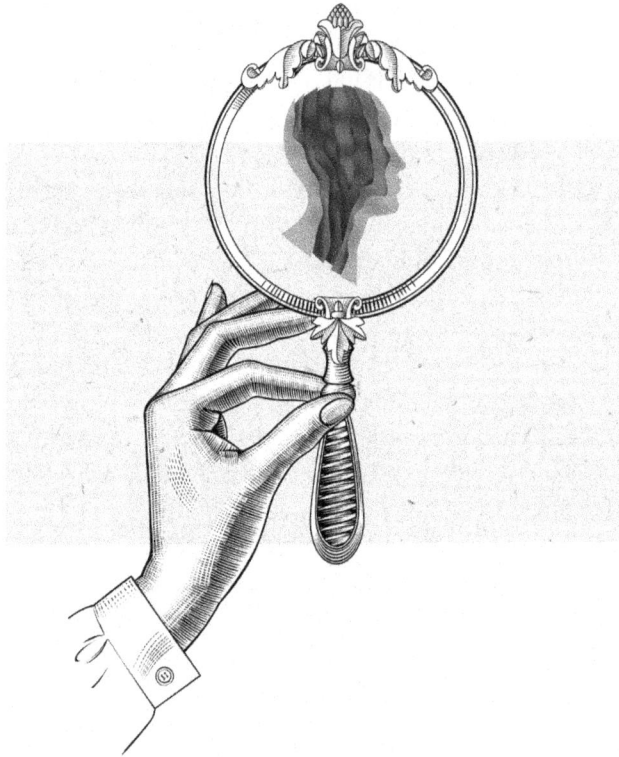

Figure 7.3   Reflexivity

In what ways do we reflect on and scrutinise our own behaviour? How does this help us to make choices and understand the reasons and structural circumstances behind them? By reflecting in this way, do we learn anything new or deeper about ourselves or society?

Focus on Facts

- Archer is an influential figure within critical realism, a philosophy of social science which tries to map the ontological character of social reality by conceptualising the causal (or 'generative') mechanisms that produce the facts and events that researchers can empirically examine.
- Archer's position is not without its critics (Akram and Hogan, 2015; Caetano, 2015; Farrugia and Woodman, 2015), who argue that the concept of reflexivity omits the role of dispositions derived from the habitus, thereby underplaying the influences of socialisation on social behaviour.

- Elder-Vass (2007b) attempts to reconcile the arguments of Archer and Bourdieu by suggesting that reflexive decision-making and dispositions are not mutually exclusive. Elder-Vass links dispositions to their neural base in human physiology, suggesting that they have emergent powers that may influence decision-making. Archer (2010) contests this position.

Case Study 7.2

Reflexivity and Educational Choice

Zoe Baker's (2019) article, 'Reflexivity, Structure and Agency: Using Reflexivity to Understand Further Education Students' Higher Education Decision-Making and Choices', presents a practical application of Archer's ideas. Drawing on various methods, including longitudinal semi-structured interviews, focus groups and audio diaries, Baker argues that Archer's modalities of reflexivity may be used to helpfully examine how young people make their educational choices and decisions. In particular, Baker shows that students adopt different modalities of reflexivity as a capability or strategy for deliberating enablements or constraints on their original intentions. For example, Baker offers the case of 'Noel', a student whose reflexive modalities shift as the context for his pursuit of a degree in higher education changes. As Baker (2019, p. 10) recalls:

> During his first year of his college studies, he demonstrated strong meta-reflexive motivations for his choice. Noel focuses on how elements of Physics are aligned with his self-perceived qualities, feeling that they were well suited to his 'inquisitive' and 'curious' disposition ... Noel made his [higher education] choices primarily consisting of 'Russell Groups'. His preferred choice was a Russell Group institution in the North, but he was uncertain of his likelihood of being awarded a place following the receipt of his AS-level results. In an attempt to compensate for his insufficient grades, Noel applied to outreach schemes delivered by his Russell Group choices ... [which provided benefits] such as extra consideration by admissions staff, as well as alternative offers.

According to Baker, Noel's reasoning demonstrates a shift towards autonomous reflexivity, in that autonomous reflexives are strategic when facing structural constraints. Noel's approach coveys this; he identifies and accesses the enablement of outreach schemes while trying to avoid the constraints of rejection by his preferred higher education institutions. From this perspective, Baker argues that Noel demonstrates a 'dual mode' of reflexivity: employing meta-reflexive tendencies when deciding on his degree subject but employing autonomous reflexive tendencies when strategically negotiating barriers to entry. Importantly, Baker (2019, p. 11) contends that not everyone will respond to these circumstances as Noel has: 'different individuals will not necessarily use the same reflexive modes as others as a means to cope and overcome situations that constrain them from reaching their goals'.

(Continued)

As such, Archer's work allows education research to account for the different ways in which students reflexively make choices about their educational futures. Baker argues that this is significant because, through Archer's modalities of reflexivity, education research can account for student decision-making without conflating it with structure. Students confront structural circumstances with personal concerns in mind, and, as such, their approaches are context-specific, where any given student is capable of multiple approaches. This position contrasts with Bourdieu, whose concept of habitus dominates education research through the understanding that student choices reflect various examples of social, cultural and economic capital (Baker, 2019, pp. 2–3). By utilising Archer, Baker suggests that research can avoid this determinism and produce essential insights into how students use reflexivity differently when facing similar circumstances that enable or constrain them into realising their higher education intentions. Indeed, Archer's work can draw attention to the enablements (such as outreach schemes) that assist students in making the 'right choices' for *them* in higher education.

Summary

- The 'problem of structure and agency' is a recurring issue within social theory, which raises important questions such as how social structures shape social behaviour, how agents reproduce or transform social structures, and how structure and agency merge (and whether they should).
- Pierre Bourdieu, Anthony Giddens and Margaret Archer are three prominent thinkers who offer different ways of conceptualising the relationship between structure and agency. Bourdieu and Giddens are 'structurationists' (emphasising that structure and agency merge at the point of practice). Archer is a 'poststructurationist' (emphasising that structure and agency must be kept analytically separate).
- Bourdieu reconciles the problem of structure and agency through the concept of habitus: the internalisation of social conditions into bodily and social practices.
- Giddens reconciles the problem of structure and agency through the concept of structuration: agents actively reproducing existing rules and resources through their social practices.
- Archer reconciles the problem of structure and agency through analytical dualism: to separate 'structure' and 'agency' and examine their interplay over time to account for their effects through distinct properties and powers.

Review Questions

- What is 'the problem of structure and agency'? Discuss with reference to the concepts of 'objectivism' and 'subjectivism' in social theory.

- Bourdieu argues that those possessing the appropriate type and amount of capital can dominate a particular field. What examples can you think of?
- What are the significant differences between Archer's view of structure and agency and those of Giddens and Bourdieu?

Annotated Reading

For a detailed look at the history of the problem of structure and agency and the similarities and differences between Giddens, Bourdieu and Archer, see John Parker's (2000) *Structuration* (Maidenhead: Open University Press).

Michael Grenfell's (2008) edited collection *Pierre Bourdieu: Key Concepts* (London: Routledge) provides a helpful introduction to Bourdieu's key ideas.

Rob Stones's (2005) *Structuration Theory* (London: Palgrave) remains an essential text for those seeking to further understand Giddens's theory of structuration.

Archer's interest in the problem of structure and agency spans almost four decades. A helpful introduction to and synopsis of Archer's key ideas is available in Tom Brock, Mark Carrigan and Graham Scambler's (2017) *Structure, Culture and Agency: Selected Papers of Margaret Archer* (London: Routledge).

For those looking for an accessible guide to critical realism, see Berth Danermark, Mats Ekstrom, Liselotte Jakobsen, and Jan Ch. Karlsson's (2002) *Explaining Society: Critical Realism in the Social Sciences* (London and New York: Routledge).

8

Feminism and Intersectionality

Chapter Objectives

This chapter will:

- Introduce feminist perspectives in social theory, including liberal, radical, Marxist, psychoanalytic, postmodern and Black feminism.
- Familiarise essential concepts, including patriarchy and intersectionality.
- Provide historical and contemporary examples of feminist politics.

Keywords

Feminism, equality, patriarchy, sexism, intersectionality, Black feminism

Introduction

How do feminists view the social world? What consequences does this perspective have for social theory and research? This chapter will introduce students to how feminist thinkers have sought to challenge social inequality and **patriarchy**. In particular, it will look at the similarities and differences between liberal, radical, Marxist, psychoanalytic and postmodern feminism and ask students to reflect on their respective political struggles through examples such as women's rights and domestic labour. This chapter will also consider intersectional perspectives, such as Black feminism, to show how relations of gender, race and class intersect to oppress women further. Examples from the Everyday Sexism Project and digital Black feminism will support students to see how society marginalises and disadvantages women.

A Brief History of Feminist Politics

We can suggest that the beginnings of feminism lie with the stirrings of 'first wave' feminists, such as English author Mary Wollstonecraft. Wollstonecraft's *A Vindication of the Rights of Women*, published in 1792, is an early example of feminist writing that seeks to challenge how society oppresses and subordinates women. Writing when the English education system prepared women for domestic roles and marriage only, Wollstonecraft calls for women to deserve the same fundamental rights and social and economic opportunities as men. Similarly, feminist writers and activists such as Barbara Bodichon, Bessie Rayner Parkes, Millicent Fawcett, Emmeline Pankhurst, Lucretia Coffin Mott, Sojourner Truth, Susan B. Anthony and Ida B. Wells were influential in the USA and the UK in fighting for social reforms, including suffrage (women's right to vote), abolitionism (ending slavery) and civil rights. These feminists were pioneers of these reforms, highlighting the contradictions between societal ideals of equality, on the one hand, and the misogynistic and racist structures and practices that were a daily reality for many, on the other.

'Second wave' feminism refers to the resurgence of feminist political action in several countries following the Second World War. It develops the focus on securing formal legal equality, as enshrined in voting rights, to recognise the broader structural and material factors in shaping women's oppression. Feminists such as Simone de Beauvoir, Betty Friedan, Gloria Steinem, Kate Millett, Carol Hanisch, Susan Brownmiller, bell hooks, Audre Lorde, Angela Davis and Alice Walker all sought to extend the scope of feminism to make equality fuller and more meaningful. Their activism was influential in raising consciousness about various issues, including inequalities in work and pay, access to reproductive health care and birth control, inequities in domestic labour, and discrimination based on gender, race and class. Several critical social movements also emerge during this time, including the National Organization for Women, the women's liberation movement, the civil rights movement, the National Black Feminist Organization, and the gay rights movement. By the end of the second wave, feminists were advancing women's interests in many aspects of contemporary life, and feminist politics became part of higher education, most notably through the teaching of feminist ideas within women's studies programmes at universities.

'Third wave' feminism describes the development of these struggles since the late 1980s. It reflects the impact of postmodernism on theories of society (see Chapter 6), encouraging people to deconstruct oppressive social categories while embracing diversity and cultural change. Tong (2009, p. 284) suggests that an essential characteristic of third-wave feminism is that it is eager to understand how gender oppression and other kinds of human oppression co-create and co-maintain each other. According to Tong (2009, p. 285), 'third-wave feminists stress that women and feminists come in many colours, ethnicities, nationalities, religions and cultural backgrounds … who represent a wide variety of multicultural perspectives'. Feminist schol ars such as Kimberlé Crenshaw, Judith Butler and Patricia Hill Collins capture this diversity by incorporating the idea of **intersectionality** into their work: a prism for understanding how different identities (such as race, class and gender) overlap to compound social injustices and human rights violations. This focus on diversity is also apparent in feminist punk culture in the 1990s, notably in the example of 'Riot Grrrl', a feminist movement that uses music to address issues such as rape, sexual harassment, racism, patriarchy, classicism and female empowerment. Importantly, these issues continue to inspire new generations of women's rights activists who now embrace popular culture and the Internet to invent new ways of thinking and doing feminism online. Laura Bates's (2014) Everyday Sexism Project is an excellent example of how today's feminists challenge **power** imbalances within contemporary culture (see Case study 8.1 below).

Finally, it is important to contest the very metaphor of feminist history as a series of successive 'waves'. Feminists suggest that this historical framing fails to make sense of the complexities of feminist history and often downplays its divisive nature. Indeed, Finlayson (2016, p. 55) characterises feminist history as neither linear nor one of steady progress but complete with many 'breaks and reversals, periods of backlash or co-option'. For example, talk of 'waves' often overlooks the political differences and disagreements within feminism, such as the marginalisation of Black feminist issues from the 'mainstream' movement or the role of colonialism in eroding women's status in Asia, Africa and Latin America. From this perspective, Delap (2020) calls for a global history of feminisms to capture the diversity of women's social and political demands outside of a (historically) white, middle-class and Euro-American historical framing. Indeed, it is crucial to recognise that, for many, feminism is not a unified political movement but a decentralised set of goals against specific experiences of different social, cultural and economic circumstances. One way to make sense of these experiences is to consider the different theoretical perspectives feminists use to conceptualise their subordination and emancipation.

Focus on Facts

Prominent among second-wave feminists is Simone de Beauvoir, whose two-volume book *The Second Sex* (1956/1949) reveals that societies historically attribute a secondary status to women. Famously, Beauvoir (1956/1949, p. 15) states:

> humanity is male and man defines women not in herself but as relative to him … She is defined and differentiated with reference to man and not he with reference to her; she is the incidental, the inessential as opposed to the essential. He is the Subject, he is the Absolute – she is the Other.

Through chapters that consider the experience of what it is like to be a woman (as a young girl, wife, lover and mother), Beauvoir reveals that men create values and practices that subordinate women by restricting their actions, representations and experiences. Indeed, Beauvoir's existentialism helps question whether women can genuinely experience themselves in a society where men confine them to certain traits, such as feminine beauty or dependence. This theme reappears throughout feminist writings.

Figure 8.1 Women as Other

In what ways are women often defined by their relationship to, or in opposition to, men? Think about the idea that it is men who create values and practices that try to control and structure women's actions.

Traditional Feminist Perspectives

A crucial beginning for understanding the different theoretical orientations of several feminisms lies in the differences between three major traditions: liberal, radical and Marxist feminism. Although these traditions are contestable and incomplete, they help mark a range of perspectives that provide a starting point for understanding how feminists conceptualise social inequality and propose solutions for its elimination.

Liberal Feminism

Liberal feminism is the most widely known form of feminist thought (Beasley, 1999, p. 51). This is because liberal feminism campaigns for equal opportunities between men and women and seeks to end the artificial barriers which prevent women's full participation in public life. As such, liberal feminism is the mainstream or moderate position within feminist thought, advocating for all kinds of rights, whether political (e.g., the right to vote), economic (financial independence), equality (equal pay legislation) or reproductive (legal rights to contraception, abortion and fertility treatment). Significantly, liberal feminism dates back at least to the time of Wollstonecraft, when there was a critical concern with humanist values, such as individual autonomy and the freedom of women from restriction by men and the state. This humanism sees liberal feminists emphasise not difference but 'sameness' between the sexes, arguing that, as rational social beings, men and women are essentially the same. Liberal feminists view any differences between the sexes as the product of defective, biased or ideological constructions that deliberately seek to disadvantage women somehow (see Abbott et al., 2005, p. 29). From this perspective, liberal feminists ask for equality of opportunity and equal treatment between men and women:

> [Liberal feminism] says: we deserve to be equal with you, for we are in fact the same. We possess the same capabilities; but this fact has been hidden, or these abilities have, while still potentially ours, been socialised, educated, 'out'. (Evans, 1995, p. 13, cited in Abbott et al., 2005, p. 32)

In arguing for equal rights, the key point here is that liberal feminism campaigns to liberate women from laws and practices that treat them as different and place them at a disadvantage to men. They also seek widespread legal and cultural changes to prevent discrimination against women, for example, by providing paid maternity leave and equal pay in the workplace. As a result, women owe liberal feminists many of the political, educational, economic and reproductive rights they currently enjoy (though, as debates over abortion in the USA in 2022 show, such rights are never fully assured).

Liberal feminism is not without its critics. For example, the Black feminist bell hooks (1984), in the book *Feminist Theory: From Margin to Centre*, argues that liberal feminism has a history of presenting women's concerns from the perspective of white, upper- and middle-class mothers and wives. hooks suggests that liberal feminists gloss over the differences and concerns of Black women, particularly poor ones. Indeed, in a particularly withering critique of the liberal feminist Betty Friedan (author of *The Feminist Mystique*), hooks (1984, pp. 1–2) notes:

> Friedan concludes her first chapter by stating: 'We can no longer ignore that voice within women that says: "I want something more than my husband and my children and my house."' That 'more' she defined as careers. She did not discuss who would be called in to take care of the children and maintain the home if more women like herself were freed from their house labor and given equal access with white men to the professions. She did not speak of the needs of women without men, without children, without homes. She ignored the existence of all non-white women and poor white women. She did not tell readers whether it was more fulfilling to be a maid, a babysitter, a factory worker, a clerk, or a prostitute, than to be a leisure class housewife. She made her plight and the plight of white women like herself synonymous with a condition affecting all American women.

What hooks is suggesting here is that liberal feminists fail to include the experiences of all women when conceptualising experiences of social inequality. Indeed, hooks insists that if feminism is ever to fulfil its revolutionary potential, then liberal feminists must redefine their theory to include the lives and ideas of women on the margins of society.

Radical Feminism

Radical feminists are sceptical of how social reforms will emancipate women from oppression. This is because they see patriarchy as the foundational structure of domination and submission through which men learn how to exercise control and power over women. Radical feminists seek to raise consciousness about patriarchy to reveal the systematic ways in which men oppress women because of their sex. For example, radical feminists employ patriarchy to trace the historical emergence of systems of male domination, such as religion, the state or the household. They also explore the sexual division of labour and how it makes women unequal to men in productive and reproductive work. Radical feminists also criticise the deep-rooted nature of women's sexual oppression by internalising social patterns in psychology and the unconscious (see Stacey, 1993, cited in Beasley, 1999, p. 55).

It is also vital to note that one of the most significant aspects of patriarchy is violence. Radical feminists examine the violent practices of men and male-dominated organisations against women. For example, Susan Brownmiller's (1975) book *Against Our Will: Men, Women and Rape* identifies and challenges many deeply ingrained myths about rape: 'that women cry rape with ease and glee' (p. 387) or 'as an instrument of vengeance' (p. 228); 'that rape is not a crime of irrational, impulsive, uncontrollable lust, but is a deliberate, hostile, violent act of degradation and possession' (p. 391); and '[t]he dogma that women are masochistic by nature and crave the "lust of pain"' (p. 315) or invite rape. Brownmiller reframes rape as an act of patriarchal power and argues that it is a conscious process by men to intimidate women and keep them in a state of fear. Of course, violence need not take this form of overt physical cruelty. It is also implicit in examples of exploitation and social control, whether through sexual harassment in the workplace (Mackinnon, 1979), financial and economic coercion (Singh, 2021), misogynistic standards in beauty and fashion (Jeffreys, 2005) or sexism within psychotherapy and gynaecology (Daly, 1978). As such, radical feminists challenge men's patriarchal power as a group wherever men seek to control women's behaviour and life chances.

This understanding of patriarchy is also why radical feminists reject the idea that men and women are 'the same'. Radical feminism encourages women to recognise and celebrate their strength and values, rejecting androgyny as a distortion of women's biological nature. Instead, radical feminists seek to establish a sisterhood of trust and support in which women work together to confront patriarchal power and reclaim the valuable qualities specific to women. There is a degree of separatism within radical feminism as women may withdraw from any facet of patriarchal domination, including intimate relationships with men (Abbott et al., 2005, p. 34). Importantly, this intense interest in asserting differences between men and women (to recover what is good about being a woman) does, in some cases, place radical feminism in contention with transgender identity and rights. As Hines (2020, pp. 35–36) notes, being transgender relates to various practices that question traditional ways of seeing gender and its relationship to sex and sexuality. However, radical feminist texts, such as Janice Raymond's (1979) *The Transsexual Empire* (cited in Hines, 2020, p. 35), maintain that sex is biologically determined and that transgender men and women reproduce gender stereotypes and forms of male power and privilege. Hines (2020, pp. 35–36) highlights how trans activists and scholars have spoken out critically against this perspective, arguing that it is an example of transphobia within anti-trans radical feminist writing. Hines (2020, pp. 35–36) asserts that feminists must continue to deconstruct the sex/gender binary if feminism is to fully account for the complexities of bodies, identities and experiences while productively agitating for social change on behalf of all women.

Marxist Feminism

Where radical feminists position patriarchy as the overarching structure of women's oppression, Marxist – or more broadly, socialist – feminists argue that it is capitalism that structures gender inequality. Marxist feminists see the accumulation and unequal distribution of wealth (through economic class relations) as a major source of women's oppression and subordination. A major reference point here is the work of Friedrich Engels (2010/1884), who suggests that capitalism exploits women through the institution of marriage. More specifically, Engels argues that, through marriage, men subordinate women into domestic roles that take control over their work and reproductive capabilities. This arrangement, Engels suggests, ensures men's dominance over women and provides the ruling class with a steady structure of inheritance that protects the accumulation of wealth and ownership of private property. From this perspective, women's subordination to the family and household structures maintains the inequalities of the capitalist economic system. Indeed, Engels argues that women's employment will help undermine the patriarchal domestic sphere while also creating new relations of solidarity between women and men to challenge the broader exploitation of workers within capitalist workplaces.

Engels' arguments were influential on the socialist feminism of Evelyn Reed (1970), who argues that with the rise of capitalism and the nuclear family,

> [w]omen were then given two dismal alternatives. They could either seek a husband as provider and be penned up thereafter as housewives in city tenements or apartments to raise the generation of wage slaves. Or the poorest and most unfortunate could go as marginal workers into the mills and factories (along with children) and be sweated as the most downtrodden and underpaid section of the labor force.

Reed resists the view that these alternatives are solely the result of patriarchy (i.e., men oppressing women *as* women), arguing that the primary enemy of women is the ruling class. Indeed, Reed (1970) was particularly critical of how ruling-class women contribute to reproducing economic inequality:

> Will the wives of bankers, generals, corporation lawyers and big industrialists be firmer allies of women fighting for liberation than working-class men, Black and white, who are fighting for theirs?

As such, Reed suggests that women must join men, together with other oppressed members of society, to create a combined anti-capitalist movement that represents the broadest range of working-class people.

One of the major criticisms of Marxist feminist theory is that it places insufficient emphasis on how men oppress women, particularly as they benefit from women's unpaid domestic labour and continue to subordinate women in ways not caused by class division (e.g., sexual harassment or violence). In response, socialist feminists began to assert that patriarchy and capitalism correspond in various ways to deepen women's oppression. For example, Juliet Mitchell (1971, cited in Tong, 2009, pp. 4–5), in *Woman's Estate*, argues that a range of structures shape women's oppression, from economic structures (as Marxists argue) to structures of reproduction and sexuality (as radical feminists argue) and structures of socialisation and education (as liberal feminists argue). Similarly, Alison Jaggar argues that where capitalism exploits women as workers, patriarchy oppresses women *as women*, that is, it affects women's identity, not just their productive activities. Adapting the concept from Marx, Jaggar (1983) argues that women will always be 'alienated' in ways that men are not. This is because men can appropriate women's bodies for pleasures and social practices that deny women the agency to experience their sexuality or child-rearing and intellectual capacities (Tong, 2009, pp. 113–115).

Figure 8.2   Patriarchy

How does society subjugate and oppress women? Reflect on how patriarchal structures attempt to 'step on' and 'crush' women's liberties and expression.

Finally, there is also the work of Iris Marion Young (1981), Heidi Hartmann (1981), and Sylvia Walby (1990), who draw on the concept of patriarchy to reveal how male power operates through the sexual division of labour, in both the home and the workplace (see also Tong, 2009, pp. 115–120). These socialist feminists reveal that women experience patriarchy in many ways, such as through uncompensated domestic work, sexual harassment in the workplace, and men's control over women's culture and sexuality. In their view, the history of women's oppression is broader and more complex than one of either class relations or sexual oppression. Indeed, these theorists draw out the historical tensions between advancing capitalist economies and misogynistic views about women's domestic duties and economic independence.

Content Warning

This case study includes examples of sexual harassment and sexually explicit and violent language, which you may find troubling or distressing.

Case Study 8.1

Everyday Sexism

The British feminist writer Laura Bates is the originator of the Everyday Sexism Project, a website that documents testimonials of sexism worldwide (https://everydaysexism.com). Bates startedw the project after experiencing a series of sexist incidents, from street harassment to workplace discrimination and sexual assault. After speaking to friends, family and even strangers in the supermarket, Bates realised that these experiences constitute a formative part of women's everyday reality. She writes:

> Every single woman I spoke to had a story. But not from five years ago, or ten. From last week, or yesterday, or 'on my way here today'. And they weren't just random one-off events ... This inequality, this pattern of casual intrusion whereby women could be leered at, touched, harassed and abused without a second thought, was *sexism*: implicit, explicit, common-or-garden and deep-rooted sexism, pretty much everywhere you'd care to look. (Bates, 2014, p. 11)

Like Bates, these women also found it difficult to speak about their experiences of sexism publicly. Bates (2014) suggests that contemporary culture makes it easy for people to readily dismiss complaints about sexism either as a 'joke' or 'banter' or as evidence that someone is 'uptight', 'humourless' and 'frigid'. In response, Bates started the website to give women a voice and space to share their stories. Indeed, within months of the site's initial launch, thousands of entries appeared, testifying to the sheer scale and breadth of the problem. Some examples include (Bates, 2014, pp. 22, 34, 99, 107, 116, 189, 267):

Called a prude for objecting to Porn Fridays where female colleagues' faces were photo-shopped onto porn pics.

Had a frightening experience with a drunk man muttering threats while sitting across from me on a train, and then following me off and throughout the station, until I literally had to run and hide to lose him. When I later told my boyfriend what happened he said: 'well I'm glad you're home safe now' and completely dismissed it.

My younger brother's 13. He had his friends round last weekend and I couldn't believe it when I heard them sitting in the front room discussing girls in their class in 3 categories 'frigid', 'sluts' and 'would like to rape'.

Told that being groped/touched/having a crotch rubbed against you unwantedly is 'a normal part of university nightlife.'

The boys who worked behind the Student Union bar used to play 'fuck a fresher' at freshers week. There was a points scoring system … bonus points if you brought the girl's knickers in, took her virginity.

Saw my hours cut every time I complained to a manager about the co-worker who sexually harassed me.

Ex told me white guys'll only date me to annoy their parents.

Bates argues that these testimonials reveal that society normalises prejudice and sexual violence against women. The Everyday Sexism Project sets out to raise awareness about these issues so people can stand up for social justice. Indeed, Bates (2014) argues that the project gives women and men the power to say 'no' to sexism by naming and identifying its indicators. Bates (2014) also suggests that the project draws attention to the need for a far more comprehensive and mandatory sex-and-relationships education, covering consent and respect, domestic violence and rape. Finally, stories from the project are helping to inform the work of the British Transport Police in how they detect sexual offences and how ministers and members of Parliament tackle sexual harassment through better policies in schools, universities, businesses and public spaces.

A related example is the #MeToo movement – a hashtag that went viral on social media platforms in 2017 as survivors of sexual harassment, sexual assault, and sexual bullying began to bond and share their stories online. The phrase has its origins in the activism of Tarana Burke, a women's advocate in the United States who coined the term in 2006 to let victims of sexual violence know that they are not alone. The term reappeared in 2017 as movie celebrities drew

(Continued)

attention to the accusations of predatory behaviour by the influential Hollywood producer Harvey Weinstein. Since then, the #MeToo movement has become a global phenomenon, affirming the widespread nature of sexism in society and the need to instil anti-harassment policies and new legal standards in work and civic life.

Psychoanalytic Feminism

Where liberal, radical and Marxist feminists root explanations and solutions for women's oppression in macropolitical and economic structures, psychoanalytic feminists suggest that oppression begins with the psyche and how women think about themselves. As Chapter 3 discusses, psychoanalysis is a school of psychology that studies human behaviour through theories of the unconscious and childhood sexual development. Psychoanalytic feminists develop these ideas to argue that gender inequality begins with early childhood socialisation, particularly as children experience gender roles and expectations through constructs such as 'femininity' and 'masculinity'. Indeed, psychoanalytic feminists argue that these constructs reinforce power imbalances between the sexes, creating and sustaining patriarchy.

A central topic of psychoanalytic feminism is care-giving. Early theorists, such as Dorothy Dinnerstein (1977) and Nancy Chodorow (1978), argue that patriarchal power begins with 'mothering' as an exclusive act of child-rearing by women. Drawing on the work of Freud, they suggest that this division of labour socialises children (on conscious and subconscious levels) to internalise power inequities between the sexes. Girls associate femininity with nurturing and primary care-giving, while boys associate masculinity with independence from and, yet, dominance over, women and the household. Dinnerstein and Chodorow suggest that 'dual parenting', which encourages men to take on more care-giving responsibilities, will unsettle this ideology and psychology of male dominance. Indeed, by 'feminising men' through changes to existing social arrangements (see Beasley, 1999, p. 67), these feminists aim to undermine the deep psychic structures that organise sexual oppression.

Also of interest to psychoanalytic feminists is the work of Jacques Lacan and Jacques Derrida (see Chapter 6). They argue that language is vital in structuring human **subjectivity**. Psychoanalytic feminists, such as Luce Irigaray (1985/1974) and Hélène Cixous (1976), develop these ideas by arguing that Western languages, in all their features, position men as the prime signifier of meaning and social relations. They offer the term 'phallogocentrism' to express this idea, suggesting that masculinity (and male genitalia, at least symbolically) sits at the core of Western linguistic and cultural assumptions. In response, Irigaray and Cixous call for *écriture féminine* – feminine writing – in which women become active subjects in constructing their subjectivity. They argue that women, in writing about themselves and their bodies, can subvert male-dominated ways of thinking, speaking and acting towards women. Indeed, these authors insist that feminine writing is a means for women to deconstruct, destabilise and decentre the idea that masculinity is the universal referent of human experience.

Postmodern Feminism

As Chapter 6 discusses, postmodern social theory emerges as part of a broader movement sceptical towards truth and the authorities that present (scientific) knowledge as objective fact rather than discourse. Postmodern feminists, such as Judith Butler, develop this thinking by challenging the view that the categories of sex and gender are in some way 'natural'. For example, in *Gender Trouble*, Butler (1999, p. 10) writes:

> Can we refer to a 'given' sex or a 'given' gender without first inquiring into how sex and/or gender is given, through what means? And what is 'sex' anyway? Is it natural, anatomical, chromosomal, or hormonal, and how is a feminist critic to assess the scientific discourses which purport to establish such 'facts' for us? Does sex have a history? Does each sex have a different history, or histories? Is there a history of how the duality of sex was established, a genealogy that might expose the binary options as a variable construction? Are the ostensibly natural facts of sex discursively produced by various scientific discourses in the service of other political and social interests?

Butler's point here is that sex and gender, rather than being natural or essential qualities following biological sex, are constructs that grow out of, reinforce and are reinforced by societal and political discourses. These discourses create the illusion of binary sex – the idea that a person is either born male or female with 'naturally' corresponding characteristics.

In Butler's view, this binary has no inherent truth – biology does not determine whether men are assertive or women kind – yet social discourses do legitimate expectations around how men and women should act. From this perspective, Butler asserts that sex and gender are not things that people 'have' but things people 'do'. Gender is a performative accomplishment: a set of stylised acts, bodily gestures and movements taken together to produce the 'illusion of an abiding gendered self' (Butler, 1999, p. 179). In other words, Butler suggests that sex and gender are not categories fixed in nature or biology but brought into existence by people drawing on existing social and political discourses. Like Foucault, Butler suggests that these discourses have the power to shape our understandings of sex and gender by limiting the 'scripts' from which actors perform. Of course, people can also actively resist these discourses, revealing the multiple meanings and shifting interpretations behind the expressions of gender identity.

Butler's insistence that sex and gender are social constructs is also relevant when considering postmodern theorising about sexuality – that is, **queer theory**. Along with other feminist writers, such as Eve Sedgwick and Teresa de Lauretis (cited in Beasley, 1999, p. 96), Butler employs a Foucauldian approach to reject any notion of a centred, stable sexual identity. According to Beasley (1999, pp. 96–97), these writers reject any notion of an 'essence' which is fixed either biologically or through social norms:

> They assert an antagonism to (biological or social) essentialism and a corresponding radical social constructivism in relation to sexuality/sexual identity which is

associated with the term 'queer theory'. Instead of assuming that one's (sexual) identity is singular and fixed, this grouping of feminists perceive identity as more incoherent and malleable, as constructed. Their approach involves a preference for considering (sexual) identity in terms of plurality and disaggregation, in terms of identities and differences.

From this perspective, queer theorists do not seek to define or categorise sexual identity (as typical of science) but research the genealogies of various constructions of selfhood. In keeping with Nietzsche and Foucault's method, these genealogies reveal the constitution of sexuality by power relations, which constrain and enable new kinds of relationships and expressions of love and desire (Beasley, 1999, p. 97). By drawing attention to this 'elasticity' of sexual identity, feminists use queer theory to destabilise fixed assumptions about women's sexual practices and resist prevailing sexual hierarchies.

Finally, these debates are also relevant to science and how its methodologies and politics (as a discourse) reproduce gendered categories. Prominent here is the work of the feminist Donna Haraway (1988a; 1988b), who exposes the subjective and personal agendas that often underwrite the 'objective' knowledge claims of the natural sciences. Haraway accuses scientific disciplines, such as primatology, biology and anthropology, of adopting a 'disembodied vision' – the idea that scientists claim a 'view from nowhere' as if they can detach from their research and remain completely neutral. Haraway argues that this perspective fails to recognise the role of white male dominance in constructing scientific knowledge, which continues to reproduce racial and gender inequalities. In the essay 'Situated Knowledges', Haraway (1988b) develops this point, arguing that scientific objectivity is a 'god trick' played upon the world to mask prejudice. Scientists occupy a space of political privilege in which they can objectify bodies without being seen or reflexively examined. The problem with this, Haraway asserts, is that science is free to reproduce binary classifications (e.g., 'male–female', 'sex–gender', 'nature–culture') as universal givens. Echoing Butler, Haraway argues that feminist politics can deconstruct these classifications to show that scientific discourses engender performativity for power and social control reasons. In 'A Cyborg Manifesto', Haraway (1991/1985) argues that new media and communication technologies will help break down these classifications even further, affording new opportunities for people to (re-)create themselves out of their otherness, difference and specificity (see also Chapter 10).

Black Feminism

Black feminism concerns the experiences of Black women as a means to understand their position concerning racism, sexism and class privilege within society. It has its origins in the activism of Black activists in the 1850s, such as Sojourner Truth, who argued that issues of race, such as the abolition of slavery, are inseparable from issues of gender, such as women's rights. The activism of this time has become the source of many intellectual, philosophical and political practices, which draw on Black women's lived experiences to challenge racist, sexist and classist discrimination in society. According to Patricia Hill Collins, there are at least four major themes in the construction of Black feminist thought (see Taylor, 1998, pp. 234–235):

- Black women empower themselves by creating self-definitions and self-valuations that enable them to establish positive, multiple images and repeal negative, controlling representations of Black womanhood.
- Black women confront and dismantle the overarching and interlocking structures of domination regarding race, class and gender oppression.
- Black women intertwine intellectual thought and political activism.
- Black women recognise a distinct cultural heritage that gives them the energy and skills to resist and transform daily discrimination.

Collins argues that these themes emerge from a 'Black women's standpoint' – an epistemological perspective – that involves self-reflection about Black women's lived experiences. Writing of America, Collins (2000, pp. 25–26) outlines some of these experiences:

> Despite differences of age, sexual orientation, social class, region, and religion, U.S. Black women encounter societal practices that restrict us to inferior housing, neighborhoods, schools, jobs, and public treatment and hide this differential consideration behind an array of common beliefs about Black women's intelligence, work habits, and sexuality. These common challenges in turn result in recurring patterns of experiences for individual group members. For example, African-American women from diverse backgrounds report similar treatment in stores. Not every *individual* Black woman consumer need experience being followed in a store as a potential shoplifter, ignored while others are waited on first, or seated near restaurant kitchens and rest rooms, for African-American women as a collectivity to recognize that differential *group* treatment is operating.

Collins's argument here is that the experiences of Black women – which can be very diverse – offer feminists a vital departure point in understanding the different struggles of Black women while also recognising the commonality of Black women's shared history. Collins (2000, p. 72) argues that examples of these shared struggles include the need to resist 'controlling images' and negative stereotypes of Black women, which represent them as outsiders or 'Others' of society. Black feminism then seeks to debunk representations of Black women from the standpoint of (white, Eurocentric) men and support Black women to vocalise their (diverse) experiences of and responses to discrimination.

Another important aspect of Black feminist thought is its critical relationship with mainstream feminist theory. While liberal and radical feminists consider women in general to be an oppressed group, Black feminists argue that this perspective ignores women's differences. For example, bell hooks (1984) argues that mainstream feminism largely ignores women's differences, presenting feminist issues solely from a white, middle-class, heterosexual perspective. hooks argues that this attitude is assimilationist, overlooking how sexist and racist attitudes, class privilege, and homophobia divide women. In response, hooks argues that Black feminists demystify the idea of a 'common oppression' by looking at the varied and complex social reality of women's lives.

This theme carries into the activism and legal scholarship of Kimberlé Crenshaw (1989). Crenshaw argues that the law discriminates against Black women in ways not the same as against white women or Black men. This is because Black women are affected by the intersectionality of two primary sources of oppression: race *and* gender. Crenshaw describes employment discrimination-based lawsuits to illustrate this point, arguing that there are numerous examples where a failure to understand intersectional issues leads to the rejection of Black women's complaints. For example, in one case, *DeGraffenreid* v. *General Motors*, Crenshaw (1989, pp. 141–142) writes:

> The district court granted summary judgment for the defendant, rejecting the plaintiffs' attempt to bring a suit not on behalf of Blacks or women, but specifically on behalf of Black women ... Although General Motors did not hire Black women prior to 1964, the court noted that 'General Motors has hired ... female employees for a number of years prior to the enactment of the Civil Rights Act of 1964.' Because General Motors did hire women – albeit *white women* – during the period that no Black women were hired, there was, in the court's view, no sex discrimination that the seniority system could conceivably have.

What this case implies, Crenshaw (1989, p. 143) argues, is that the law only protects Black women when their experiences coincide with the interests of white women or Black men. There was no term to describe the double set of prejudices that affect Black women's employment opportunities. Indeed, the law does not recognise or understand that Black women's lived experiences reflect racial and gender-based issues. Crenshaw (1991) argues that the same issue affects cases of violence against Black women – that single-issue analyses marginalise Black women's experiences of the gendered *and* racial dimensions of rape and domestic abuse.

What Black feminism offers, then, is a means to unearth, critique and challenge the forces of gendered racism. It confronts white patriarchy but is also critical of misogyny and sexual violence within the Black community. In each case, it offers feminists a way to vocalise their experiences of and responses to oppression while contributing to creating more humane societies (see also Luna and Pirtle, 2022).

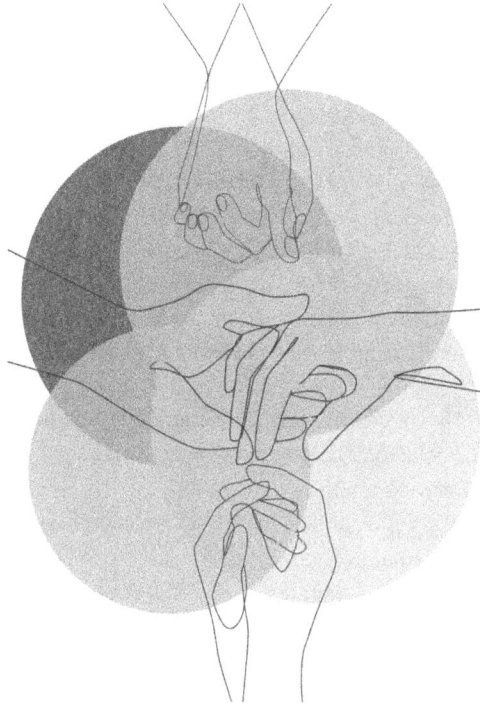

Figure 8.3 Intersectionality

Consider how people's historical and structural positions (based on race, class, gender, etc.) shape their experiences of social injustice and how they mobilise resistance.

Case Study 8.2

Digital Black Feminism

Researchers must recognise and engage with the work of digital Black feminists who challenge the disproportionate impact digital technologies have on Black women. Safiya Noble's (2018) book *Algorithms of Oppression* is a good example. Noble explains that Internet search engines, like Google, are not an innocent or neutral technology through which to search for information. Instead, they are designed and maintained by programmers – predominantly white heterosexual males – who have prejudices and motivations that skew the representations of Black women on the Internet. Noble offers some examples here:

(Continued)

- Googling 'Black girls' yields pornographic websites and escort-related services among its top listings. The same is also true of searches for 'Asian girls', 'Asian Indian girls', 'Hispanic girls', 'Latina girls' and 'American Indian girls' but not 'white girls'.
- Google image searches for 'Black girls' return hypersexualised and commodified representations of African-American women.
- When searching the phrase 'why are Black women so…', Google autosuggest results include 'angry', 'loud', 'mean', 'attractive', 'lazy', 'annoying', 'confident', 'sassy', 'insecure' and 'bitter'.
- Googling 'unprofessional hairstyles for work' features all Black women, while 'professional hairstyles for work' only features white women.
- Google video search results on 'Black girls' return a range of negative stereotypes about African-American women, including acts of violence and theft.

While it may be possible to 'fix' these individual incidents of racist and sexist discrimination, Noble suggests that the historical, social, political and economic processes of the Internet will continue to marginalise Black women. Drawing on Black feminist thought, Noble argues that it is impossible to decouple racist and patriarchal representations of Black women from capitalist interests. Indeed, Google's algorithms reflect a market economy that structures and presents knowledge to generate profit through ad-driven, click-based search results. From this perspective, Internet companies will always benefit from creating media spectacles, no matter how divisive or devastating the consequences. As such, Noble argues that digital Black feminists must resist and mobilise collectives that dismantle these systems of exploitation while working towards an ethical algorithmic future.

Another example of digital Black feminism is Kishonna Gray's (2020) book *Intersectional Tech*, which interrogates the marginalisation of Black women in digital gaming through intersections of race, gender, sexuality and (dis)ability. Gray argues that digital games are a space where the normalisation of whiteness and masculinity inevitably leads to the isolation, exclusion and punishment of Black women. In one compelling example, Gray (2020, p. 147) recalls her personal experiences of playing *Gears of War* online, in which criticism of her in-game performance quickly deteriorates into racist and sexist slurs:

> I start off by apologizing for my failures and pledge to do better. However, this conversation shifts away from my poor performance within battle to attacks against me as a person …
> 'Wait wait wait. You're not just any girl. You're black. Get this black bitch off my team. Did you spend all your welfare check buying this game? Why aren't you doing what you love? Get back to your crack pipe with your crack babies.'

Gray argues that these slurs are an example of the 'misogynoir' that characterises digital gaming culture, in which men regularly project negative stereotypes and tropes onto Black women. Gray argues that misogynoir is not limited to examples of white supremacy and anti-Black racism. Instead, Black masculinity and patriarchy also play a role in normalising the gendered and racial hierarchies in digital gaming, often through the sexualisation and objectification of Black women. Gray argues that testifying to these experiences is an essential tool in Black women's activism and can help establish intersectional counter-publics.

Summary

- Feminism has its origins in a series of 'waves' of political action that challenge various manifestations of social inequality and patriarchy. This metaphor of waves is problematic, downplaying the divisive and intersectional nature of feminist politics.
- Different theoretical perspectives inform feminist politics, from liberal, radical and Marxist theories to psychoanalytic, postmodern and Black feminist theories. These perspectives draw out different feminist issues, from women's rights and social inequality to resisting patriarchy and identifying intersectional causes of oppression.
- Contemporary examples of feminist theory and politics include analyses of everyday sexism, algorithmic bias, and racism online.

Review Questions

- Describe the different 'waves' of feminist politics concerning its diverse and contested history.
- To what extent do the concerns of liberal, radical and Marxist feminists remain today? Discuss with reference to examples of feminist activism.
- 'Women experience oppression in different ways.' What evidence can you provide to support this argument?

Annotated Reading

For a detailed look at feminist thought and its relationship to politics, see Rosemarie Tong's (2009) *Feminist Thought: A More Comprehensive Introduction* (3rd edition) (Boulder, CO: Westview Press).

Manon Garcia (2021) examines the challenging question of 'what role do women play in the perpetuation of patriarchy?' in *We Are Not Born Submissive: How Patriarchy Shapes Women's Lives* (Princeton, NJ: Princeton University Press).

For those looking to consider the impact of feminism on (digital) media, see Claire Sedgwick's (2020) *Feminist Media: From Second Wave to the Digital Age* (Lanham, MD: Rowman and Littlefield).

Zakiya Luna and Whitney N. Laster Pirtle's (2022) edited collection *Black Feminist Sociology: Perspectives and Practice* (New York and Abingdon: Routledge) offers contemporary examples of Black feminist struggles towards social justice.

Catherine Steele's (2021) *Digital Black Feminism* (New York: New York University Press) offers an insightful history of Black feminist techno culture and its ability to challenge patriarchy and white supremacy, particularly within the United States.

9

Postcolonial Theory

Chapter Objectives

This chapter will:

- Introduce postcolonial perspectives in social theory through Franz Fanon, Edward Said, Homi Bhabha and Gayatri Spivak.
- Familiarise essential concepts, including colonialism, imperialism, decolonisation, Orientalism and the subaltern.
- Provide historical and contemporary examples of postcolonial theory and activism.

Keywords

Colonialism, imperialism, decolonisation, Orientalism, subaltern, apartheid, epistemic violence

Introduction

This chapter introduces students to postcolonial thinkers who have sought to critique the global inequalities forged by the colonial empires of Anglo-European societies in the past. In particular, it will support students to reflect critically on social scientific knowledge (including social theory!) and its historical relation to imperialism. Starting with the arguments and examples of 'first-wave' thinkers, such as Frantz Fanon, students will see the importance of early anti-colonial activism in establishing a political response to the racism embedded within colonial states *and* the need to problematise European philosophy and its relationship to imperial domination. Through examples of orientalism, this chapter will introduce students to how 'second-wave' thinkers, such as Edward Said, critique Western **discourse** for naturalising social inequalities between the coloniser and colonised. Examples from American foreign policy will show how Western discourse oppresses today. Finally, students will also learn of the Subaltern Studies Group who argue that historical writings of colonialism often repress the voices and experiences of disenfranchised groups, such as the poor and women.

Colonialism, Imperialism and Decolonisation

Postcolonial theory emerges within the context of two significant historical developments. The first is European colonialism: a period in which European nations, such as Britain, France, Spain, Belgium and the Netherlands, extended their control over people of other societies by establishing settler colonies in regions such as Africa, Asia and the Americas. These colonies were a means for these nations to secure economic wealth by creating new international trade routes or securing the natural resources and labour of different lands and people. One example is the construction of sugar plantations in Jamaica, Barbados and other smaller islands by British colonists in the mid-seventeenth century. These colonists adopted a model of transporting and using enslaved Africans to plant and harvest sugar in favourable environmental conditions at minimal financial cost. Many British elites made their fortunes by exploiting enslaved people and foreign land while contributing to destroying the islands' indigenous population and culture. Indeed, a key characteristic of colonialism is the replacement of indigenous populations with an invasive settler society that maintains and protects lucrative commercial operations while generating wealth for merchants and influential business owners (such as the ruling class in the British political system).

'Colonialism' closely relates to another fundamental concept: **imperialism**. Imperialism describes the broader ideological project that seeks to use military, political or economic force to exercise control over a foreign land or people. According to Young (2016, pp. 16–17), imperialism is not strictly concerned with the issue of colonial settlement or the direct conquest or political control of another country. Instead, imperialism refers to the larger structure of **hegemony** (see Chapter 2) that legitimates the continuing exploitation of foreign nations for wealth and **power**. One example of modern imperialism is the United States, which uses its economic, cultural and militaristic influence to promote its interests and position as a global 'superpower'. Indeed, US diplomacy continues to focus on controlling the economic resources of other nations through institutions such as the International Monetary Fund and the World Bank. These institutions intervene in the governance of heavily indebted countries by imposing financial regulations that result in profitable loans and assets for imperialist powers. From this perspective, debt servicing becomes a way for the USA to maintain economic dominance by making other nations dependent on foreign financial assistance. US imperialism also comes through aggressive military interventions, such as the US-led invasion of Iraq in 2003 and the broader 'war on terror' from 2001 onwards. Here, the USA not only displays its military power to secure absolute control over strategic resources in other countries but also establishes global political influence.

The second significant historical development is decolonisation: a period in which former European colonies achieve independence through acts of resistance and self-governance. Resistance to colonial rule grew as the remaining colonial powers lost much of their reach and status towards the end of the Second World War. Within this context, there were several mass revolutionary movements in the colonial world, some of which involved violent conflict. Of particular note is the Algerian War of 1954–1962 which led to Algeria winning its independence back from France, but at the cost of many lives. The outbreak of war was partly due to an increasing resentment of the **subjugation** of Muslim-Arab Algerians by French authorities, including deplorable living conditions and open discrimination. Other examples include the decolonisation of India from British rule in 1947, following prolonged non-violent civil disobedience by Mahatma Gandhi, and anti-colonial rebellions against the British throughout the Caribbean, resulting in independence from 1962 onwards. Importantly, this anticolonial activism saw its intellectual expression through crucial works, such as W.E.B. Du Bois's (2007/1903) *The Souls of Black Folk*, Gandhi's (2021/1909) *Indian Home Rule*, C.L.R. James's (1989/1938), *The Black Jacobins*, Aimé Césaire's (2013/1956) *Return to My Native Land* and Franz Fanon's (2008/1952) *Black Skin, White Masks* (to name a few). These texts are examples of 'first wave' postcolonial theory, offering insights into the experience of colonial domination from the standpoint of the colonised. They theorise colonialism as a psychological, political and economic force, excavating the extent of imperial history and empire while considering its means of disassembly through critical inquiry.

Figure 9.1 Imperialism

Think about the power of the British Empire to take control of and effectively consume various colonies and territories around the world by placing them under British rule.

Frantz Fanon

Fanon's (2008/1952) first book, *Black Skin, White Masks*, is an excellent place to start thinking about postcolonial theory. In a partly autobiographical text, Fanon narrates his experiences as a medical student in France coming from the French colony of Martinique. Fanon uses these experiences to testify about the effects of racism and dehumanisation inherent in situations of colonial domination. In particular, Fanon argues that French colonial culture constructs crude racial lines that polarise Black and white people at the level of the human psyche. This is evident, Fanon suggests, in the processes of objectification and internalisation (or 'epidermalisation') by which reductive stereotypes circumscribe Black identity. For example, Fanon (2008/1952, p. 84) describes his experiences on a train, where a young white boy exclaims to his mother, 'Look, a Negro! Mama, see the Negro! I'm frightened!' Fanon reacts:

> Frightened! Frightened! Now they were beginning to be afraid of me. I made up my mind to laugh myself to tears, but laughter had become impossible. I could no longer laugh, because I already knew that there were legends, stories, history, and above all *historicity* … I was responsible at the same time for my body, for my race, for my ancestors. I subjected myself to an objective examination, I discovered my blackness, my ethnic characteristics; and I was beaten down by … cannibalism, intellectual deficiency, fetishism, racial defects [and] slave-ships. (Fanon, 2008/1952, pp. 84–85; see also Go, 2016, p. 21)

Fanon describes here his experience of colonialism from the perspective of the dominated. On his arrival in France, he is not treated as a French citizen but objectified by his skin colour, which carries various racial prejudices resulting from colonial history. Fanon argues that this history allows others to project an inferior status onto him, making him feel both foreign and subordinate in French society. He writes:

> The white world, the only honorable one, barred me from all participation. A man was expected to behave like a man. I was expected to behave like a black man – or at least like a nigger. I shouted a greeting to the world and the world slashed away my joy. I was told to stay within bounds, to go back where I belonged. (Fanon, 2008/1952, p. 86)

Fanon narrates his difficulty developing his identity outside of this colonial and racial consciousness. He suggests that his self-perception becomes dependent upon his coloniser, who not only determines the language he must speak but also has colonised his native culture, thereby denying him access to his origins. Without these roots, Fanon finds himself struggling with a contradiction: he must participate in French society and use its language, but by doing so he adopts a 'white mask' that screens out his Black identity. Fanon is critical of how colonial ideology seizes the human psyche in this way. Indeed, he recognises that the loss of native culture creates an ambivalence in which colonial rule encourages subjects to appropriate and imitate 'whiteness'.

Fanon (1963) extends this analysis in *The Wretched of the Earth*. This book presents a compelling description of the dehumanising effects of colonialism while considering the broader social, cultural and political implications of decolonisation. Looking to the conflict in Algiers as an example, Fanon argues that the use of violence or the threat of violence creates and maintains colonial states. He suggests that this obstinate force must be met with equal antagonism if the colonised wish to reverse these power inequalities. In this sense, the message of his second book is unequivocal: 'decolonization is always a violent phenomenon' (Fanon, 1963, p. 35). The seriousness of Fanon's message reflects his views about the underlying structure of colonial ideology. Fanon argues that colonialism segregates Algerian society along racial lines, compartmentalising the colonised from the coloniser through the threat of force, denial of education, and separation of living arrangements. This system of **apartheid** places the coloniser and colonised in a rigid binary opposition. Drawing on Marxist and psychoanalytic thinking, Fanon suggests that this opposition will result in a revolutionary response:

> And it is clear that in the colonial countries the peasants alone are revolutionary, for they have nothing to lose and everything to gain. The starving peasant, outside the class system, is the first among the exploited to discover that only violence pays. For him there is no compromise, no possible coming to terms; colonisation and decolonisation are simply a question of relative strength. The exploited man sees that his liberation implies the use of all means, and that of force first and foremost. (Fanon, 1963, p. 61)

What Fanon is suggesting here is that the fight against racial segregation links closely to capitalist exploitation. Through violent revolt, Fanon sees the possibility of a postcolonial world in which countries gain their independence by redistributing wealth. He cautions against those anti-colonial movements that would compromise with colonial powers and emulate capitalist societies. Instead, he aligns his critique with socialism, arguing that the end of colonial rule offers humanity a chance to create something different and dispense with racial hatred and economic exploitation.

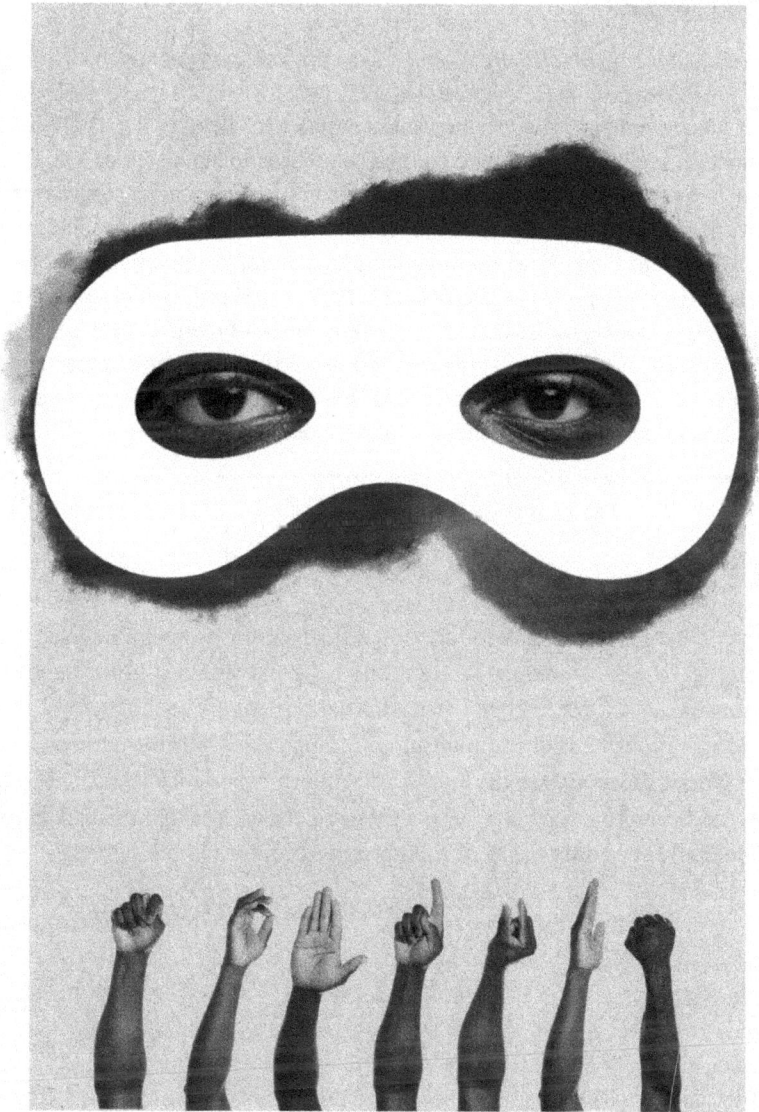

Figure 9.2 Black skin, white masks

Reflect on Fanon's discussion of 'white masks' as an example of 'covering up' Black identity to conform with a society that robs Black people of their cultural history and marginalises their opportunities for resistance.

┌─ Focus on Facts ───

Just as Fanon's (2008/1952) *Black Skin, White Masks* captures the experiences of racialised sub-jugation in the French empire, W.E.B. Du Bois's (2007/1903) *The Souls of Black Folk* conveys the experiences of African-Americans within the United States (Go, 2016, p. 22). Du Bois's work was one of the first major sociological research studies, interrogating the idea that African-Americans are a 'problem' to be 'governed' and shifting the focus to the experiences of racism in post-Civil War American society. Du Bois draws on his own experiences as a schoolteacher in Tennessee to escort the reader into Black rural life, revealing its cultural formations, triumphs and inner conflicts (Go, 2016, p. 22). In particular, Du Bois (2007/1903, p. 8) argues that racialised structures in America generate a 'double consciousness' whereby African-Americans are 'always looking at one's self through the eyes of others, ... measuring one's soul by the tape of a world that looks on in amused contempt and pity'. In other words, Du Bois suggests that American racial prejudice denies Black people true self-consciousness and self-realisation (Go, 2016, p. 22).

Edward Said

Edward Said's (1979) *Orientalism* is a foundational text within postcolonial theory that initi-ates the 'second wave' of postcolonial studies. The book moves away from the revolutionary passions igniting Fanon's work to create a substantial postcolonial scholarship that describes the ideological operations behind colonialism and imperialism. More specifically, *Orientalism* examines 'the Orient's special place in European Western experience' (Said, 1979, p. 1). Said suggests that 'the Orient' (which refers to peoples and societies in places such as Asia, Africa and the Middle East) is not only adjacent to Europe geographically but

> it is also the place of Europe's greatest and richest and oldest colonies, the source of
> its civilisations and languages, its cultural contestant, and one of its deepest and most
> recurring images of the Other ... the Orient has helped to define Europe (or the West)
> as its contrasting image, idea, personality and experience. (Said, 1979, pp. 1–2)

Said argues that the term 'Orientalism' has three meanings. First, it refers to the academic study of 'the Orient' through disciplines such as sociology, anthropology, history and philol-ogy. Second, it is also 'a style of thought based upon an ontological and epistemological distinc-tion between "the Orient" and (most of the time) "the Occident"' (Said, 1979, p. 2). What Said means here is that many writers, from poets and novelists to philosophers and economists, have come to accept an essential distinction between the East and the West. This distinc-tion becomes the starting point for their theories, novels, and social and political accounts concerning the Orient and often reinforces misleading or harmful understandings about its peoples and customs (see also **Eurocentrism**). Third, Orientalism names a discourse that supports the diffusion of colonial and imperial power. Said (1979, p. 3) writes:

Taking the late eighteenth century as a very roughly defined starting point Orientalism can be discussed and analyzed as the corporate institution for dealing with the Orient – dealing with it by making statements about it, authorizing views of it, describing it, by teaching it, settling it, ruling over it: in short, Orientalism as a Western style for dominating, restructuring, and having authority over the Orient. … My contention is that without examining Orientalism as a discourse one cannot possibly understand the enormously systematic discipline by which European culture was able to manage – and even produce – the Orient politically, sociologically, militarily, ideologically, scientifically, and imaginatively during the post-Enlightenment period.

Said's point here is that European culture reinforces itself as a site of power through academic writings, imaginative images, and preconceptions of the East. He draws on Foucault to expose this 'episteme' (see Chapter 6) or knowledge as it designates the East as a 'sort of surrogate or underground self' (Said, 1979, p. 3) to Western values. He also draws on Gramsci (see Chapter 2) to argue that this knowledge has become hegemonic (see hegemony): Western views of the Orient assure widespread consent that European culture is superior to its Eastern 'Other'. Indeed, Said (1979, p. 7) writes that Orientalism is never far from the 'idea of Europe' which refers to a 'collective notion identifying "us" Europeans against all "those" non-Europeans', the purpose of which is to reiterate 'European superiority over Oriental backwardness'. It is important to note that this concept of 'the Other' becomes a vital part of postcolonial theorising, referring to the social and psychological ways in which one group excludes or marginalises another by focusing on what makes them different or opposite.

Said evidences this orientalist discourse by examining a range of historical, literary and media texts from antiquity to the modern day. He shows how these texts repeat and reproduce specific ideas about the Orient, such as stereotypes about its 'depravity' and 'despotism', which Said suggests are 'steeped in racial and geographical platitudes' (Said, 1979, p. 102). For example, Said suggests that western literature often presents 'the Arab mind' as 'depraved, anti-Semitic to the core, violent, unbalanced' (Said, 1979, p. 307). He argues that such views are readily apparent in film and television, which reduces Arab people to representations such as an 'oil supplier' or as a 'bloodthirsty' 'slave trader', 'camel driver', 'money changer' or 'colourful scoundrel' (Said, 1979, pp. 286–287). Said (1979, p. 287) continues:

The Arab leader (of marauders, pirates, 'native' insurgents) can often be seen snarling at the captured Western hero and the blond girl (both of them steeped in wholesomeness), 'My men are going to kill you, but – they like to amuse themselves before.' … In newsreels or news-photos, the Arab is always shown in large numbers. No individuality, no personal characteristics or experiences. Most of the pictures represent mass rage and misery, or irrational (hence hopelessly eccentric) gestures. Lurking behind all of these images is the menace of *jihad*. Consequence: a fear that the Muslims (or Arabs) will take over the world.

Said (1979, p. 7) is making an important argument here. These stereotypes ensure the West's 'flexible *positional* superiority'; orientalist discourse represents the West as the very antithesis of the East. The Orient is irrational, primitive and depraved; the West is rational, modern and virtuous. Through this positioning, Said argues that orientalist discourse serves to justify colonial and imperial ambitions, particularly the assumption that the Arab world is a 'danger' and in need of Western 'enlightenment'. This imperialist assumption is a crucial feature of American and European foreign policy, which draws on orientalist stereotypes to help legitimate the invasion and occupation of 'enemy' nations (see Little, 2008). Indeed, Said concludes by suggesting that orientalist discourse is often ignorant of Islam, presenting it as a religion of terror, which only contributes to further hostility, fear and prejudice worldwide.

Content Warning

This case study includes graphic descriptions of violence, torture and sexual abuse, which you may find troubling or distressing.

Case Study 9.1

Orientalism and the 'War on Terror'

In the chapter 'Cannibalizing Iraq: Topos of a New Orientalism', Moneera Al-Ghadeer (2013) examines how American orientalist discourse is intertwined with discursive violence against the Middle East. Al-Ghadeer argues that following the events of 9/11, America adopted a new rhetoric, both at home and abroad, that was replete with symbolic attacks and descriptions of the Middle East as an elusive yet dangerous enemy. Evidence of this rhetoric is found within Presidential decrees, which mark out the contours of the 'war on terror' by threatening to 'hunt down' and 'punish' those 'cowards', 'barbarians' and 'evil-doers' hiding in the 'shadows' or burrowed away in 'caves' (see Brown, 2005, cited in Al-Ghadeer, 2013, p. 118). As with Said, Al-Ghadeer suggests that this orientalist discourse renders the enemy in terms of a binary opposition between the civilised world and the barbaric 'Other'. In Al Ghadeer's (2013, p. 118) own words, 'the Arab or Muslim, seen without culture and outside civilization, epitomizes savagery … transformed into a distant other … marked for annihilation and destruction'.

Al-Ghadeer refers to some deeply concerning anecdotes from the Iraq war, including the description of a soldier who kept a human finger in their locker throughout their tour of duty and a soldier who ate the charred flesh of an Iraqi civilian following an improvised explosive device attack aimed at American forces. Al-Ghadeer argues that such cannibalistic gestures illustrate the desire within American imperialism to 'devour the Other' or, at the very least, assert dominance alongside existing understandings of colonialism. Such is the power of this orientalist discourse that Al-Ghadeer argues that it instigates the disfiguration of the enemy through the 'spectacle of cannibalism'.

This theme of disfiguration also continues in the context of 'the Abu Ghraib photos', images that show American soldiers participating in the abuse and torture of Iraqis at Abu Ghraib prison during the 'war on terror'. According to Al-Ghadeer (2013, p. 119), the Abu Ghraib photos are a chilling example of how America's orientalism legitimates violence by 'righteously and schematically dividing the world into good and evil, civilized and primitive'. Al-Ghadeer (2013, p. 122) suggests that American imperialism often manufactures the Middle East as full of monsters – 'terrorists' – that must be destroyed for fear of imminent attack. Such a horror-movie-like discourse invites Americans to indulge in ritualistic acts of tribal violence against the 'outsider'. As Al-Ghadeer (2013, p. 119–120) writes, 'the Abu Ghraib photos also generate associations with rites, secret rituals, ceremonies of religious sacrifice, covert operations and fraternity or fight clubs … performed under the motto "God bless America"'.

Such ritualistic acts of violence include 'attaching electric wires to different parts of the body, including male genitals; punching; beating with hard objects; slapping; kicking, pouring cold water; "isolating detainees 'in the hole' for thirty days with possible thirty days extension"; and using dogs to attack them' (Al-Ghadeer, 2013, p. 123). Al-Ghadeer argues that these acts were as much about humiliating Iraqis as exacting punishment. Indeed, many images depicted Iraqi men in sadomasochistic and pornographic settings where sexual abuse and rape prevailed. Al-Ghadeer (2013, pp. 123–124) notes:

> Some detainees were forced to masturbate in front of other detainees, the soldiers and the camera. Others were thrown into sexual positions with other naked male prisoners or were threatened with rape; a soldier was 'sodomizing a detainee with a chemical light' and a 'broom stick.' One detainee explains that the soldiers forced him to rape a 15-year-old, then went further to crush him morally and psychologically by inscribing 'I'm a rapist' on his leg and taking pictures of him naked. Most of the detainees' statements indicate that they were exposed to these sexual violations during the holy month of Ramadan. In addition to the centrality of the materiality of body for the torturer, the detainee's moral values were stripped of their context, appropriated, displaced and emptied out, rendering them an indispensable site for torture.

Al-Ghadeer reveals an alarming feature of American Orientalism: American soldiers are ready to weaponise a prisoner's culture, sacred rituals, and identity to assert their ideological dominance. Al-Ghadeer argues that we are witnessing the replaying of orientalist discourse upon Iraqi flesh. American soldiers participate in communal humiliation and abuse based on orientalist assumptions about religious and cultural differences. As Said notes, it is a fear about the dangers of the 'Arab mind' and a host of other clichés that permit atrocious acts of violence. From this perspective, Al-Ghadeer warns against the very material consequences of American orientalist discourse and the 'war on terror' rhetoric.

Homi Bhabha

Homi Bhabha is another influential postcolonial theorist who developed Said's analysis of Oriental discourse by asking supplementary questions about the nature of colonial power and resistance. In particular, Bhabha queries whether orientalist discourse is as sure of itself as one might first presume. In a critical reply to Said, Bhabha argues that even the most orientalist text can contain moments where colonial power must confront alternative perspectives. Indeed, Bhabha draws on poststructuralism (see Chapter 6) to question the stability and conviction of orientalist discourse, suggesting that the discourse of colonialism is often pulling in two contrary directions at once. This 'ambivalence' becomes clearer through Bhabha's (1994, pp. 81–82) account of colonialist stereotyping:

> The problem of origin as the problematic of racist, stereotypical knowledge is a complex one … Stereotyping is not the setting up of a false image which becomes the scapegoat of discriminatory practices. It is a much more ambivalent text of projection and introjection, metaphoric and metonymic strategies, displacement, overdetermination, guilt, aggressivity; the masking and splitting of 'official' and phantasmic knowledges to construct the positionalities and oppositionalities of racist discourse.

Bhabha's argument here (if a bit wordy!) has far-reaching implications. Bhabha (1994, p. 70) suggests that, like Said, the objective of colonial discourse is to justify colonial conquest by constructing the colonised as a population of 'degenerate types' based on their racial origin. The purpose of this is to establish a fundamental difference between 'the Orient' and 'the Occident' (to borrow from Said's phrasing) by representing the former as essentially outside of Western culture and comprehension. Yet, Bhabha (1994, pp. 70–71) argues that this distinction operates in a contrary sense because it also makes 'the Other' 'entirely knowable and visible'. Colonial discourse brings 'the Other' inside its modes of representation, thus lessening its radical difference. Bhabha argues that this contrary nature reflects the ambivalence and instability of colonial discourse.

As an example of this ambivalence, Bhabha considers the contrary ways colonial discourse represents the Black colonised subject:

> The black is both savage (cannibal) and yet the most obedient and dignified of servants (the bearer of food); he is the embodiment of rampant sexuality and yet innocent as a child; he is mystical, primitive, simple-minded and yet the most worldly and accomplished liar, and manipulator of social forces. (Bhabha, 1994, p. 82; see also Go, 2016, p. 43)

Like Said, Bhabha recognises that these images of depravity and savagery populate colonial discourse. Yet, they are antagonistic to the idea that the colonised subject *may also* be domesticated and understood. Bhabha argues that this ambivalence reveals the limits and shortcomings of colonial reason, which fails to achieve a stable definition of difference between the coloniser and colonised. Drawing on psychoanalysis (see Chapter 3), Bhabha argues that these stereotypes reveal deep-seated anxiety within colonial power, which desperately tries to confine populations into essential categories through repetitive (racist) stereotypes. Bhabha argues that this attempt to secure the colonised subject within the coloniser's modes of representation is only ever partially successful. Indeed, he argues that there are 'gaps' in colonial discourse that the oppressed may exploit.

According to Go (2016, pp. 44–45), Bhabha opens up this question of agency and resistance through two essential concepts. The first is 'mimicry'. Bhabha argues that colonial discourse insists that the colonised mimic their masters by becoming 'Western' and more 'civilised'. The irony here, Bhabha notes, is that if the colonised become more 'Western' and 'civilised', the distinction and self-proclaimed superiority of colonial power is invalidated (Go, 2016, p. 44). Indeed, Bhabha (1994, p. 88) suggests that mimicry is a subtle form of resistance to colonial power, calling it a 'menace' that uses the ambivalence within colonial discourse to 'disrupt its author'. In one example, Bhabha discusses the idea that Indian natives must learn English if they are to be employed by British authorities. He argues that these 'Anglicised' people would be neither exclusively native nor quite English, but something in-between: a menace whose resemblance would threaten to collapse understandings of difference within orientalist discourse (Bhabha, 1994, p. 87). Indeed, Bhabha (1994, p. 89) views mimicry as a way to disturb the normality of colonial discourse by suggesting that the colonial subject is 'almost the same but not white'.

Bhabha's second concept is 'hybridity'. Drawing on Derrida (see Chapter 6), Bhabha argues that stereotypes are like linguistic signs, which establish their meaning only through chains of **signification**. Bhabha argues that while colonial authority depends on the continual repetition of stereotypes, no reiteration of the stereotype is ever the same: new meanings and interpretations always emerge (Go, 2016, p. 45). Bhabha draws on the example of English missionaries in the early nineteenth century trying to convert Hindus in India to Christianity. Bhabha suggests that these attempts required translating the Bible from English to Hindi, resulting in a 'hybrid' text with two different voices (Go, 2016, p. 45). In Bhabha's view, such a translation undermined the fixed opposition between coloniser and colonised while drawing attention to the ambivalence within colonial discourse. Indeed, he argues that the translated Bible 'estranges' a once familiar symbol of English national authority by creating a new representation that reflects the 'uncanny forces of race, sexuality, violence, cultural and even climatic differences' (Bhabha, 1994, p. 113; see also Go, 2016, p. 45). In other words, hybridity opens up a space within colonial discourse that unsettles assumptions about the homogeneity of colonial identity and authority.

Focus on Facts

Sociologists Stuart Hall and Paul Gilroy take the concept of hybridity further by suggesting that Black migrant experiences can undermine and subvert colonial formations of ethnicity and identity. In particular, they speak of a hybrid position they call 'Black British' – a mode of self-representation that interrogates 'white' understandings of British national identity by infusing it with elements of Black film, art, music and style. Hall and Gilroy argue that this politics of hybridity helps to decentre exclusionary conceptions of Britishness as essentially 'white' by celebrating the impurity, intermingling and transformations that come out of new and unexpected combinations of human beings, cultures and ideas (see Mercer, 1994).

Subaltern Studies and Gayatri Spivak

This issue of agency is also a key area of concern for several scholars known collectively as the Subaltern Studies Group, including Ranajit Guha (1988), Dipesh Chakrabarty (2000) and Partha Chatterjee (1999). Drawing on the ideas of Antonio Gramsci (see Chapter 2), these critics explore how historical representations of India fail to account for the 'subaltern' consciousness that characterises local forms of Indian experience. More specifically, they argue that written accounts of India's history are often elitist, dominated by English historians or an English-trained Indian bourgeoisie, which represses the voices and experiences of a colonised Indian peasantry. Guha (1988), in particular, critiques the idea that India's history is one of an indigenous elite leading the Indian people away from colonial rule. Instead, Guha suggests that such an idealist story effectively erases the activities, efforts and struggles of the subaltern classes, whose insurgency and anticolonial resistance also form part of (post)colonial knowledge. Subaltern studies, then, emphasises the agency of the colonised. It seeks to recover the history-making power of those 'from below' (see Thompson, 2008/1978) by questioning how we might access the experiences and consciousness of the subaltern within colonial history.

Gayatri Spivak's (2003/1988) work makes a critical intervention here. In the essay, 'Can the Subaltern Speak?', Spivak draws on poststructuralist thinking (see Chapter 6) to question the assumption, within subaltern studies, that one can retrieve from colonial history the consciousness of the oppressed. Spivak argues that any representation of the subaltern is a discursive construct that discourses of power and knowledge constitute. For this reason, the intellectual is not a transparent medium through which to represent subaltern voices or experiences. Indeed, Spivak resists the suggestion that we can ever encounter the subaltern on their own terms, arguing that any attempt to render their consciousness visible will do so with recourse to dominant understandings of human **subjectivity** (McLeod, 2010, p. 129). Like Foucault (see Chapter 6), then, Spivak recognises that the very act of creating knowledge exists within discursive frameworks that authorise (and give visibility to) certain voices and experiences.

Spivak argues that issues of gender further deepen these problems because representations of the subaltern tend to prioritise men. Spivak (cited in McLeod, 2010, p. 129) writes:

> As object of colonialist historiography and as subject of insurgency, the ideological construction of gender keeps the male dominant. If, in the context of colonial production, the subaltern has no history and cannot speak, the subaltern as female is even more deeply in shadow.

From Spivak's perspective, subaltern and postcolonial studies are gendered in worrying ways, giving little attention to female oppression and the suffering of subaltern women.

Figure 9.3 Can the subaltern speak?

In what ways are the voices of marginalised women 'locked away' (particularly in the historical archive, as Spivak suggests)? Who has the 'key', and what does this say about the power of trying to 'rescue' subaltern testimonies?

This position does not lead Spivak to suggest, as subaltern studies might, that historical research may recover oppressed women's voices from colonial history. On the contrary, Spivak warns against 'hunting' for women's 'lost voices' in the archive, suggesting that it will likely result in dominant discourses speaking *for* them (McLeod, 2010, p. 129). In Spivak's view, it is better to acknowledge women as 'unrepresentable in discourse' as any attempt to retrieve their voices will likely disfigure their speech (McLeod, 2010, p. 130). In other words, Spivak is offering a critique here of those who would claim to rescue or understand the 'authentic' voice of the subaltern as female (McLeod, 2010, p. 130).

Spivak (2003/1988) considers this issue by discussing controversies surrounding the practice of *sati* in India, which refers to the act of 'widow sacrifice' (whereby a wife would throw herself on her husband's funeral pyre and burn to death). Spivak suggests that official accounts of this practice fail to represent the testimony of women's voices and consciousness. Indeed, British colonial officials took *sati* as evidence of the uncivilised and barbaric 'backwardness' of Hindu culture, criminalising it in 1829 (Go, 2016, pp. 53–54). Spivak queries this imperialist logic and argues that *sati* was a far more nuanced and disputed act than the British attitude would allow. By outlawing it, the British not only erased some significant complexities within Hindu culture, such as its patriarchal nature, but also failed to account for women's own interests, motivations, politics and agency (Go, 2016, p. 54). Spivak refers to this as an example of **epistemic violence**: the idea that subaltern experiences, knowledge and understandings are marginalised, if not effaced, by the discourses of the powerful.

Case Study 9.2

Decolonising Sociology

The impact of postcolonial theory is evident in recent calls for the need to decolonise university curricula. In *Decolonizing Sociology*, Ali Meghji (2021) argues that sociology as a discipline must reflexively assess its relationship with processes of colonialism and imperialism. Meghji (2021, p. 2) writes:

> although we are regularly presented with a picture of sociology as being one of the most 'critical' of the social sciences, sociology became formally institutionalised in the nineteenth century at the height of global colonialism, imperialism and empires. This world of colonialism and empires was not merely background noise to sociology, but rather the discipline came to internalise colonial ways of thinking and representing the world.

These ways of thinking, Meghji suggests, are evident in early examples of sociological research, which (re)produce ideas and knowledge about colonial differences while benefiting from the spoils of empire. For example, Meghji (2021, pp. 9–10) examines the work of Durkheim, suggesting that his typologies regarding 'primitive' and 'advanced' cultures (see

Chapter 4) were based on a comparative distinction between colonised and European societies. Meghji (2021, pp. 9–10) suggests that this distinction reflects the broader 'civilising mission' of French colonialism, which, at the time, sought to characterise colonies as 'backward' and in need of 'enlightenment'. Indeed, Durkheim's characterisation of colonial societies as 'primitive' conveys no mention of the fact that the French empire was violently dispossessing and subjugating these local populations (see Connell, 1997). Such disclosures raise essential questions about Durkheim's claim that sociology is an objective and authoritative 'science of society'. Indeed, his empirical research methods are intractably tied to the geopolitics of colonisation (see Kurasawa, 2013).

Through this example and many others, Meghji (2021) critiques early sociological research for establishing a 'colonial episteme' that originates in the Global North and primarily reflects the interests and concerns of influential or privileged white male thinkers. Moreover, Meghji is critical of the extent to which this episteme dominates the sociological canon, making it difficult to recognise the experiences of those from the Global South. Meghji (2021) argues that there is an 'intellectual imperialism' within sociology that forces writers in the Global South to engage with Northern theories and institutions if their work is to be valued. From this perspective, Meghji (2021, p. 148) articulates a decolonial approach that focuses on rendering sociology more inclusive by 'fostering horizontal conversations across different epistemic traditions'. Meghji asserts (2021, p. 96):

> this sociology is built on the epistemic principle that we ought to ultimately work together – between frameworks, traditions, concepts and so on – to achieve the most critical paradigms of social thought. Some have labelled this epistemological approach 'pluriversality' … [or] what Bhambra (2014) terms 'connected sociologies'.

Meghji suggests that the process of decolonisation is not about creating a bifurcated view of sociological theories and methods. One does not necessarily need to abandon the teaching and concepts of white male authors, such as Durkheim, Marx and Weber. Instead, Meghji (2021, p. 96) asserts that a decolonial sociology must

> look to the conversations between the apparently opposite sides of the sociological coin. While it is essential to highlight the provincial nature of sociology embracing the Eurocentric standpoint, and while it is equally essential to highlight the attempts to ground approaches built from a Southern standpoint it is also a disservice to decolonial sociology to avoid the links between different sociological traditions that have resulted in critical paradigms of social thought.

In other words, Meghji argues that sociology is at its best when it represents the *situated nature* of knowledge and examines how the geopolitics of coloniality and imperialism continue to position what is valued in the sociological canon.

Summary

- Postcolonial theory has its origins in the context of two significant historical developments: European colonialism and decolonisation. The term 'colonialism' closely relates to another fundamental concept, 'imperialism'.
- Historical processes of decolonisation occur alongside the emergence of influential postcolonial thinkers, such as Franz Fanon and Edward Said. These theorists draw attention to the divisive and dehumanising effects of orientalist discourse and the possibilities for resistance.
- Poststructuralism has had a significant impact on postcolonial thinking, particularly the arguments of Homi Bhabha, who raises questions about 'ambivalence' within colonial power.
- A group of Indian historians known as the Subaltern Studies Group suggest that historical writings of colonialism often repress the voices and experiences of the most disenfranchised. Gayatri Spivak suggests this is particularly true of women and questions whether historical research can find a unified or 'authentic' female voice in the archive.

Review Questions

- Describe the origins of postcolonial theory with reference to European colonialism and decolonisation processes.
- Said suggests that the term 'Orientalism' has three meanings. What are they?
- What is the main argument of Gayatri Spivak's (2003/1988) essay 'Can the Subaltern Speak?'

Annotated Reading

For a detailed introduction to postcolonial theory, see Julian Go's (2016) *Postcolonial Thought and Social Theory* (Oxford: Oxford University Press).

Ania Loomba (2005) also provides a helpful introduction to postcolonial thinking in *Colonialism/Postcolonialism* (London: Routledge).

Patrick Williams and Laura Christian (2013) provide a selection of key readings within postcolonial thinking in *Colonial Discourse and Post-Colonial Theory* (London: Routledge).

For those interested in learning more about Homi Bhabha's key concepts, see David Huddart's (2006) *Homi K. Bhabha* (London: Routledge).

Gurminder K. Bhambra and John Holmwood's (2021) *Colonialism and Modern Social Theory* (Cambridge: Polity Press) is an essential resource for decolonising modern social theory.

Gurminder K. Bhambra, Kerem Nişancıoğlu and Dalia Gebrial's (2018) edited collection *Decolonising the University* (London: Pluto Press) offers insightful examples of contemporary decolonial political activism.

10

New Materialism and Posthumanism

Chapter Objectives

This chapter will:

- Introduce new materialist and posthumanist perspectives in social theory through Bruno Latour, Gilles Deleuze and Félix Guattari, and Rosi Braidotti.
- Describe key concepts, including assemblages, affect and posthumanism.
- Show the relevance of actor-network theory and posthumanism through examples such as love and human–animal relations.

Keywords

New materialism, assemblages, actants, affect, posthumanism, humanism, anthropocentrism

Introduction

What is next for social theory? How will it shape the future? This chapter addresses these questions by introducing readers to essential discussions on new materialism – a collective term that describes an emerging field of inquiry that studies the role of materiality in social and cultural life. A key feature of new materialism is that it challenges some core assumptions within mainstream social theory, notably the centrality of the 'human' in social and cultural analyses and the divisive nature of its 'irresolvable' debates (see Chapter 7). This chapter will draw on thinkers such as Bruno Latour, Gilles Deleuze and Félix Guattari, and Rosi Braidotti to show how new materialists attempt to cut across these problematic assumptions by examining what matter 'is' and what matter 'does'. More specifically, readers will learn about the importance of networks and **assemblages** in rethinking and tracing the associations between social and technical actors and the potential for non-human entities to **affect** physical, biological, psychological, social, political and emotional change. These considerations will prompt readers to recognise the call of **posthumanism**, which promises to usher in a new way of thinking about social and cultural life that is practically, publicly and politically engaged.

New Materialism: What Is It?

New materialism refers to a range of interdisciplinary perspectives that share an interest in discussing the properties of material things in terms of agency and ethical responsibility. It denotes a 'return to matter', which means that new materialism raises essential ontological and epistemological questions about how humans relate to the material world. A key claim of new materialism is that existing social theories treat material things – such as the natural environment, technology, space and inanimate organisms – as passive substances that are empty of meaning. Their response is to suggest that matter is 'alive', 'vibrant', and 'agentive' – bringing a new, active understanding of the role of material effects in shaping human and non-human interactions. Indeed, new materialists ask us to reconsider the nature of human and non-human material relations to challenge **anthropocentrism** within traditional and contemporary social thought.

Like debates concerning structure and agency, new materialism has its beginnings in critiques of objectivist and subjectivist perspectives in social thought (see Chapter 7). New materialists reject some of the foundational propositions in sociology, including traditional concerns with realism and idealism, structure versus agency, and the extent to which macro-explanations have causal primacy over micro-explanations (or vice versa). Instead, new materialists focus on what matter is and what matter does as a means to cut across many of these theoretical dilemmas. They shift the argument away from some of sociology's most entrenched **dualisms** (structure and agency, mind and body, social and natural, human and non-human) by suggesting that relational networks or assemblages of affect guide human and non-human behaviour. This position implies that no single causal law governs social action (like the economy for Marxists) but a variety of forces that can act as 'agents' to make things happen. Indeed, what is most distinctive about new materialism is that it does not distinguish between the natural and the social world: it recognises the materiality of all things and argues that they can act.

According to Fox and Alldred (2017, p. 5), one crucial repercussion of this perspective is that new materialists reject any sense of social structures (like class or patriarchy) as explanations for how societies and cultures work. New materialists do not subscribe to the idea that causal structures or mechanisms exist 'at depth' nor that the practice of social research can help explain them (see **realism**). On the contrary, what interests new materialists are 'events' – 'an endless cascade of events compromising the material effects of both nature and culture that together produce the world and human history' (Fox and Alldred, 2017, p. 5). In other words, new materialists explore the relational character of events to reveal their physical, biological and expressive arrangements. This enables them to describe the various forces that produce the social world, such as the assemblages of human and non-human 'agents' that make things possible.

It follows logically, then, that new materialism is also 'post-anthropocentric' (Braidotti, 2013): it shifts the focus away from human beings as the central or most significant entities in the world towards a recognition of the intrinsic value of non-human entities, including animals, plants and other material resources. This shift is timely because it reflects a rising interest in the ethical underpinnings of animal rights and welfare (Singer, 1977; Peggs, 2012), biological conservation (Cafaro et al., 2017; Sanborn and Jung, 2021), climate change (Barry et al., 2013; Dietz et al., 2020) and sustainable development (Fox and Alldred, 2021). Indeed, new materialists precisely think about the agency of matter and materiality to seek justice in these contemporary contexts (Coole and Frost, 2010). This means that new materialists, despite their rejection of conventional sociological concepts, continue to pursue critical analyses, particularly of the discriminatory and violent effects of human activity on this planet (Braidotti, 2019).

What new materialism offers is a new way to conceptualise 'agency' that extends beyond human actors to the non-human and inanimate. This proposition radically shakes up traditional assumptions within social theory, namely that the 'social' and 'natural' worlds are somehow distinct with their own causal laws (see Chapters 2, 4 and 7) or only open to human interpretation and experience (see Chapter 5). On the contrary, new materialism suggests that the social and natural both have material effects and that these effects consistently produce events in an ever-changing world (Fox and Alldred, 2017, p. 4). This perspective opens up social theory to recognise the effects of humans on non-humans and vice versa.

The next section of this chapter will introduce some key concepts within new materialism through the writings and ideas of four crucial thinkers: Bruno Latour, Gilles Deleuze and Félix Guattari, and Rosi Braidotti.

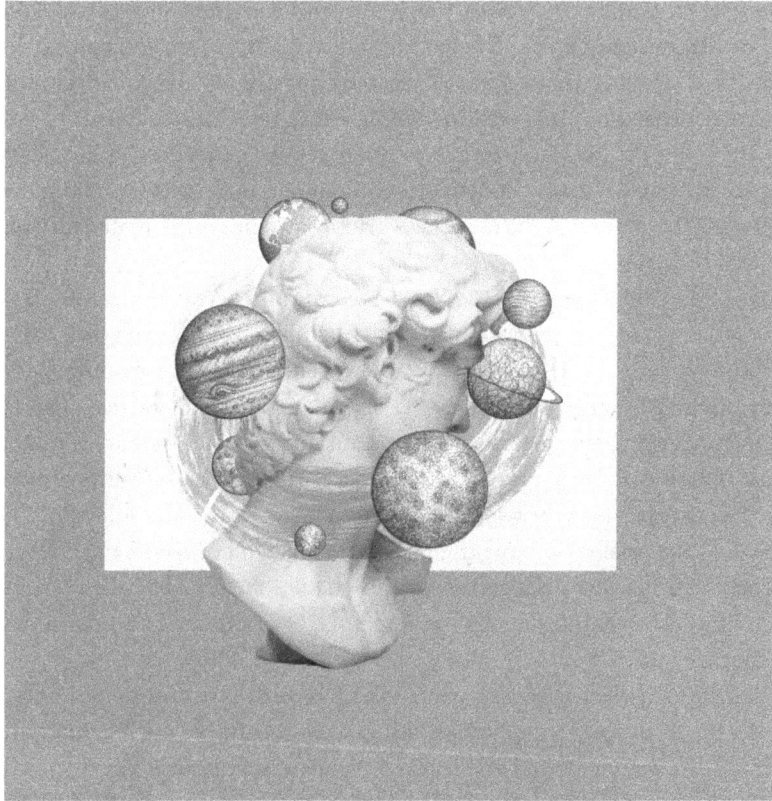

Figure 10.1 Anthropocentrism

In what ways do our perspectives and theories about the world place us at the 'centre of the universe'? Think about what this means for our treatment of the natural environments on this planet as well as other non-humans, such as animals.

Bruno Latour and Actor-Network Theory

Some of the earliest stirrings of new materialism begin in the writings of the French philosopher, anthropologist and sociologist Bruno Latour. Alongside other key figures, such as Michael Callon and John Law, Latour was influential in developing a new approach in the social sciences known as 'actor-network theory' (ANT). ANT is a theoretical and methodological approach for exploring the social and technical ('sociotechnical') processes that guide scientific and technical knowledge. It has its origins in the social studies of science and technology, where thinkers like Latour sought to challenge the conventional idea that producing scientific facts was somehow an extraordinary pursuit, existing outside of daily practices. In early works, such as *Laboratory Life*, Latour and colleagues (Latour and Woolgar, 1986, p. 239) question this assumption by undertaking ethnographic research to describe how scientists 'fabricate' these facts 'out of circumstance'. More specifically, Latour traces the social and technical aspects of laboratory science, including how texts, materials and skills combine to form the basis of objective knowledge claims. This is particularly apparent, Latour suggests, in how scientific research reports enrol other actors, such as research collaborators, funders, regulators and publics, into accrediting facts. What is essential about this analysis is that it reveals that the work of science is no different from other social activities. ANT scholars assert that all activity is a process of 'negotiation' across various social, technical, conceptual and textual apparatuses (Latour and Woolgar, 1986, p. 40). Indeed, what makes something 'factual' is how scientists work to 'stabilise' certain statements about how the world works (Latour and Woolgar, 1986, pp. 176–177).

Three key assumptions emerge from this approach. First, ANT is not a conventional social theory. As Couldry (2008, p. 93) writes:

> [ANT] seeks to explain social order not through an essentialized notion of 'the social' but through the networks of connections among human agents, technologies, and objects. Entities (whether human or non-human) within those networks acquire power through the number, extensiveness, and stability of the connections routed through them .... Such connections are contingent and emerge historically (they are not natural) but, if successful, a network acquires the force of 'nature'.

Couldry's point here is that ANT extends 'the social' to studying associations between human and non-human actors. Latour adopts the term 'actants' to encourage researchers to move away from assuming that only humans act in the world. Indeed, ANT looks at actants to stress the material and non-human factors in any interaction. Actants can be anything as long as they are a source of action, from microbes (Latour, 1988) and sea scallops (Callon, 1984) to gymnastics equipment (Kerr, 2014) and the procedural rules of video games (Johnson, 2019). The critical point is that material causes and human actors may be the determinants of social interactions and outcomes.

Second, ANT does not subscribe to traditional sociological concerns about the causal importance of structure and agency (see Chapter 7). There are no such things as 'structures' or 'agents' nor the 'micro' or 'macro' workings of particular individuals or collectives. Instead, Latour (2005) adopts the term 'network' to help describe the web of relations within which and through which actants act. Notably, the term network does not designate a 'thing' that exists 'out there', perhaps with the shape of interconnected points, much like a telephone, motorway or sewage 'network' (Latour, 2005, p. 129). Instead, for Latour, the term 'network' is what ANT researchers use to describe the relations through which actants achieve the social. This means that analysts observe and follow the associations and disassociations of actants as they do things, including making others act. From this perspective, networks are a way of describing the arrangements of human and non-human relations rather than explaining the causes of a particular interaction. Indeed, ANT thinkers consider networks and actants to be constantly emerging and shifting, making it difficult to identify examples of 'structure' and 'agency'.

Third, ANT involves rethinking how social **power** operates in society. Latour (2005, p. 22) writes:

> When sociologists of the social pronounce the words 'society', 'power', 'structure', and 'context', they often jump straight ahead to connect vast arrays of life and history, to mobilize gigantic forces, to detect dramatic patterns emerging out of confusing interactions, to see everywhere in the cases at hand yet more examples of well-known types, to reveal behind the scenes some dark powers pulling the strings ... the time has come to have a much closer look at the type of aggregates thus assembled and at the ways they are connected to one another.

Latour's point is that ANT seeks to move beyond the conventional understanding of power in sociology. ANT does not seek to explain power as hidden 'at depth' but proposes a 'flat' conception of the social. This is a view of society where everything that exists does so on the surface. The social is made up of networks of actants whose associations and disassociations have no primary *cause* structuring them. Instead, ANT views power as a *consequence* of the arrangements of actants within a network. This means that power does not belong to a single entity (i.e., a structure or individual persons), but is distributed throughout a network as all sorts of human and non-human actants are assembled. The power of a government to rule a nation, for example, does not reside with one person or an office or building. Instead, it involves various institutions, laws, policies, technologies and objects. It is these (material) things that help hold actor-networks together.

Importantly, Latour does describe how actor-networks can evoke power, though again, this is not in the traditional sense of a single 'top-down' authority. Instead, Latour suggests that actor-networks can grow through the number of associations they make and by recruiting actors into their networks. These networks evoke power as they stabilise into large, almost irreversibly linked elements (Michael, 2017, p. 33). For Latour, many of the processes of well-established actor-networks remain opaque and obscure. Indeed, the more robust a network becomes, the harder it is to understand its contents and processes; it is as if 'scientific and technical work is made invisible by its own success' (Latour, 2000, p. 304). ANT then aims to 'unpack' these networks to make the scientific and technical construction of knowledge more transparent.

Latour's ANT offers new materialism a way of moving beyond traditional sociological concerns with cause and effect, structure and agency, and human-only interactions. It encourages social researchers to recognise and describe all aspects of human and non-human relations and the arrangements through which they are assembled. This provides a very different understanding of power for social inquiry, which is less concerned with what 'pulls the strings' of society and more with making visible processes of knowledge construction.

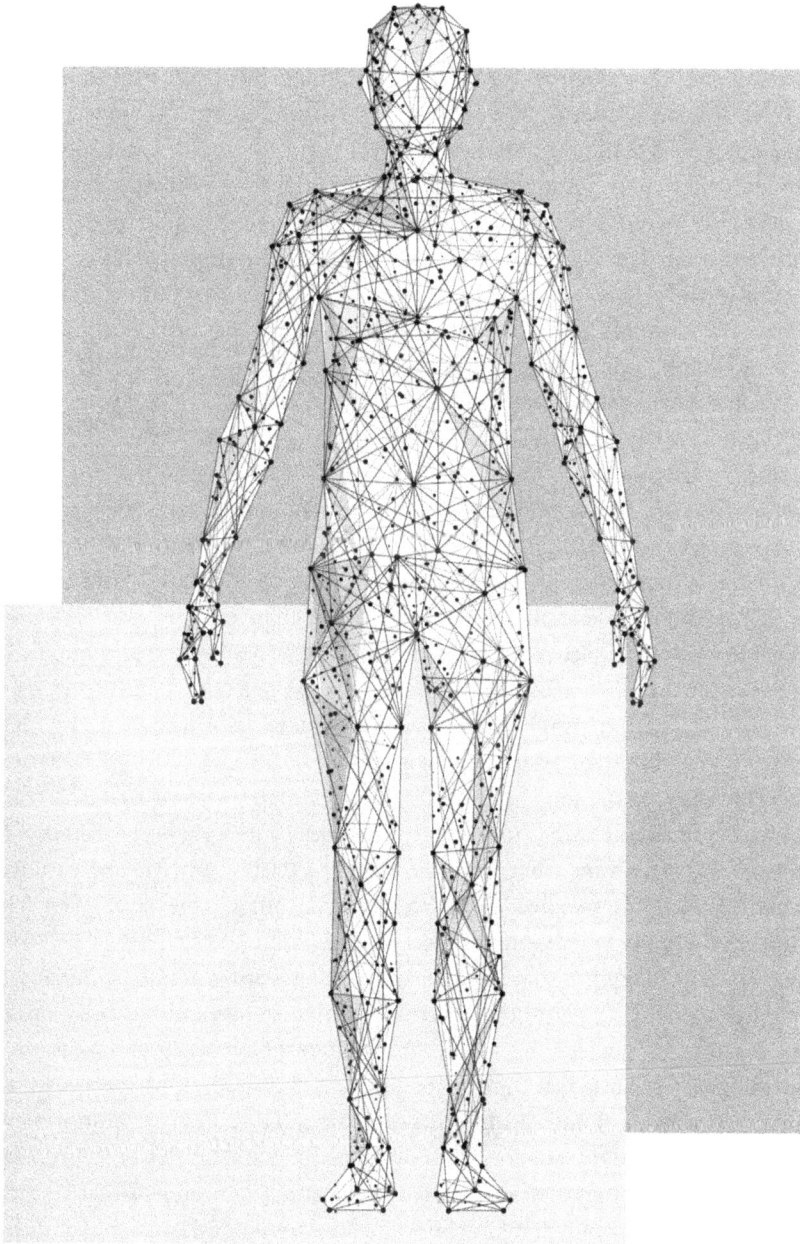

Figure 10.2 Actor-networks

Think about the networks or 'web of relations' within which people act. How do they connect with other human and non-human actants? How do these associations and disassociations make things happen?

Gilles Deleuze and Félix Guattari

Gilles Deleuze is another influential French scholar within new materialism who, alongside his colleague Félix Guattari (discussed below), raises important questions about the nature of reality and the foundations of philosophical inquiry. Like Latour and other ANT theorists, Deleuze has an interest in the materiality of life and seeks to understand how the relations between physical and social phenomena ('materialities') produce events and experiences. However, what is different about Deleuze is the influence of poststructuralism on this materialist ontology (see **social ontology**). As Chapter 6 discusses, poststructuralist thinkers point to the idea that language and meaning are in constant flux. There is always the possibility that other words (or signs) may appear to change how we interpret or understand a given phenomenon. This makes it difficult to grasp at anything 'real' or 'true' as meaning is always deferred in an ongoing process of **signification**. Deleuze shares many of these concerns but suggests that we must examine the materiality of life, not just language, to understand the temporal processes by which change occurs. Deleuze simply offers poststructuralism concepts like assemblage and affect to help understand how change takes place or, indeed, how certain things develop into new things. From this perspective, it is a little easier to grasp at the substance of physical and social processes without understating the possibilities of change.

We can get insight into Deleuze's thinking by looking at one of his most important works: *Difference and Repetition* (2001/1968). In this book, Deleuze sets out what he sees as a common problem within Western philosophy: that it views ontology as a way to simply define *what exists* in the world rather than asking questions about *how* things change. Deleuze criticises philosophers such as Aristotle and Kant for this way of thinking, arguing that they comprehend life by repeatedly classifying things into stable categories of thought and substance. Consider, for example, how we determine what something is, like a telephone – we might list its physical characteristics, like its power source, dialler, ringer, transmitter, or receiver. We can even use these attributes to identify whether that object *is* a telephone or something else, like a cricket bat or a dog. The critical point is that this type of thinking helps us rationally judge what exists in the world by describing the attributes essential to its existence. Deleuze has a problem with this type of thinking. He suggests that it cannot account for how things change in the world or how certain things develop into new things over time. So, for example, consider how the telephone evolves from, say, a landline into an internet-enabled smartphone. We cannot explain such change only by referring to the telephone's internal features, like its power source, because the smartphones of today are the result of all kinds of social, technological and historical developments, including computer programming, microchips, satellite technology, consumer culture, and the military development of the Internet. As such, Deleuze invites us to think about how the relations between materialities change and configure over time. He argues that the 'difference' between things, not their 'repetition', produces change. Indeed, we should conceptualise things as always in motion, converging (or not) to create new possibilities, events and experiences. From this perspective, Deleuze distances himself from the idea that 'anything goes' (present within more radical framings of postmodern theory) by arguing that change, while a vital feature of life, only presents itself through a finite number of (material) possibilities.

The concept of assemblage is essential here. It comes from Deleuze's collaboration with Félix Guattari in the book *A Thousand Plateaus* (1987) and describes how materialities gain shape and substance as they are drawn into arrangements or layouts of various elements. Deleuze and Guattari use the concept of assemblage to explore an alternative way of conceptualising 'unity' within **social systems.** Consider, for example, in Chapter 4, how functionalists talk about society as operating like the organs of the human body. Durkheim and others suggest that society produces 'unity' through a set of relations between people and its parts, such as social roles, which ensure the integration of members into a functioning 'whole'. For Deleuze and Guattari, this arrangement is far too static or fixed to account for the change and difference that takes place over time (as discussed above). In their view, society comprises a multiplicity of relations – assemblages – always in composition, mixture and aggregation. From this perspective, there is no single principle guiding the organisation of social systems, like social cohesion, but a series of interlocking moments as materialities combine to form events and experiences before then diverging and going on to create new things. Assemblages, then, are a way of understanding how things come together without assuming that any particular social system is the final outcome or independent of physical, social and historical processes.

Finally, what holds assemblages together is affect: an essential concept for Deleuze and Guattari, which refers to 'a force that achieves some kind of change of state or capabilities in a relation' (Fox and Alldred, 2017, p. 18). Deleuze and Guattari take the idea of affect from the philosopher Baruch Spinoza, who suggests there are certain states of mind, particularly related to emotions and desire, which can modify and (dis)empower how people experience the world and live their lives. Deleuze and Guattari develop this perspective by suggesting that affect can also become independent from subjects, intersecting with various materialities to shape how social and historical processes unfold. For example, consider the capacity of social media to produce intense feelings of belonging or loneliness. Here all sorts of biological, psychological, social and technological materialities converge to affect human thoughts, beliefs and feelings. For Deleuze and Guattari, this capacity of affect to flow through human and non-human relations gives assemblages their holding power (even if momentarily). Indeed, it can be said that affect influences the arrangement of assemblages.

Focus on Facts

- The philosopher Manuel DeLanda (2006) develops Deleuze and Guattari's concept of assemblage in the book *A New Philosophy of Society: Assemblage Theory and Social Complexity*. In this book, DeLanda revisits the problem of structure and agency (see Chapter 7) to suggest that assemblages offer a 'third way' to conceptualise the relationship

(Continued)

between individual and society-level phenomena. More specifically, DeLanda focuses on the 'emergent properties' (see **emergence**) of assemblages, arguing that the interactions between materialities are complex and cannot be reduced to any single entity or the internal relations between things. Put simply, DeLanda argues that change and stability in the arrangement of assemblages are due to the contexts in which phenomena occur. For example, consider all the relations that comprise a 'work-assemblage'; what constitutes work is not just the relationship between an employee and employer but all the ideas, people, networks and resources that affect how businesses and organisations operate. Significantly, these external relations may affect how a work-assemblage is held together, such as when an economic downturn produces a change in staff workload or job security.

- Deleuze and Guattari's work is also very influential in the so-called 'affective turn' in the social sciences (Clough and Halley, 2007; Clough, 2008), which uses the concept of affect to explore new ways of understanding 'experience' not limited to human sensibilities and emotion.

- The feminist writer Sara Ahmed (2010) suggests that happiness is an example of affect, pushing people towards or away from specific experiences, objects and behaviours. Ahmed argues that happiness 'sticks' people to certain things – 'happy objects' – which then acquire a positive value as a social good. Ahmed suggests one example of this kind of 'happy object' is the family. The family is a primary indicator of happiness because it is connected to happy memories, activities, practices and ideals, including marriage and parenthood. Importantly, as these objects become inundated with affect, Ahmed (2010, p. 44) notes that they also become 'sites of personal and social tension'. Writing of 'feminist killjoys' and 'unhappy queers', Ahmed considers how activists disrupt dominant understandings of family happiness and allow women to rethink the objects that make them happy beyond the 'happy housewife' figure.

Case Study 10.1

The Love-Assemblage

We can further explore the idea of an assemblage through Fox and Alldred's (2017) study of 'love' and the sexualities of young men (see also Alldred and Fox, 2015). Fox and Alldred suggest that traditional sociological accounts of 'love' often fail to appreciate the range of human and non-human relations that assemble to produce the 'affective flows' that we associate with love and its social, psychological and physical consequences (Fox and Alldred, 2017, p. 120). Indeed, they develop a new materialist perspective on 'love' – which they call a 'love-assemblage' – to account for the many relations and affects that produce loving actions and feelings, some of which are physical, others of which are social and cultural. As an example, Fox and Alldred (2017, p. 120) refer to the experiences of one young man, Neil, who talks about love in the following way:

… I fell in love with this girl. It was like our first love kind of thing. … It's like, it's like a, it's like a bubble amongst the ah … I don't know, because the world's pretty … I don't want to say, dark, because that's unfair. But it's not … it's kind of like … scary sometimes … when you think about how much shit is going on on the earth, and how many wars and all that. And I think loving… one other person is a, it's a good way of just, kind of, finding a meaning. You know, it feels like it's not all for nothing, and that there is a point.

Fox and Alldred (2017, pp. 120–121) suggest that we can consider the different relations and affects that populate a 'love-assemblage' from this and other parts of Neil's interview. A love-assemblage is not just Neil's relationship with his girlfriend but also the other circumstances in Neil's life, such as his concern with world events, like 'war', or the influence of former sexual relations on his perceptions of male and female sexuality. Fox and Alldred (2017, p. 121) suggest that these relations sit alongside many others, such as the public and private spaces where lovers meet; the food, drink and other consumables that form the backdrop to intimate relations; and the social norms and practices that encircle loving relationships, such as ideals concerning marriage and parenthood or the commercialisation of love through gift-giving. In each case, no single relation determines what love 'is' but rather various relations that affect each other to produce an arrangement of 'love' that is different from, say, how we might understand an assemblage of 'hate' or 'shame'.

What is significant about the love-assemblage, Fox and Alldred (2017, p. 121) suggest, is that it helps uncover all sorts of different capacities for action, desire and feeling. Some affects, for example, are physical: a kiss or a hug from a lover can produce feelings which, in turn, generate further affects such as sexual arousal. Other affects are social and cultural, such as norms regarding sexual behaviour or concepts concerning 'romance' and 'dating'. Significantly, these affects arrange in different ways to produce, for example, a decision to take a partner out for a romantic meal or create a subject-position like 'boyfriend', 'partner' or 'couple'. These different capacities also help cut across various dualisms within social theory, like the idea that there is a fundamental difference between the natural and social worlds or individual and collective-level phenomena or public or private realms of social life. For example, Fox and Alldred (2017, p. 122) suggest that

a love-assemblage may link the bedroom to the boardroom of Valentine's Day card companies; the clubs and pubs where attachments form, morph and evaporate; the legislatures and courts where the cultural limits on love are demarcated from stalking, sexual harassment and worse; the manufacturers and retailers of alcohol, beauty products and sex aids; even the pages of academic and medical journals and books that discuss sexuality or emotions.

From this perspective, the concept of assemblage helps us to understand how love flows across many different social forms, bodies and things. 'Love' is not just a biological feeling or a cultural construct – it can entangle all sorts of human and non-human relations, from physical processes of the body to the materiality of objects and broader social, cultural and economic processes. The new materialist, then, cannot single out one explanation of 'love' but seeks to describe these relations and how their affects are assembled as such.

Rosi Braidotti and Posthumanism

Another influential new materialist is the feminist philosopher Rosi Braidotti, whose work is crucial in understanding the development of 'posthumanism' in social theory. Posthumanism refers to a series of theoretical and practical developments across the social sciences, arts and humanities that critique the legacy of humanism within social thought. More specifically, posthumanists set about to problematise, deconstruct or supersede the **Enlightenment** conception of the human as an autonomous, exceptional or rational agent at the organising centre of the world (Nimmo, 2019). Posthumanists suggest that this vision of the human typically results in 'anthropocentrism': a view that relegates non-humans (including animals and the environment) to a passive context or stage for human thought and action. Posthumanists argue that this thinking has (un)intended consequences, generating all kinds of natural and social injustices, including current global ecological and environmental disasters. As such, posthumanists develop a 'post-anthropocentric ontology' (Nimmo, 2019, p. 2) that suggests that humans are but one actor among many others in a living and materially varied world that is neither reducible to human beings nor their linguistic or conceptual constructs. From this perspective, we cannot talk of humans as autonomous from non-human entities. Indeed, they are constituted 'through perpetually unfolding relations with multiple other agents and forces which transgress and confound the imagined boundaries of the human individual, the human self, and the human social domain' (Nimmo, 2019, p. 2).

Braidotti's work furthers this perspective by considering what a post-anthropocentric subject might look like. In her book, *The Posthuman*, Braidotti (2013) explores how the posthuman subject can displace some of the more problematic aspects of traditional humanist thought by developing a worldview that values life in all of its iterations. Importantly, Braidotti's arguments draw from a range of influential thinkers, including Nietzsche (see Chapter 3), Beauvoir and Haraway (see Chapter 8), Foucault (see Chapter 6), Fanon and Said (see Chapter 9) and Deleuze and Guattari (see above). Braidotti's theoretical engagements here are far-reaching, but they recognise that humanism has its historical roots in European colonialism and a conception of the individual that is often responsible for humanity's more self-destructive tendencies, including war, genocide and material exploitation. Braidotti's (2013, p. 14) stance suggests that we must move away from a self-centred view of the human as 'the measure of all things' towards a new understanding that resituates humanity within nature and planet Earth as a whole. From this perspective, Braidotti (2013, p. 66) outlines a three-phase process that reconfigures the human into a posthuman subject, which she labels 'becoming-animal', 'becoming-earth' and 'becoming-machine'.

The first process that Braidotti (2013, pp. 66–67) discusses is 'becoming-animal', which refers to an axis of transformation [that] entails the displacement of anthropocentrism and the recognition of trans species solidarity on the basis of our being environmentally based, that is to say embodied, embedded and in symbiosis with other species.

In other words, Braidotti sets out to challenge humanist assumptions concerning how humans distinguish themselves apart from and above animals. In particular, Braidotti (2013, p. 68) considers how we typically classify animals into one of three groups: those with whom we watch television; those that we eat; and those that we are scared of. Braidotti suggests that each of these categories confines the human–animal interaction into problematic relations, such as a possessive relation (pet ownership), an instrumental relation (food consumption) or a fantastical relation (exotic entertainment).

For example, in the context of pet ownership, Braidotti (2013, p. 68) observes that the relationship between humans and animals is 'unequal and framed by the dominant human and structurally masculine habit of taking for granted free access to and the consumption of the bodies of others'. In other words, Braidotti (2013, p. 68) points out how pet ownership is an example of the 'human subject's sense of supreme ontological entitlement'. Such entitlement is evident not only in ownership over animals but also in how we reduce them to metaphors of human vice or virtue. So, for example, we readily refer to rats and rodents as 'vermin', often destroying them without any real or meaningful understanding of how they live and survive. Such a violent imposition, Braidotti asserts, emerges from how humans *impose* values on animals as a means to reaffirm their centrality in the universe. Braidotti (2013, p. 70) suggests that we must devise 'a system of representation that matches the complexity of contemporary non-human animals and their proximity to humans'. In this sense, Braidotti's work echoes that of other ecofeminists and environmentalists who wish to promote animal conservation and revaluate how humans relate to animals on a day-to-day basis (see McKenna, 2020; Plumwood, 2002).

Braidotti's analysis also considers the other relationships humans have to animals, including food and sustenance ('those we eat') and as a form of spectacle ('those we are scared of'). Braidotti (2013, p. 70) argues that these categories are clearly 'linked to the market economy and labour force ... [in which] animals have constituted a sort of zoo-proletariat, in a species hierarchy run by the humans'. In other words, Braidotti suggests that animals continue to be exploited not only for their resources, whether in terms of milk, edible meat, tusks, wool, oil and fat, etc., but also for their entertainment value, such as through petting zoos, aquarium displays or even as funny or emotional moments on social media. From this perspective, people only view animals as products or commodities within a capitalist marketplace – to be traded, consumed and disposed of depending on their market value. Braidotti (2013, p. 71) calls for a 'qualitative shift' here, arguing that we need an ethical appreciation of animals that affirms them as distinct living things, neither reducible to the rationalities of the market nor consumer desires or fantasies.

Braidotti also considers two other processes by which we can reconfigure the human into a posthuman subject: 'becoming-earth', an axis that stresses environmental and social sustainability issues, and 'becoming-machine', an axis that highlights the interrelations of humans and technology. 'Becoming-earth' captures the idea that we need to develop new alliances between the natural, social and human sciences to find solutions to complex problems, such as climate change, extinction threats, the exhaustion of natural resources and issues concerning global migration and global social justice. Braidotti (2013, p. 89) argues that we can no longer think of these challenges as just an ordinary 'human' concern. Instead, we need the transformative imaginings of an interrelational, trans-species subject – someone who can make a habitable environment for all by moving away from anthropocentric thinking toward planetary-level concerns. The other process, 'becoming-machine', provides the conditions for thinking through the posthuman as an 'extended, relational self' (Braidotti, 2013, p. 90) with one's technologically mediated environments. Like Haraway's discussion of 'cyborgs' (see Chapter 8), Braidotti observes that technology opens up new ways of thinking about humans with positive and negative consequences.

Figure 10.3 Human–machine assemblage

What is a human? Reflect on this question while also thinking about the intrinsically connected ways humans are shaped by non-humans, such as machines and technology. Are we some form of hybrid or 'cyborg'?

For example, on the one hand, technologies push the boundaries of what it means to be human, challenging the idea that we are a set of 'fixed' properties, characteristics or bodily actions. Indeed, through all sorts of emerging biological and technological enhancements, from genetic engineering, neurotechnology, nanomedicine and bioprinting, we are refiguring the very possibilities of what humans can do and achieve. For Braidotti, there is the potential that such technological innovations (and others in the future) will help create a world that breaks down any remaining exploitation or discrimination of humans and non-humans. On the other hand, Braidotti also recognises that information technology is deeply implicated in violence and killing. Speaking of the US use of drones, Braidotti (2013, pp. 125–126) argues that digital surveillance technologies enable the pursuit of a new kind of 'tele-thanatological' warfare, which sees the tracking down and assassination of people from thousands of miles away. This administration of death from afar reveals the capacity of the posthuman also to open up new relations for *in*humanity. Indeed, Braidotti recognises that our current transition into the posthuman only furthers the violent legacies of colonialism and imperialism.

Altogether, then, Braidotti's work contributes to new materialism by inviting us to consider the problems with anthropocentrism from a posthumanist perspective. This encourages researchers to think through the limits of humanism and the possibilities of who we are capable of becoming while taking a planetary view of the challenges that humans and non-humans face.

Case Study 10.2

Animals and Posthumanism

Pramod Nayar (2014) invites us to consider the impact of posthumanism on social theory by questioning the relationship between humans and animals and, in particular, how humans *think* about animals through the lens of the 'autonomy' and 'uniqueness' of human life. Nayar (2014, p. 121) begins by presenting a thought experiment that asks us to consider whether we would eat a cow if we thought the cow could think like a human. Nayar suggests that, as humans, we have particular assumptions about what 'to think' means, and rarely do these assumptions extend to how and what a cow's 'thoughts' might be. Indeed, Nayar argues that humans are willing to consume cows often because they do not consider cows to exist on the same level as humans – thinking or being like 'us'. This is an example of anthropocentrism: humans do not treat animals as equals because it is the human's definition of rationality and autonomy that constitutes the defining principles of life (and death). Indeed, Nayar asserts that, historically, humans use qualities like 'thought', 'reason' and 'language' to bestow upon themselves a uniqueness that distinguishes them from animals. This is particularly apparent in how humans extend themselves certain rights, such as the right to life or the freedom from forced labour, while incorporating animals into the capitalist marketplace as commodities. So, for example, in contemporary culture, people use animals for meat or for products such as leather or for sports

(Continued)

such as horse racing. For Nayar (2014, p. 121), this exploitation of animals (and their suffering) results from an anthropocentric worldview that assigns animals lesser value simply because they do not 'think' like humans.

Nayar suggests that posthumanism can transform how we think about animals by asking very different questions or redirecting or critiquing the very concepts and ideas that have come to define human–animal relations. For example, consider the question 'is a dog a person?' Typically, we might answer that dogs do not present with the notions of self-reflexivity, intelligence or consciousness that humans understand as the characteristics of personhood. However, as Nayar suggests, posthumanists ask questions that decentre the human to challenge our perspective or understanding of these things. So, for example, rather than focusing on intelligence as an indicator of personhood, we might ask whether suffering is an index of personhood instead (Sztybel, 2008, cited in Nayar, 2014, p. 126). Indeed, as Nayar probes, if humans could experience an animal's pain, would we consider it a 'personal' experience? How might this change our understanding of animals? Could we consider them to be persons who suffer? For Nayar, these are the questions that posthumanists ask to disrupt anthropocentric ways of thinking. Indeed, they help to reveal the limits of human knowledge and the possibility that there are wholly other origins and ways of understanding and addressing the social and natural world.

Summary

- New materialism refers to a range of perspectives that share an interest in discussing the properties of material things in terms of agency and ethical responsibility. New materialists raise ontological and epistemological questions about how humans relate to the material world and non-humans, such as animals, technology and the natural environment.
- Actor-network theory (ANT) is a crucial perspective in new materialism that stresses how material and non-human factors or 'actants' shape social interactions and the construction of (scientific) knowledge.
- The work of Deleuze and Guattari is also influential in new materialism because they challenge how we think of the world – not as something to be defined through classification and categorisation but as something in movement as assemblages of relations (of humans and non-humans) configure and reconfigure over time.
- New materialists are also critical of the anthropocentrism in much thinking about the social and natural world. Posthumanists like Rosi Braidotti share this view and challenge the idea that humans are the central organising feature of planet Earth. This perspective raises critical questions about the relationship that humans have with animals and the environment.

Review Questions

- What is new materialism? Discuss with reference to 'actor-networks', 'assemblages' and 'affect'.
- What is Deleuze's main argument in *Difference and Repetition* (2001/1968)?
- Braidotti outlines three phases that reconfigure the human into a posthuman subject. What are they?

Annotated Reading

For an introduction to new materialism, see Nick J. Fox and Pam Alldred's (2017) *Sociology and the New Materialism: Theory, Research, Action* (London: Sage).

Mike Michael's (2017) *Actor-Network Theory: Trials, Trails, and Translations* (London: Sage) is an essential resource for those looking to learn more about the history of ANT and its relationship to big sociological questions.

Todd May (2005) provides a helpful introduction to Deleuze's work in *Gilles Deleuze: An Introduction* (Cambridge: Cambridge University Press).

See Pramod K. Nayar's (2014) *Posthumanism* (Cambridge: Polity Press) to learn more about posthumanism.

Rosi Braidotti's (2019) *Posthuman Knowledge* (Cambridge: Polity Press) offers an insightful discussion about current debates in posthumanism and the environmental and ethical challenges facing humans and non-humans.

GLOSSARY

Affect   A force that transitions a thing from one state to another.

Agency   The capacity of human (and non-human) individuals and groups to exercise autonomy in the context of social structures and cultural beliefs, norms and values.

Alienation   Workers do not gain fulfilment at work or feel estranged from their productive activities due to limits on their creativity and autonomy.

Analytical dualism   Recognises that structure and agency have distinct properties and powers, which requires analysing their interplay rather than conflating them together (as is the case with Pierre Bourdieu's concept of 'habitus' or Anthony Giddens's concept of 'structuration').

Anthropocentrism   The view that humans alone possess intrinsic value above and beyond other entities, such as animals or the environment.

Apartheid   A form of political, legal, economic or social discrimination based on race often referred to in the context of South Africa, where historical colonial arrangements upheld segregationist policies.

Assemblage(s)   An arrangement or configuration of human and non-human relations which is always open to change.

Biopower   The regulation and administration of human life through technologies that manage and control the population to maximise health and economic productivity.

Capital   (1) Money and other assets or resources owned by a person or organisation, often used to invest in the production of commodities for sale to generate profit. (2) Pierre Bourdieu extends the notion of capital beyond its economic conception to emphasise other kinds of exchanges, including social, cultural and symbolic.

Capitalism   An economic and political system in which individuals and private companies sell products, goods and services to generate profit in a competitive marketplace.

Class   A group of people within a society who occupy the same social and economic statuses, such as the working class who sell their labour for wages or the capitalist class who own the means of producing and distributing goods.

Collective conscience   Refers to regulating social life through shared beliefs and values.

Critical realism   A philosophy of (social) science that focuses on questions of ontology and epistemology to understand matters of causation, emergence, structure and agency.

Cultural capital   Pierre Bourdieu's concept to describe an individual's social assets (education, skills, taste, posture, clothing) that promote social mobility within society.

Deconstruction   A method for analysing and critiquing the assumptions, judgements and values within texts, paying particular attention to the arrangement of words, ideas and meanings.

Dialectic   A method of conversation or debate to discover philosophical truths, often by exchanging opinions through a series of questions and answers.

Discourse   Refers to ways of thinking, communicating and constituting knowledge about people and things, which, together with social practices, form the basis for subjectivity and power relations.

Disenchantment   The progressive decline and devaluation of religion and mysticism in modern society due to science, secularism and bureaucracy.

Dramaturgical   A concept that uses a theatrical metaphor to describe social life and identity formation.

Dualism   The idea that we can analyse or explain reality through two opposing (but sometimes complementary) principles, such as structure and agency, subject and object, natural and social, and mind and body.

Emergence   A way of thinking about social and/or natural complexity by recognising that, as things interact, they generate properties or capabilities not possessed by their individual parts. A typical example is water, an emergent property of hydrogen and oxygen elements. Neither hydrogen nor oxygen shares the characteristics of water until they are arranged in a particular way, thereby generating this substance.

(The) Enlightenment   An intellectual and cultural movement during the seventeenth and eighteenth centuries emphasising science, reason and logic over and against non-rational beliefs and forms of social organisation (e.g., religion or monarchy).

Epistemic violence   Gayatri Spivak's concept to describe how non-Western methods and forms of knowledge are obstructed, undermined, excluded, distorted, misrepresented or silenced by imperialist discourse.

Ethnomethodology   An approach to studying the practices, procedures and sources that people use to make sense of and navigate their everyday experiences and settings.

Eurocentrism   A view that assumes the superiority of European cultural values while viewing the histories and cultures of non-Western societies from a European perspective.

Existentialism   Represents a philosophical belief that each person is responsible for creating purpose and meaning in their life.

Exploitation   A process by which capitalists unfairly appropriate the value workers produce, often through limited wages, long working hours, or poor working conditions.

Fascism   A form of violent, authoritarian and ultra-nationalist government that became particularly prominent in Europe during the early twentieth century.

Feudalism   A hierarchical social system common to medieval Europe in which people (vassals or serfs) were bound to cultivate their lord's land in exchange for military protection.

Genealogy   A method of historical analysis that is suspicious and critical of the origins or meanings of particular ideas.

Governmentality   The use of subtle methods of power by governments to control their populations, often through social institutions, practices or procedures that regulate conduct.

Habitus   Refers to relatively enduring embodied dispositions that individuals acquire through experience and socialisation, particularly concerning social class position.

Hegemony   Refers to cultural institutions, such as mass media, exercising authority over people and encouraging consent to the status quo.

Idealism   A perspective in philosophy that reality is dependent upon the mind rather than existing independently (or objectively) of it.

Ideology   A set of beliefs that appear normal but obscure the true nature of reality, such as ideas that legitimate class or gender-based inequalities.

Imperialism   When a country extends its influence or power over another through military conquest or political or economic pressure.

Individualism   A set of beliefs and practices that emphasise the moral worth of the individual over the needs of a group as a whole.

Industrialisation   A period or process in which societies undergo social and economic change as technology and machinery cause a shift from agricultural output to mass production and industry.

Intentionality   Humans ascribe meaning to objects or things as they direct their consciousness or thoughts towards them.

Interpellation   A concept in Marxist theory whereby individuals acknowledge and internalise cultural or ideological values.

Intersectionality   Refers to the multiple, intersecting ways that different histories and structural positions (based on class, gender, race, etc.) shape people's experiences and life chances.

Intersubjectivity   Refers to sharing thoughts, feelings, experiences and expectations between two or more people.

Language game   Ludwig Wittgenstein's analogy for the idea that the meaning of words is always context-dependent and, like games, relies on a set of rules (of language) to exist.

Lifeworld   Refers to the taken-for-granted routines, habits, and knowledge of everyday life.

McDonaldisation   George Ritzer's concept for describing how contemporary society adopts the characteristics of a fast-food restaurant by focusing on efficiency, calculability, predictability and control.

Neoliberalism   A theory of economics and social policy that advocates free market competition and the shift of economic power from the public to the private sector.

Objectivism   The notion that there is an objective reality independent of our modes of comprehending it, but that through science and verifiable facts we may be able to describe it accurately.

Patriarchy   Refers to when men exercise power over women due to their privileged position in society, which is historically grounded in social institutions, norms and values.

Pluralism   A diversity of different ideas or people coexisting simultaneously.

Posthumanism   Focuses on critiquing the humanist ideal of 'Man' as the universal representative of the human.

Power   (1) The capacity of an individual, group or institution to exercise control over people and bring about the desired outcome, despite possible resistance (Max Weber). (2) Power is not restricted to individuals or institutions nor reducible to them but circulates and reproduces the relations in which people are enmeshed (Michel Foucault).

Pragmatism   A philosophy that considers the practical consequences or actual effects of social action and interaction to be vital components of meaning and truth.

Queer theory   Refers to critical perspectives that challenge the dominant position of heterosexuality in society and critiques the idea of stable, binary sexual and gender identities.

Rationalisation   Refers to when rationality, reason and efficiency replace traditions, values and beliefs as the basis for human behaviour in society.

Realism   Implies that the world is separate from the theories we use to describe it and that these theories can help us generate facts and explanations about it.

Reflexive modernisation   A concept developed by Ulrich Beck, Anthony Giddens and Scott Lash, which suggests that a defining characteristic of modern societies is the rapidity of social change and the many risks (ecological, environmental, technological) that this brings. These risks generate a complex and uncertain world in which individuals and institutions must engage in an ongoing process of self-monitoring and risk management.

Reflexivity   The capacity of a person to evaluate their thoughts, feelings, beliefs and surroundings and consider how these contexts influence their actions.

Reification   The mistake of treating a social construct, such as money, as though it were a natural or absolute thing.

Repression   (1) The use of force to control, subdue or suppress individuals or groups. (2) A concept in psychoanalysis that refers to the unconscious blocking of unpleasant memories, emotions and thoughts from the conscious mind.

Scepticism   An attitude or perspective that doubts the possibility of truth or questions the adequacy or reliability of knowledge claims by challenging their foundational principles.

Secularism   The separation of religious affairs from state institutions and governance, related to the decline in the social significance of religious thinking and practices.

Self   Refers to an individual's sense of their own being or distinct identity or personality, usually established through interactions with others.

Signification   The act or process of establishing the meaning or representation of a word, sign or symbol within language.

Simulacra   The experience of virtual or simulated realities as more real than the ones they substitute.

Social epistemology   A branch of philosophy that concerns the study of knowledge, seeking ways to explain knowledge production and how or whether it is possible to 'know' anything.

Socialisation   The acquisition of values, habits and attitudes within society for social cohesion.

Social ontology   A branch of philosophy that concerns the nature of being and existence, seeking ways to classify and explain social phenomena.

Social solidarity   Émile Durkheim's concept for the social cohesion that comes from sharing social bonds and ties.

Social stratification   Refers to how differences in economic resources or social and cultural status generate inequalities between groups of people in society.

Social structure   Characterises the fundamental or relatively enduring features that constitute society, enabling and constraining social behaviour in different ways, such as social institutions, rules, roles, statuses and norms.

Social system(s)   Refers to interrelated parts of society, such as individuals, groups and institutions, operating as an organised whole.

Stigma   Refers to discriminating against members of society based on undesired social characteristics that serve to distinguish them from the general population.

Structuration Anthony Giddens's concept that society should be understood as a 'duality of structure', where structure and agency are intimately tied in the creation and reproduction of social systems (not analytically distinct).

Subjectivism Refers to when knowledge is limited to the subjective experiences of the self, so there can be no objective truth nor absolute moral values.

Subjectivity Refers to an individual's perspectives, values, social experiences and viewpoints.

Subjugation The act of dominating a group of people by taking away their freedom, whether by exercising physical or psychological control over them.

Typifications Refers to people's customary knowledge and practices that are used to construct ideas about the world and those within it.

Unconscious Sigmund Freud's concept which refers to the repository of thoughts, memories, feelings and instinctual desires that guide a person's behaviour without conscious awareness.

Verstehen Means 'understanding' in German and refers to interpreting the subjective meanings that individuals and groups attribute to their behaviour.

Wage labour refers to a social and economic relationship in which workers sell their labour to an employer for pay through a formal or informal employment arrangement.

REFERENCES

Abbott, P., Wallace, C. and Tyler, M. (2005) *An Introduction to Sociology: Feminist Perspectives* (3rd edn). London and New York: Routledge.

Adorno, T. and Horkheimer, M. (1997/1944) *Dialectic of Enlightenment*. London and New York: Verso.

Ahmed, S. (2010) *The Promise of Happiness*. Durham, NC: Duke University Press.

Akram, S. and Hogan, A. (2015) On reflexivity and the conduct of the self in everyday life: reflections on Bourdieu and Archer. *British Journal of Sociology*, 66(4), 605–625.

Alatas, S.F. and Sinha, V. (2017) *Sociological Theory Beyond the Canon*. London: Palgrave Macmillan.

Alexander, J. (2003) *The Meanings of Social Life: A Cultural Sociology*. Oxford: Oxford University Press.

Al-Ghadeer, M. (2013) Cannibalizing Iraq: Topos of a new Orientalism. In Z. Elmarsafy, A. Bernard and D. Attwell (eds), *Debating Orientalism* (pp. 117–133). Basingstoke: Palgrave.

Alldred, P. and Fox, N. (2015) The sexuality-assemblage of young men: A new materialist analysis. *Sexualities*, 18(8), 905–920.

Allen, K. (2004) *Max Weber: A Critical Introduction*. London: Pluto Press.

Althusser, L. (2001/1971) *Lenin and Philosophy and Other Essays*. New York: Monthly Review Press.

Appelrouth, S. and Edles, L. (2021) *Classical and Contemporary Sociological Theory*. London: Sage.

Archer, M. (1982) Morphogenesis versus structuration: On combining structure and action. *British Journal of Sociology*, 33(4), 455–483.

Archer, M. (1988) *Culture and Agency: The Place of Culture in Social Theory*. Cambridge: Cambridge University Press.

Archer, M. (1995) *Realist Social Theory: The Morphogenetic Approach*. Cambridge: Cambridge University Press.

Archer, M. (2000) *Being Human: The Problem of Agency*. Cambridge: Cambridge University Press.

Archer, M. (2003) *Structure, Agency and the Internal Conversation*. Cambridge: Cambridge University Press.

Archer, M. (2007) *Making Our Way through the World*. Cambridge: Cambridge University Press.

Archer, M. (2010) Can reflexivity and *habitus* work in tandem? In M. Archer (ed.), *Conversations about Reflexivity*. London: Routledge.

Archer, M. and Morgan, J. (2020) Contributions to realist social theory: An interview with Margaret S. Archer, *Journal of Critical Realism*, 19(2), 179–200.

Artz, L. and Murphy, O.B. (2000) *Cultural Hegemony in the United States*. London: Sage.

Arvidsson, A. (2006) *Brands: Meaning and Value in Media Culture*. New York: Routledge.

Baker, Z. (2019) Reflexivity, structure and agency: Using reflexivity to understand Further Education students' Higher Education decision-making and choices. *British Journal of Sociology of Education*, 40(1), 1–16.

Barry, J.A., Mol, P.J. and Zito, A.R. (2013) Climate change ethics, rights and policies: An introduction. *Environmental Politics*, 22(3), 361–376.

Barthes, R. (1991/1957) *Mythologies*. New York: Noonday Press.

Bates, L. (2014) *Everyday Sexism*. London: Simon & Schuster.

Beauvoir, S. de (1956/1949) *The Second Sex*. London: Jonathan Cape.

Beasley, C. (1999) *What is Feminism? An Introduction to Feminist Theory*. London: Sage.

Becker, H. (1963) *Outsiders: Studies in the Sociology of Deviance*. New York: Free Press.

Beer, D. (2016) *Metric Power*. London: Palgrave.

Bellah, R. N. (1967) Civil religion in America. *Daedalus*, 96(1), 1–21.

Bellah, R. N., Madsen, R., Sullivan, W., Swidler, A. and Tipton, S. M. (1985) *Habits of the Heart: Individualism and Commitment in American Life*. Berkeley: University of California Press.

Bennett, J. (2001) *The Enchantment of Modern Life: Attachments, Crossings, and Ethics*. Princeton, NJ: Princeton University Press.

Bergen, D.V., Johannes, H.S., Balkon, A. and Sawitiri, S. (2009) Suicidal behaviour of young immigrant women in the Netherlands. Can we use Durkheim's concept of 'fatalistic suicide' to explain their high incidence of attempted suicide? *Ethnic and Racial Studies*, 32, 302–322.

Berger, P., and Luckmann, T. (1991/1966) *The Social Construction of Reality: A Treatise in the Sociology of Knowledge*. London: Penguin.

Bernard, T. (1983) *The Consensus-Conflict Debate: Form and Content in Social Theories*. New York: Columbia University Press.

Best, S. and Kellner, D. (1991) *Postmodern Theory: Critical Interrogations*. Basingstoke: Macmillan Education.

Bhabha, H.K. (1994) *The Location of Culture*. London and New York: Routledge.

Bhambra, G. (2007) *Rethinking Modernity: Postcolonialism and the Sociological Imagination*. Basingstoke: Palgrave Macmillan.

Blumer, H. (1969) *Symbolic Interactionism: Perspective and Method*. Berkeley: University of California Press.

Boag, S. (2012) *Freudian Repression, the Unconscious, and the Dynamics of Inhibition*. London: Karnac Books.

Bocock, R. (2002) *Sigmund Freud*. London: Routledge.

Boltanski, L. and Chiapello, E. (2007) *The New Spirit of Capitalism*. London: Verso.

Boucher, G. (2012) *Understanding Marxism*. Durham: Acumen.

Bourdieu, P. (1992) *The Logic of Practice*. Cambridge: Polity Press.

Bourdieu, P. (2013/1977) *Outline of a Theory of Practice*. Cambridge: Cambridge University Press.

Bourdieu, P. and Eagleton, T. (1992) Doxa and common life. *New Left Review*, 191, 111–121.

Bourdieu, P. and Passeron, J.C. (1990/1977) *Reproduction in Education, Society and Culture*. London. Sage.

Braidotti, R. (2013) *The Posthuman*. Cambridge: Polity Press.

Braidotti, R. (2019) *Posthuman Knowledge*. Cambridge: Polity Press.

Brock, T. (2021) Counting clicks: Esports, neoliberalism and the affective power of gameplay metrics. In D. Y. Jin (ed.), *Global Esports: Transformation of Cultural Perceptions of Competitive Gaming*. London and New York: Bloomsbury Academic.

Brock, T., Carrigan, M. and Scambler, G. (eds) (2016) *Structure, Culture and Agency: Selected Papers of Margaret Archer*. London: Routledge.

Brownmiller, S. (1975) *Against Our Will: Men, Women and Rape*. New York: Fawcett Columbine.

Butler, J. (1999) *Gender Trouble: Feminism and the Subversion of Identity*. London and New York: Routledge.

Caetano, A. (2015) Defining personal reflexivity: A critical reading of Archer's approach. *European Journal of Social Theory*, 18, 60–75.

Cafaro, P.J., Butler, T., Crist, E., Cryer, P., Dinerstein, E., Kopina, H., Noss, R., Piccolo, J., Taylor, B., Vynne, C. and Washington, H. (2017) If we want a whole earth, nature needs half. A response to Büscher et al. *Oryx – The International Journal of Conservation*, 51(3), 400.

Caillois, R. (2001/1961) *Man, Play and Games*. Urbana: University of Illinois Press.

Callon, M. (1984) Some elements of a sociology of translations: Domestication of the scallops and the fishermen at St Brieuc Bay. *Sociological Review*, 32(1), 196–233.

Cant, C. (2020) *Riding for Deliveroo: Resistance in the New Economy*. Cambridge: Polity Press.

Césaire, A. (2013/1956) *Return to My Native Land*. New York: Archipelago Books.

Chakrabarty, D. (2000) *Provincializing Europe: Postcolonial Thought and Historical Difference*. Princeton, NJ: Princeton University Press.

Chatfield, T. (2017) *Critical Thinking*. London: Sage.

Chatterjee, P. (1999) *The Partha Chatterjee Omnibus: Nationalist Thought in the Postcolonial World, The Nation and its Fragments, A Possible India*. Oxford: Oxford University Press.

Chodorow, N. (1978) *The Reproduction of Mothering: Psychoanalysis and the Sociology of Gender*. California: University of California Press.

Cixous, H. (1976) The laugh of the Medusa. *Signs*, 1(4), 875–893.

Cline, E. (2011) *Ready Player One*. London: Century.

Clough, P. (2008) The affective turn: Political economy, biomedia and bodies. *Theory, Culture and Society*, 25(1), 1–22.

Clough, P. and Halley, J. (2007) *The Affective Turn: Theorizing the Social*. Durham, NC: Duke University Press.

Cohen, A. K. (1955) *Delinquent Boys: The Culture of the Gang*. New York: Free Press.

Collins, P. H. (2000) *Black Feminist Thought: Knowledge, Consciousness, and the Politics of Empowerment*. London and New York: Routledge.

Connell, R. (1997) Why is classical theory classical? *American Journal of Sociology*, 102, 1511–1557.

Connell, R. (2007) *Southern Theory*. Cambridge: Polity Press.

Coole, D. and Frost, S. (2010) *New Materialisms: Ontology, Agency and Politics*. Durham, NC: Duke University Press.

Corsini, R. and Wedding, D. (2008) *Current Psychotherapies*. Belmont, CA: Thomson Brookes/Cole.

Couldry, N. (2008) Actor-network theory and the media: Do they connect and on what terms? In A. Hepp, F. Krotz, S. Moores and C. Winter (eds), *Connectivity, Networks and Flows: Conceptualizing Contemporary Communications*. New York: Hampton Press.

Craib, I. (1992) *Modern Social Theory: From Parsons to Habermas*. Hemel Hempstead: Harvester Wheatsheaf.

Craib, I. (1997) *Classical Social Theory*. Oxford: Oxford University Press.

Crenshaw, K. (1989) Demarginalizing the intersection of race and sex: A black feminist critique of antidiscrimination doctrine, feminist theory and antiracist politics. *University of Chicago Legal Forum*, 1989(8), 139–167.

Crenshaw, K. (1991) Race, gender, and sexual harassment. *Southern California Law Review*, 65(3), 1467–1476.

Crotty, M. (1998) *The Foundations of Social Research: Meaning and Perspective in the Research Process*. London: Sage.

Cruickshank, J. (2003) *Realism and Sociology: Anti-foundationalism, Ontology and Social Research*. London: Routledge.

Daly, M. (1978) *Gyn/ecology: The Metaethics of Radical Feminism*. Boston: Beacon Press.

Danaher, G., Schirato, T. and Webb, J. (2000) *Understanding Foucault*. St. Leonards, New South Wales: Allen & Unwin.

Danermark, B., Ekstrom, M., Jakobsen, L. and Karlsson, J. (2002) *Explaining Society: Critical Realism in the Social Sciences*. London: Routledge.

DeLanda, M. (2006) *A New Philosophy of Society: Assemblage Theory and Social Complexity*. London and New York: Continuum.

Delap, L. (2020) *Feminisms: A Global History*. London: Penguin.

Deleuze, G. (2001/1968) *Difference and Repetition*. London: Continuum.

Deleuze, G. and Guattari, F. (1987) *A Thousand Plateaus: Capitalism and Schizophrenia*. Minneapolis: University of Minnesota Press.

Dietz, T., Shwom, R. L. and Whitley, C. T. (2020) Climate change and society. *Annual Review of Sociology*, 46, 135–158.

Dillon, M. (2009) *Introduction to Sociological Theory: Theorists, Concepts, and Their Applicability to the Twenty-First Century*. Chichester: Wiley-Blackwell.

Dinnerstein, D. (1976) *The Mermaid and the Minotaur: Sexual Arrangement and Human Malaise*. New York: Harper and Row.

Du Bois, W.E.B. (2007/1903) *The Souls of Black Folk*. Oxford: Oxford University Press.

Durkheim, E. (2002/1925) *Moral Education*. New York: Dover Publications.

Durkheim, E. (2006/1897) *Suicide: A Study in Sociology*. London and New York: Routledge.

Durkheim, E. (2008/1912) *The Elementary Forms of Religious Life*. Oxford: Oxford University Press.

Durkheim, E. (2014/1893) *The Division of Labour in Society*. New York: Free Press.

Durkheim, E. (2014/1895) *The Rules of Sociological Method*. New York: Free Press.

Eagleton, T. (2011) *Why Marx was Right*. New Haven, CT: Yale University Press.

Elder-Vass, D. (2007a) For emergence: Refining Archer's account of social structure. *Journal for the Theory of Social Behaviour*, 37(1), 25–44.

Elder-Vass, D. (2007b) Reconciling Archer and Bourdieu in an emergentist theory of action. *Sociological Theory*. 25(4), 325–346.

Engels, F. (2010/1884) *The Origin of the Family, Private Property and the State*. London: Penguin.

Fanon, F. (1963) *The Wretched of the Earth*. New York: Grove Press.

Fanon, F. (2008/1952) *Black Skin, White Masks*. London: Pluto Press.

Farrugia, D. and Woodman, D. (2015) Ultimate concerns in late modernity: Archer, Bourdieu and reflexivity. *British Journal of Sociology*, 66(4), 626–644.

Finlayson, L. (2016) *An Introduction to Feminism*. Cambridge: Cambridge University Press.

Foucault, M. (2001/1961) *Madness and Civilization*. London: Routledge.

Foucault, M. (2002/1969) *The Archaeology of Knowledge*. London: Routledge.

Foucault, M. (2020/1975) *Discipline and Punish: The Birth of the Prison*. London: Penguin.

Foucault, M. (2020/1976) *The History of Sexuality, Volume 1: The Will to Knowledge*. London: Penguin.

Fox, N. and Alldred, P. (2017) *Sociology and the New Materialism: Theory, Research, Action*. London: Sage.

Fox, N. and Alldred, P. (2021) Economics, the climate change policy-assemblage and the new materialisms: Towards a comprehensive policy. *Globalizations*, 18(7), 1248–1258.

Freud, S. (1997/1899) *The Interpretation of Dreams*. Ware, Hertfordshire: Wordsworth Editions.

Freud, S. (2002/1930) *Civilization and Its Discontents*. London: Penguin.

Fromm, E. (2001/1955) *The Sane Society*. London: Routledge.

Fulcher, J. (2004) *Capitalism: A Very Short Introduction*. Oxford: Oxford University Press.

Gandhi, M. (2021/1909) *Hind Swaraj or Indian Home Rule*. Berkeley, CA: West Margin Press.

Garfinkel, H. (1967) *Studies in Ethnomethodology*. Englewood Cliffs, NJ: Prentice-Hall.

Giddens, A. (1968) 'Power' in the recent writings of Talcott Parsons. *Sociology*, 2(3), 257–272.

Giddens, A. (1979) *Central Problems in Social Theory: Action, Structure and Contradiction in Social Analysis*. London: Macmillan.

Giddens, A. (1998) An interview with Anthony Giddens. *Irish Journal of Sociology*, 8, 113–123.

Go, J. (2016) *Postcolonial Thought and Social Theory*. Oxford: Oxford University Press.

Goffman, E. (1959) *The Presentation of Self in Everyday Life*. New York: Anchor Books.

Goffman, E. (1961) *Asylums: Essays on the Social Situation of Mental Patients and Other Inmates*. New York: Doubleday.

Goffman, E. (1963) *Stigma: Notes on the Management of Spoiled Identity*. Englewood Cliffs, NJ: Prentice-Hall.

Gray, K. (2020) *Intersectional Tech: Black Users in Digital Gaming*. Baton Rouge: Louisiana State University Press.

Green, E.M. (2015) Gramsci and subaltern struggles today: Spontaneity, political organization and Occupy Wall Street. In M. McNally (ed.) *Antonio Gramsci* (pp. 156–178). Basingstoke: Palgrave Macmillan.

Guha, R. (1988) On some aspects of historiography of colonial India. In R. Guha and G. Spivak (eds), *Selected Subaltern Studies* (pp. 37–44). Oxford: Oxford University Press.

Habermas, J. (1984/1981) *The Theory of Communicative Action, Vol. 1: Reason and the Rationalization of Society*. Boston: Beacon Press.

Hagan, F.E. and Daigle, L.E. (2020) *Introduction to Criminology: Theories, Methods, and Criminal Behaviour* (10th edn). London: Sage.

Hall, S. (1987) Gramsci and us. *Marxism Today* (June), pp. 16–21.

Hall, S. (2001/1973) Encoding/decoding. In M. Durham and D. Kellner, D. (eds), *Media and Cultural Studies: Keyworks*. Oxford: Blackwell.

Haraway, D. (1988a) *Primate Visions: Gender, Race, and Nature in the World of Modern Science*. London: Routledge.

Haraway, D. (1988b) Situated knowledges: The science question in feminism and the privilege of partial perspective. *Feminist Studies*, 14(3), 575–599.

Haraway, D. (1991/1985) A cyborg manifesto: Science, technology, and socialist-feminism in the late twentieth century. In *Simians, Cyborgs, and Women: The Reinvention of Nature* (pp. 149–181). New York: Routledge.

Hartmann, H. (1981) The unhappy marriage of Marxism and Feminism: Towards a more progressive union. In L. Sargent (ed.), *Women and Revolution* (pp. 1–42). Boston: South End Press.

Hawkes, T. (1977) *Structuralism and Semiotics*. Berkeley: University of California Press.

Heidegger, M. (1996/1927) *Being and Time*. New York: State University of New York Press.

Hines, S. (2020) Feminist and gender theories. In D. Richardson and V. Robinson (eds), *Introducing Gender and Women's Studies* (pp. 24–39). London: Red Globe Press.

Hochschild, A. (2003/1983) *The Managed Heart: Commercialisation of Human Feeling*. Berkeley: University of California Press.

Holligan, C. and McLean, R. (2019) A Durkheimian theorization of Scottish suicide rates, 2011–2017. *Social Sciences*, 8(10), 1–12.

hooks, b. (1984) *Feminist Theory: From Margin to Centre*. Boston: South End Press.

Inglis, D. with Thorpe, C. (2019) *An Invitation to Social Theory* (2nd edn). London: Polity.

Ingraffia, B. (1995) *Postmodern Theory and Biblical Theology: Vanquishing God's Shadow*. Cambridge: Cambridge University Press.

Irigaray, L. (1985/1974) *Speculum of the Other Woman*. New York: Cornell University Press.

Jaggar, A. (1983) *Feminist Politics and Human Nature*. Brighton, Sussex: Harvester Press.

James, C.L.R. (1989/1938) *The Black Jacobins*. New York: Vintage.

Jeffreys, S. (2005) *Beauty and Misogyny: Harmful Cultural Practices in the West*. London: Routledge.

Johnson, M. (2019) *The Unpredictability of Gameplay*. New York: Bloomsbury.

Jones, P. and Bradbury, L. (2018) *Introducing Social Theory*. Cambridge: Polity Press.

Kant, I. (1998/1781) *Critique of Pure Reason*. Cambridge: Cambridge University Press.

Kerr, R. (2014) From Foucault to Latour: Gymnastics training as a socio-technical network. *Sociology of Sport*, 31, 85–101.

Kirkpatrick, G. (2002) The hacker ethic and the spirit of the information age. *Max Weber Studies*, 2(2), 163–185.

Kivisto, P. (2020) *Social Theory: Roots and Branches*. Oxford: Oxford University Press.

Klesse, C. (2007) *The Spectre of Promiscuity*. Aldershot, Hampshire: Ashgate.

Kurasawa, F. (2013) The Durkheimian School and colonialism: Exploring the constitutive paradox. In G. Steinmetz (ed.), *Sociology and Empire: The Imperial Entanglements of a Discipline* (pp. 188–210). Durham, NC: Duke University Press.

Laclau, E. and Mouffe, C. (1985) *Hegemony and Socialist Strategy*. London: Verso.

Latour, B. (1988) *The Pasteurization of France*. Cambridge, MA: Harvard University Press.

Latour, B. (2000) *Pandora's Hope: Essays on the Reality of Science Studies*. Cambridge, MA: Harvard University Press.

Latour, B. (2005) *Reassembling the Social: An Introduction to Actor-Network Theory*. Oxford: Oxford University Press.

Latour, B. and Woolgar, S. (1986) *Laboratory Life: The Construction of Scientific Facts*. Princeton, NJ: Princeton University Press.

Launer, J. (2005) Anna O and the 'talking cure'. *QJM: An International Journal of Medicine*, 98(6), 465–466.

Layder, D. (2006) *Understanding Social Theory*. London: Sage.

Lechte, J. (2007) *Fifty Contemporary Thinkers: From Structuralism to Post-Humanism*. London: Routledge.

Liberman, K. (2013) *More Studies in Ethnomethodology*. New York: State University of New York Press: New York.

Little, D. (2008) *Orientalism: The United States and the Middle East since 1945*. Chapel Hill: University of North Carolina Press.

Luna, Z. and Pirtle, W.N.L. (eds) (2022) *Black Feminist Sociology: Perspectives and Praxis*. New York and Abingdon: Routledge.

Lyotard, J.-F. (1984/1979) *The Postmodern Condition: A Report on Knowledge*. Minneapolis: University of Minnesota Press.

Mackinnon, C.A. (1979) *Sexual Harassment of Working Women: A Case of Sex Discrimination*. New Haven, CT: Yale University Press.

Maffesoli, M. (1996) *The Time of the Tribes*. London: Sage.

Marcuse, H. (1987/1955) *Eros and Civilisation: A Philosophical Inquiry into Freud*. London: Routledge.

Marx, K. (1843) Justification of the correspondent from the Mosel. https://marxists. architexturez.net/archive/marx/works/1843/01/15.htm, accessed 26 April 2022.

Marx, K. (1844) *Estranged Labour*. https://www.marxists.org/archive/marx/works/1844/ manuscripts/labour.htm, accessed 26 April 2022.

Marx, K. (1845) *Theses on Feuerbach*. https://www.marxists.org/archive/marx/works/1845/ theses/theses.htm, accessed 26 April 2022.

Marx, K. (1852) *The Eighteenth Brumaire of Louis Bonaparte*. https://www.marxists.org/archive/ marx/works/1852/18th-brumaire/ch01.htm, accessed 26 April 2022.

Marx, K. (1867) *Capital: Volume 1*. https://www.marxists.org/archive/marx/works/1867-c1/ index.htm, accessed 26 April 2022.

Marx, K. (1973/1939) *Grundrisse: Introduction to the Critique of Political Economy*. New York: Vintage.

McKenna, E. (2020) *Rights, Responsibilities and Respect*. Lanham, MD: Rowman and Littlefield.

McLeod, J. (2010) *Beginning Postcolonialism*. Manchester: Manchester University Press.

Mead, G. H. (1934) *Mind, Self and Society*. Chicago: University of Chicago Press.

Meghji, A. (2021) *Decolonizing Sociology*. Cambridge: Polity Press.

Mercer, K. (1994) *Welcome to the Jungle: New Positions in Black Cultural Studies*. London and New York: Routledge.

Merchant, B. (2017) *The One Device: The Secret History of the iPhone*. London: Transworld.

Merleau-Ponty, M. (2012/1945) *Phenomenology of Perception*. London and New York: Routledge.

Merton, R. K. (1938) Social structure and anomie, *American Sociological Review*, 3(5), 672–682.

Messner, S.F. and Rosenfeld, R. (2013) *Crime and the American Dream* (5th edn). Belmont, CA: Wadsworth Cengage Learning.

Michael, M. (2017) *Actor-Network Theory: Trials, Trails and Translations*. London: Sage.

Miles, S. (2001) *Social Theory in the Real World*. London: Sage.

Miller, R. and Rose, N. (2008) *Governing the Present: Administering Economic, Social and Personal Life*. Cambridge: Polity Press.

Moran, D. (2000) *Introduction to Phenomenology*. London and New York: Routledge.

Myles, J. (1999) From habitus to mouth: Language and class in Bourdieu's sociology of language. *Theory and Society*, 28(6), 879–901.

Nayar, P.K. (2014) *Posthumanism*. Cambridge: Polity Press.

Nietzsche, F. (1966/1886) *Beyond Good and Evil*. New York: Vintage Books.

Nietzsche, F. (1968/1901) *The Will to Power*. New York: Vintage.

Nietzsche, F. (1974/1882) *The Gay Science*. New York: Vintage.

Nietzsche, F. (1989/1887) *On the Genealogy of Morals and Ecce Homo*. New York: Vintage Books.

Nietzsche, F. (1992/1872) *The Birth of Tragedy*. Cambridge: Cambridge University Press.

Nietzsche, F. (2005/1888) The Anti-Christ: A curse on Christianity. In A. Ridley and J. Norman (eds), *The Anti-Christ, Ecce Homo, Twilight of the Idols and Other Writings*. Cambridge: Cambridge University Press.

Nietzsche, F. (2006/1883) Thus spoke Zarathustra: A book for all and none. In A. Del Caro and R. Pippin (eds), *Nietzsche: Thus Spoke Zarathustra*. Cambridge: Cambridge University Press.

Nimmo, R. (2019) *Posthumanism*. London: Sage.

Noble, S. (2018) *Algorithms of Oppression*. New York: New York University Press.

Outhwaite, W. (2015) *Social Theory*. London: Profile Books.

Parker, I. (2000) *Structuration*. Maidenhead: Open University Press.

Parker, I., Georgaca, E., Harper, D. and McLaughlin, T. (1995) *Deconstructing Psychopathology*. London: Sage.

Parsons, T. and Bales, R. (1956) *Family Socialization and Interaction Process*. London: Routledge.

Peggs, K. (2012) *Animals and Sociology*. Basingstoke: Palgrave Macmillan.

Peräkylä, A. (2004) Conversational analysis. In C. Seale, G. Gobo, J.F. Gubrium and D. Silverman (eds), *Qualitative Research Practice*. London: Sage.

Plumwood, V. (2002) *Environmental Culture: The Ecological Crisis of Reason*. London and New York: Routledge.

Reay, D. (1995) They employ cleaners to do that: Habitus in the primary classroom. *British Journal of Sociology of Education*, 16(3), 353–371.

Reed, E. (1970) Women: Caste, class, or oppressed sex. *International Socialist Review*, 31(3), 15–17, 40–41. https://www.marxists.org/archive/reed-evelyn/1970/caste-class-sex.htm, accessed 26 April 2022.

Reeves, A., McKee, M. and Stuckler, D. (2014) Economic suicides in the Great Recession in Europe and North America. *British Journal of Psychiatry*, 205(3), 246–247.

Riley, A.T. (2005) The theory of play/games and sacrality in popular culture: The relevance of Roger Caillois for contemporary Neo-Durkheimian cultural theory. *Durkheimian Studies / Études Durkheimiennes*, 11, 103–114.

Ritzer, G. (2008) *Classical Sociological Theory* (5th edn). New York: McGraw-Hill.

Ritzer, G. (2013) The Weberian theory of rationalization and the McDonaldization of contemporary society. In P. Kivisto (ed.), *Illuminating Social Life: Classical and Contemporary Theory Revisited*. London: Sage.

Ritzer, G. (2015/1993) *The McDonaldization of Society*. London: Sage.

Royce, E. (2015) *Classical Social Theory and Modern Society: Marx, Durkheim, Weber*. Lanham, MD: Rowman and Littlefield.

Said, E. (1979) *Orientalism*. New York: Vintage.

Saler, M. (2012) *As If: Modern Enchantment and the Literary Prehistory of Virtual Reality*. Oxford: Oxford University Press.

Sanborn, T. and Jung, J. (2021) Intersecting social science and conservation. *Frontiers in Marine Science*, 8.

Sarup, M. (1993) *An Introductory Guide to Post-Structuralism and Postmodernism.* London: Harvester Wheatsheaf.

Saussure, F. de (2011/1916) *Course in General Linguistics* (P. Miesel and H. Saussy, eds). New York: Columbia University Press.

Schütz, A. (1972/1967) *The Phenomenology of the Social World.* Evanston, IL: Northwestern University Press.

Schütz, A. (1970) *On Phenomenology and Social Relations.* Chicago: University of Chicago Press.

Singer, P. (1977) *Animal Liberation: A New Ethics for Our Treatment of Animals.* New York: Random House.

Singh, S. (2021) *Domestic Economic Abuse: The Violence of Money.* New York: Routledge.

Southwell, G. (2009) *A Beginner's Guide to Nietzsche's Beyond Good and Evil.* Chichester: Wiley-Blackwell.

Spivak, G. (2003/1988) Can the subaltern speak? In P. Williams and L. Chrisman (eds), *Colonial Discourse and Post-Colonial Theory.* London: Routledge.

Stack, S. (2004) Émile Durkheim and altruistic suicide. *Archives of Suicide Research,* 8(1), 9–22.

Stones, R. (2005) *Structuration Theory.* London: Palgrave.

Storr, A. (2001) *Freud: A Very Short Introduction.* Oxford: Oxford University Press.

Sturrock, J. (2008) *Structuralism.* Oxford: Blackwell.

Tallis, R. (2003) *Philosophical Inquiry into Human Being.* Edinburgh: Edinburgh University Press.

Taylor, U. (1998) The historical evolution of black feminist theory and praxis. *Journal of Black Studies,* 29(2), 234–253.

ten Have, P. (2004) *Understanding Qualitative Research and Ethnomethodology.* London: Sage.

Thompson, E.P. (2008/1978) *The Poverty of Theory or An Orrery of Errors.* New York: Monthly Review Press.

Thompson, K. (2002) *Émile Durkheim.* London: Routledge.

Thorpe, R. and Holt, R. (2008) Existential phenomenology. In *The SAGE Dictionary of Qualitative Management Research.* London: Sage.

Thurschwell, P. (2000) *Sigmund Freud.* London: Routledge.

Tong, R. (2009) *Feminist Thought: A More Comprehensive Introduction* (3rd edn). Boulder, CO: Westview Press.

Tyler, I. (2020) *Stigma: The Machinery of Inequality.* London: Zed Books.

Wacquant, L. (2001) Whores, slaves and stallions: Languages of exploitation and accommodation among boxers. *Body and Society,* 7(2–3), 181–194.

Walby, S. (1990) *Theorizing Patriarchy.* Oxford: Blackwell.

Weber, M. (1978) *Economy and Society.* Berkeley: University of California Press.

Weber, M. (2002/1905) *The Protestant Ethic and the Spirit of Capitalism.* London: Penguin.

Wollstonecraft, M. (2014/1972) *A Vindication of the Rights of Women: With Strictures on Political and Moral Subjects.* Toronto: HarperCollins.

Woodcock, J. and Graham, M. (2020) *The Gig Economy: A Critical Introduction.* Cambridge: Polity Press.

Young, I.M. (1981) Beyond the unhappy marriage: A critique of the dual systems theory. In L. Sargent (ed.), *Women and Revolution* (pp. 43–70). Boston: South End Press.

Young, R.J.C. (2016) *Postcolonialism: An Historical Introduction.* Oxford: Blackwell.

Zahavi, D. (2018) *Phenomenology: The Basics.* Abingdon: Routledge.

INDEX

Page numbers in *italics* refer to figures.